COMMONLY MISUNDERSTOOD BIBLE VERSES

RON RHODES

HARVEST HOUSE PUBLISHERS

EUGENE, OREGON

Cover by Dugan Design Group, Bloomington, Minnesota

Cover photos © iStockphoto

Emphasis and inserts in Scripture quotations are added by the author.

COMMONLY MISUNDERSTOOD BIBLE VERSES
Copyright © 2008 by Ron Rhodes
Published by Harvest House Publishers
Eugene, Oregon 97402
www.harvesthousepublishers.com

Library of Congress Cataloging-in-Publication Data
  Rhodes, Ron.
  Commonly misunderstood Bible verses / Ron Rhodes.
    p. cm.
  Includes bibliographical references.
  ISBN-13: 978-0-7369-2175-6 (pbk.)
  ISBN-10: 0-7369-2175-3
  1. Bible—Criticism, interpretation, etc.—Miscellanea. I. Title.
  BS511.3.R49 2008
  220.6—dc22

                                                                          2008001768

Printed in the United States of America

08 09 10 11 12 13 14 15 16 / VP-SK / 10 9 8 7 6 5 4 3 2 1

To David and Kylie

Acknowledgments

This book is decades in the making. Over the course of many years, I've appeared on innumerable radio and television shows; spoken at many churches, conferences, rallies, and seminars; and answered countless letters and e-mails. Most of these have one thing in common. At some point in the process, someone asked me to explain a difficult Bible verse. I must therefore give a hearty thanks to the thousands of people I've interacted with over these decades—many of whom simply asked, "What do you think this verse means?" This book has emerged out of all those interesting interactions.

I want to express deepest appreciation to my wife, Kerri, and our two children, David and Kylie, for their never-ending support, their encouragement, and their constant prayers! I couldn't have accomplished this work without them. Thanks also to all my friends at Harvest House Publishers.

Contents

The New Testament

Understanding Hard Sayings

Some Bible verses are not as easy as others to understand. Peter once said of the apostle Paul, "His letters contain some things that are hard to understand, which ignorant and unstable people distort, as they do the other Scriptures, to their own destruction" (2 Peter 3:16). We learn two things here: Some verses are in fact hard to understand, and misunderstanding such verses can be destructive.

For example, Philip, an apostle, came upon an Ethiopian eunuch who was reading from Isaiah, and Philip asked him, "Do you understand what you are reading?" The eunuch responded: "How can I, unless someone explains it to me?" So Philip sat with him and explained everything to him (Acts 8:27-31).

You may have read certain verses that you find hard to understand. If so, this book is for you. Of course, no single book could examine every hard saying in the Bible. However, this book contains some of the most common ones. I've included those that I've been asked about most often through my years of ministry. My hope and prayer is that this book will guide your understanding so that you attain a better grasp of God's Word. For those who seek even further information on Bible difficulties, I've included a select bibliography of helpful books at the end of this book.

Meanwhile, let's set the stage for the rest of the book by briefly noting some important guiding principles for interpreting Scripture. For decades, these principles have guided me in dealing with Bible difficulties.

1. When the plain sense makes good sense, seek no other sense.
A plain reading of Genesis indicates that when God created

Adam in His own rational image, He gave Adam the gift of intelligible speech. This enabled him to use words to communicate objectively with his Creator and with other human beings (Genesis 1:26; 11:1,7). Scripture shows that God sovereignly chose to use human language as a medium of revelational communication, often through the "Thus saith the Lord" pronouncements of the prophets (such as Isaiah 7:7 and many others).

If God created language primarily so He could communicate with human beings and so human beings could communicate with each other, then He would naturally use language and expect human beings to use it in its normal and plain sense. This view of language is a prerequisite to understanding not only God's spoken word but also His written Word (Scripture).

2. Submit all "preunderstandings" to Scripture. Theological preunderstandings—doctrinal opinions we have previously formed—should not bias our interpretation of Scripture. Any preunderstandings that the interpreter brings to Scripture should be in harmony with scriptural teaching and be subject to correction by it. We must avoid interpreting Scripture through an alien grid or filter that obscures or negates its true message. To avoid misinterpreting Scripture, students must be careful to examine their presuppositions in the light of Scripture. Only preunderstandings that are compatible with Scripture are legitimate.

3. Pay close attention to the context. Each statement in Scripture must be taken in its proper context. Every word in the Bible is part of a sentence, every sentence is part of a paragraph, every paragraph is part of a book, and every book is part of the whole of Scripture. The interpretation of a specific passage must not contradict the complete teaching of Scripture on a point. Individual verses do not exist as isolated

fragments, but as parts of a whole. The exposition of these verses, therefore, must keep them in right relation both to the whole and to each other. Scripture interprets Scripture.

4. Make a correct genre judgment. The Bible contains a variety of literary genres, each of which has certain peculiar characteristics that we must recognize in order to interpret the text properly. Biblical genres include history (such as Acts), the dramatic epic (Job), poetry (Psalms), wise sayings (Proverbs), and apocalyptic writings (Revelation). An incorrect genre judgment will lead one far astray in interpreting Scripture. A parable, for example, should not be treated as history, nor should poetry or apocalyptic literature (both of which contain many symbols) be treated as straightforward narrative. When the psalms refer to God as a rock (Psalm 18:2; 19:14), we should not understand this literally but as a symbol of God's sturdiness: God is our rock-solid foundation. The psalms often use such metaphors.

The wise interpreter allows his knowledge of genres to guide his approach to each individual biblical text. In this way, he can accurately determine what the biblical author was intending to communicate to the reader.

5. Consult history and culture. The interpreter of Scripture must seek to step out of his Western mind-set and into a first-century Jewish mind-set, paying special attention to such things as Jewish marriage rites, burial rites, family practices, farm practices, business practices, the monetary system, methods of warfare, slavery, the treatment of captives, and religious practices. Such detailed historical information helps us understand the world of the biblical writers, and so interpreting the Bible correctly becomes a much easier task.

6. Interpret the difficult verses in light of the clear verses. Let

us never forget that being clear on the straightforward verses helps us make sense of the difficult verses.

7. Interpret the Old Testament in light of the New Testament. God gave revelation to humankind progressively throughout Old and New Testament times. He didn't just give His entire revelation for all time to our first parents, Adam and Eve, or to Moses, the lawgiver. Rather, as the centuries slowly passed, God provided more and more revelation that became progressively full so that by the time the New Testament was complete, God had told us everything He wanted us to know. In view of this, a key interpretive principle is that we should always interpret the Old Testament in view of the greater light of the New Testament.

8. Distinguish between the descriptive and the prescriptive. When reading the Bible, a key question to ask is this: Is the Bible verse in question merely *describing* something that took place in biblical times, or is it *prescribing* something that Christians should be doing for all time?

9. Realize that some biblical truths are explicit; others are implicit. *Explicit* refers to that which is fully and clearly expressed, leaving nothing implied; *implicit,* by contrast, refers to that which is implied or understood though not directly expressed. For example, the Bible explicitly teaches that God created the heavens and the earth (Genesis 1:1). By contrast, the Bible implies but never directly states some truths, such as the doctrine of the Trinity—the doctrine that there is one God, but that within the unity of the one God are three co-equal and co-eternal persons: the Father, the Son, and the Holy Spirit (Matthew 28:19; 2 Corinthians 13:14).

10. Distinguish between promises and principles. We must be cautious to distinguish between promises and principles in the Bible. Many wisdom sayings in the book of Proverbs,

for example, are not intended to be promises. The book of Proverbs is a wisdom book and contains maxims of moral wisdom intended to guide one's life.

11. Affirm the benefit of proper interpretation. Since God is the ultimate author of Scripture (2 Timothy 3:16), we should do everything in our power to make sure we understand it rightly. After all, God's Word shows us how to live optimally during our time on earth and how to ensure eternal life in God's presence following the moment of death. Join me in resolving to make every effort to correctly understand every verse in the Bible.

Let's proceed to make sense of some of the difficult verses of Scripture.

The
OLD TESTAMENT

Genesis

Genesis 1—*Are the days of creation 24-hour periods or long ages?*

Many today find theological support for the idea that the days in Genesis are long periods of time. For example, in Genesis 2:4 (KJV) *day* refers to the entire time frame during which God created. In Job 20:28 *day* refers to the time of God's wrath. In Psalm 20:1 (KJV) *day* refers to a time of trouble. Moreover, in Psalm 90:4 and 2 Peter 3:8 we are told, "With the Lord a day is like a thousand years, and a thousand years are like a day." Besides, the sun was not created until the fourth day of creation, so the first three days couldn't have been literal 24-hour solar days.

Contrary to this position, many other Christians provide substantive arguments that the days of Genesis 1 are literal 24-hour periods:

1. The Genesis account makes reference to evening and morning, indicating that literal days are meant (Genesis 1:5).

2. Genesis tells us that God created the sun to rule the day and the moon to rule the night. This would seem to indicate that the days were literal solar days (Genesis 1:16).

3. Solar days seem to be implied in Exodus 20:11, where we are told that "in six days the LORD made the heavens and the earth, the sea, and all that is in them, but he rested on the seventh day."

4. Whenever a number is used with the Hebrew word for *day* (*yom*), it always refers to a literal solar day (without exception in the Old Testament). Genesis says that God created the universe in six days, so it must have meant literal solar days.

5. If Genesis had intended to communicate that God created

in long periods, a perfectly acceptable Hebrew word would have been ideal to communicate this concept: *olam*. But this word is not used. *Yom* is used, and as noted above, *yom* with a number always refers to a 24-hour day.

6. Second Peter 3:8 does not indicate that a day for God actually lasts a thousand years. Rather it says that a day is *like* a thousand years. God is above the limitations of time.

7. The Genesis account indicates that Adam was created on day six, and he then lived on through day seven and continued to live in the days that followed. If the days of Genesis were long ages, how can these many thousands of years be reconciled with the biblical statement that Adam died at age 930 (Genesis 5:5)?

8. The argument that the first three days could not have been literal days because the sun was not created until day four is not convincing. The first three days were probably the same length of time as the last four days. The exact same kinds of descriptive words are used to describe *all* the days—words like *evening* and *morning*. Some believe God created a temporary localized source of light in heaven (see Genesis 1:3) which, as the earth rotated, gave the appearance of light for the day and darkness for the night, all within a 24-hour period. God Himself could have been the light (see Revelation 21:23; 22:5).

Genesis 1—*How can the creation account be reconciled with what scientists say about the immense age of the universe?*

Scientists typically argue for the theory of uniformitarianism—the idea that the geological, biological, and astronomical processes that we now observe in our present universe operated identically in the past at the same strength and intensity. If this is correct, this would seem to indicate that millions of years would have been necessary to produce such things as fossils, volcanoes, and mountains.

Creationists suggest that one ought not to quickly assume uniformitarianism for earth's past. They suggest that the overwhelming force of a universal flood during Noah's time, combined with the rapid extermination of innumerable plants and animals, was undoubtedly a voluminous producer of thick sediments that entrapped plants and animals. The fossils formed quickly. They thus suggest that the geological column is a record of what transpired in rapid fashion during the flood, not over millions of years.

Genesis 1—*Is the creation account compatible with theistic evolution?*

Theistic evolutionists argue that God began creation and then directed and controlled the processes of evolution to produce the universe as we know it today. He allegedly entered into the process of time on occasion to modify what was developing. Most theistic evolutionists hold to the day-age theory—the idea that each of the days of Genesis refer to a long age of time.

Theistic evolutionists typically deny the historicity of Adam and Eve. They generally argue that at some point in the process of evolution, God modified an already-existing higher primate (an ape), put a soul within it, and transformed it into Adam "in the image of God." In this view, then, God directly created the spiritual nature of humanity, but the physical nature was a product of evolution.

This view has several problems:

1. Theistic evolution makes a complete allegory out of Genesis 1–2. However, nothing in the context of Genesis indicates it is to be taken as anything less than history.

2. The suggestion that humanity is derived from a nonhuman ancestor cannot be reconciled with a correct understanding of Genesis 2:7. God created Adam's material nature from the dust of the ground. This indicates that God formed Adam from inorganic material rather than obtaining it from some previously living form (like an ape). God then breathed the breath of life into Adam.

3. Christ, as God, is all-knowing. Christ, as God, is also the Creator of the universe (see John 1:3; Colossians 1:16; Hebrews 1:2,10). Jesus the Creator affirmed that Adam was created not only in the image and likeness of God (spiritually) but also male and female (physically) (Matthew 19:4). This affirmation from Christ would be quite misleading if in fact the physical nature of man was actually derived from a higher primate that was modified.

4. The apostle Paul teaches in 1 Corinthians 15:39 that "all flesh is not the same: Men have one kind of flesh, animals have another, birds another and fish another." Man was not created from an ape. Rather, humans and apes have an entirely different "flesh." This verse cannot be made to agree with theistic evolution.

Genesis 1–2—*Were human beings or animals created first?*

Some argue that in Genesis 1 the animals are portrayed as being created before man, whereas Genesis 2 says that man was created before the animals. There is no real contradiction, however, since Genesis 2 does not affirm precisely when God created the animals. All it says is that God brought the animals to Adam so Adam might name them. The proper way to understand Genesis 2 is that God brought the animals He had formerly created to Adam so Adam could name them.

Genesis 1:1—*How could the author of Genesis know how the universe was created if he wasn't there to witness it?*

The Bible is a book of divine revelation. God Himself gave special revelation to Moses (the author of Genesis) regarding how He created the universe.

Genesis 1:14—*How could there be light prior to the appearance of the sun on the fourth day?*

This light may be totally unrelated to the sun. The universe includes a number of sources of light, and God Himself is a source of light (Revelation 21:23; 22:5). Some Bible expositors believe the sun existed from the first day, but its light appeared on the fourth day as the mist of creation dissipated.

Genesis 1:26-27—What does "in the image of God" mean?

Scripture indicates that man was created in God's image in the sense that he is a finite reflection of the infinite God in his rational nature (Colossians 3:10), in his moral nature (Ephesians 4:24), and in his dominion over creation (Genesis 1:27-28). In the same way that the moon reflects the brilliant light of the sun, so finite man—as created in God's image—is a reflection of God in these aspects.

Genesis 1:26-27—Why are plural pronouns used in reference to God?

In this passage we read: "Then God said, 'Let us make man in our image, in our likeness.'" The word used of God in Genesis 1:26-27 is *Elohim,* and it has a plural ending (*-im*). This is a "plural of majesty"— pointing to the majesty, dignity, and greatness of God. The plural pronouns *us* and *our* are grammatical necessities required by the plural Hebrew noun *Elohim.* In other words, the plural pronoun *us* corresponds grammatically with the plural form of the Hebrew word *Elohim.* One demands the other.

Genesis 1:26-27—Does this passage indicate God has a physical body?

Man is physical, and man is made in God's image (Genesis 1:26-27), so does this verse mean God has a physical body? No! A fundamental interpretive principle is that Scripture interprets Scripture. John 4:24 indicates that God is Spirit. Luke 24:39 tells us that a spirit does not have flesh and bones. Man was created in God's image in the sense that he is a finite reflection of God in his rational nature (Colossians 3:10), moral nature (Ephesians 4:24), and dominion over creation (Genesis 1:27-28).

Genesis 2:2—*Does the fact that God had to rest after six days of creation mean He is not all-powerful?*

God didn't have to rest in the sense that His physical energy had become depleted and He needed to recuperate. Rather, the Hebrew word for rest communicates the idea of ceasing from activity. Genesis 2:2 is simply saying that God completed His work of creation and then stopped. There was nothing further to do. The job was done.

Genesis 2:17—*Did Adam die the same day he sinned, as God promised?*

Genesis 5:5 says Adam lived to the age of 930 years. So, Adam did not die physically the same day he sinned. There is no real contradiction, however, since Adam and Eve did die spiritually the day they ate the fruit.

The word *death* carries the idea of separation. Physical death involves the separation of the soul or spirit from the body. Spiritual death involves the separation of the human being from God. When Adam and Eve partook of the forbidden fruit, they were immediately separated from God in a spiritual sense. Their consequent action of trying to hide from God in the Garden of Eden indicates their awareness of this spiritual separation. The moment of their sin, they became "dead...in transgressions and sins" (Ephesians 2:1-3). Their spiritual separation from God eventually led to their physical deaths.

Genesis 4:3-5—*Why did God accept Abel's offering but reject Cain's?*

The answer to this question is found in the attitude that each displayed in regard to their respective offerings. Abel gave not only the firstborn of his flock but also the choicest of the firstborn (Genesis 4:4). He gave the "best of the best" that was in his possession. By contrast, Cain brought "some of the fruits of the soil" (verse 3). One gets the feeling that Cain routinely gathered some fruit and offered it to the Lord to outwardly fulfill his obligation.

Abel's faith in God was another key factor (Hebrews 11:4). Cain, by contrast, was apparently characterized by unbelief.

Genesis 4:13-16—*What was the mark of Cain?*

This passage tells us that God put a mark on Cain so no one who encountered him would kill him. Scripture does not specify what this mark was. Scripture's omission in informing us about the nature of the mark is probably meant to point us away from the mark itself and to the graciousness of God in protecting someone who didn't deserve it. In other words, God and His graciousness are on center stage, not the mark.

Sadly, we must note that this passage has been misused in church history in a variety of ways. At one time during the Middle Ages, for example, people who called themselves Christians labeled Jews as "murderers of Christ" and forced them to wear a "mark of Cain." What a tragic misapplication.

Genesis 4:17—*Where did Cain get his wife?*

The biblical text implies that Cain married one of his sisters. Several facts lead us to this conclusion. First, Adam and Eve had a number of children. Genesis 5:4 says, "After Seth was born, Adam lived 800 years and had other sons and daughters." Adam and Eve were the first man and woman, and God had commanded them (and their descendants) to be fruitful and multiply (Genesis 1:28), so we can reasonably conclude that Cain married one of his many sisters. He possibly could have married a niece or even a grandniece.

One must keep in mind that in the early years of the human race, no genetic defects had yet developed as a result of the fall of man. By the time of Abraham, God had not yet declared this kind of marriage to be contrary to His will (see Genesis 20:12). Laws governing incest apparently did not become enacted until the time of Moses (Leviticus 18:7-17; 20:11-12,14,17,20-21). No prohibition regarding marrying a sister (or a niece or grandniece) existed in the days of Cain.

Genesis 5—*Did people actually live for centuries in the early years of humanity?*

In Genesis 5 we read that Adam lived 930 years, Seth lived 912 years, Enosh lived 905 years, and so on. Nothing in Genesis 5 indicates this chapter is to be taken less than literally. We are left to conclude that people really did live that long during the early years of humanity. As to why this was the case, many have suggested that prior to the flood, a water canopy surrounded the earth (Genesis 1:7), and this canopy served to protect the inhabitants of earth from harmful radiation in outer space. People accordingly lived longer. Also, prior to the flood, people may primarily have been vegetarians and not meat eaters (see Genesis 9:3), and perhaps this too contributed to the longer lives. All this points to the truth of Psalm 139:14 that human beings are fearfully and wonderfully made.

Genesis 6–8—*What was the actual source of the floodwaters?*

One verse in Genesis tells us the floodwaters came from rain, while another says the floodwaters came from rain *and* the waters of the earth (Genesis 7:4; 8:2). Correctly interpreted, there is no contradiction. These verses would contradict if Genesis 7:4 said rain would be the *only* source of water, but it does not say that. Taken together, these are complementary verses.

Genesis 6–9—*Was the flood universal or local?*

The flood appears to have been universal. The waters climbed so high on the earth that "all the high mountains under the entire heavens were covered" (Genesis 7:19). They rose so greatly on the earth that they "covered the mountains to a depth of more than twenty feet" (verse 20). The floodwaters prevailed for nearly 54 weeks, indicating more than just local flooding.

The Bible also says that every living thing that moved on the earth perished, "the creatures that swarm over the earth, and all mankind. Everything on dry land that had the breath of life in its nostrils died. Every living thing on the face of the earth was wiped out...Only Noah was left, and those with him in the ark" (verses 22-23). The language of Genesis 6–9 clearly points to a universal flood.

The universal view best explains the source of the worldwide distribution of diluvia deposits. A universal flood would also explain the sudden death of many woolly mammoths frozen in Alaskan and Siberian ice. Investigation shows that these animals died suddenly by choking or drowning and not by freezing.

Genesis 6:2—*Are the "sons of God" evil angels?*

This verse tells us that "the sons of God saw that the daughters of men were beautiful, and they married any of them they chose." There is much debate as to the identity of these sons of God. A common view is that some evil angels cohabited with human women. These facts support this position:

1. Some manuscripts of the Septuagint (an early Greek translation of the Hebrew Old Testament) have the phrase "angels of God" instead of "sons of God." The early Jews understood this phrase to be referring to angels.

2. The Hebrew phrase for "sons of God" (more literally, "sons of Elohim") always refers to angels when used elsewhere in the Old Testament (see Job 1:6; 2:1; 38:7, KJV).

3. The "evil angel" interpretation of Genesis 6 may give us a clue as to why some angels are presently bound in prison and others are not (2 Peter 2:4).

Another view is that some fallen angels possessed human men. This view has the merit of providing a good explanation of how angels who are bodiless (Hebrews 1:14) and sexless (Matthew 22:30) could cohabit with human women.

Still another common interpretation is that the phrase "sons of God" refers to members of the godly line of Seth (the Redeemer's line—Genesis 4:26) who intermingled with the godless line of Cain. Instead of remaining true to God and loyal to their spiritual heritage, they allowed themselves to be enticed by the beauty of ungodly women who followed the tradition and example of Cain. In support of this view, God sometimes calls men His sons (Isaiah 43:6).

Genesis 6:3—*Does this verse mean man's life span is 120 years?*

In this verse the Lord affirms, "My Spirit will not contend with man forever, for he is mortal; his days will be a hundred and twenty years." This is not likely to refer to man's life span, for people later than this time lived up to 600 years. Apparently, the 120 years refers to the time God would allow before He sent the flood on humankind. God thus provided plenty of time for humans to repent before sending judgment.

Genesis 6:6—*In what sense did God repent?*

In this verse we read, "It repented the LORD that he had made man on the earth, and it grieved him at his heart" (KJV). God does not repent in the human sense of turning from sin. The word *repent,* when used of God, generally refers to a change in God's course of action due to something human beings have done. For example, God promised to judge the Ninevites, but then God changed His mind (repented) and withheld judgment after the entire city itself repented (Jonah 3:10 KJV). Many people fail to realize that God has what we might call a built-in repentance clause to His promises of judgment. This clause is found in Jeremiah 18:7-10:

> If at any time I announce that a nation or kingdom is to
> be uprooted, torn down and destroyed, and if that nation I
> warned repents of its evil, then I will relent and not inflict
> on it the disaster I had planned. And if at another time I
> announce that a nation or kingdom is to be built up and
> planted, and if it does evil in my sight and does not obey me,
> then I will reconsider the good I had intended to do for it.

So God changes His policy toward man when He sees a change in their actions.

Genesis 6:14-17—*How could Noah's Ark hold enough animals?*

The ark was an extremely large vessel—450 feet long, 75 feet wide, and 45 feet high. It had 1.5 million cubic feet, with three stories. It therefore had plenty of room to carry a very large body of animals.

Genesis 7:24—*Did the flood rains fall for 40 days or 150 days?*

Genesis 7:24 speaks of waters on the earth for 150 days, but other verses say 40 days (7:4,12,17). Actually, these numbers are referring to different things. The rain fell for only 40 days (7:12), but the water flooded the earth for 150 days (7:24). After the 150 days, the waters began to decrease (8:3). During the fifth month after the flood began, the ark rested on the mountains of Ararat (8:4).

Genesis 9:6—*How can capital punishment be justified in view of God's command not to murder (Exodus 20:13)?*

In Genesis 9:6 capital punishment was instituted in view of the sanctity of human life. The underlying basis for this severe punishment is the fact that man was made in the image of God (Genesis 1:26). Man is so valuable as an individual that anyone who tampers with his sacred right to live must face the consequences of losing his own life. The worth of the individual is so great that the highest penalty is attached to those who tamper with the life of even one man. This was true in the Old Testament, and it is true today. Murder is an outrage against God.

Certainly the death penalty was incorporated into the Mosaic code (see Exodus 21:12; Numbers 35:16-31). And in Romans 13:1-7 the apostle Paul taught that human government has a God-given right to use force in its resistance of evil and to take the life of a criminal. Second Peter 2:13 indicates that one of the purposes of government is to punish those who do evil, and capital punishment is evidently one of the ways this purpose is to be carried out.

It is true that one of the Ten Commandments says we are not to murder (Exodus 20:13). However, a murder by a citizen and an execution by the government are two different things in Scripture. One is a premeditated crime; the other is a deserved punishment. Government is set up by God (Romans 13:1-7), so capital punishment may be viewed as the enacting of divine judgment through the instrumentality of human government.

Genesis 12:10-20—*Why did God allow Abraham to prosper by lying?*

The biblical text does not say Abraham prospered at God's hand by lying. The text reveals that Pharaoh gave Abraham material gifts probably to make amends for unwittingly taking his wife into his palace. After all, adultery was condemned by Egyptian religious law. We might also note that some of the trouble Abraham experienced in the years that ensued may have been a direct result of his failure to trust in God's protective power instead of lying.

Genesis 15:17—*Is the Bible not to be trusted since it uses unscientific language such as "the sun went down" (KJV)?*

We all know the sun does not literally go down. The earth revolves and merely gives the appearance of the sun going down. However, even modern meteorologists refer to sunrise and sunset. The Bible also uses this nonliteral language as an accepted means of communication.

Genesis 16:1-4—*Why did Abraham agree to sire a son with Hagar when Sarah was still alive?*

What Abraham did was wrong and was not sanctioned by God. In their limited understanding, however, Abraham and Sarah may have thought it was the right thing to do. One primary purpose of marriage in Abraham's day was to give birth to a son. Abraham was 85 years old and did not have one. Moreover, women during that time either attained or lost status depending on whether they had children. Such facts may have led Abraham and Sarah to conclude that perhaps a son through Hagar would solve all their problems. In this case, Hagar would essentially act as a surrogate mother who would bear a child, after which time the child would be raised by Sarah. Of course, Scripture goes on to indicate that Hagar's offspring was not the child of promise (Genesis 17:21).

Genesis 19:8—*Was the sin of Sodom homosexuality or inhospitality?*

In this verse we read Lot's words to some wicked men regarding Lot's male visitors: "Look, I have two daughters who have never slept with a man. Let me bring them out to you, and you can do what you like with them. But don't do anything to these men, for they have come under the protection of my roof." Some have argued that the sin of Sodom and Gomorrah was inhospitality, not homosexuality. The request of the men of the city to "know" the men in Lot's house allegedly means they wanted to get acquainted (Genesis 19:5 KJV) because the Hebrew word for *know* (*yadha*) generally has no sexual connotations whatsoever (see Psalm 139:1).

It is true that the Hebrew word *yadha* does not necessarily mean, to have sex with; nonetheless, in the present context of Sodom and Gomorrah, it clearly has this meaning. This is evident for several reasons. First, 10 of the 12 times this word is used in Genesis it refers to sexual intercourse (see Genesis 4:1,25 KJV). Second, it means to know sexually in this very chapter, for Lot refers to his two virgin daughters as not having known a man (19:8 KJV), which is an obvious sexual use of the word. Third, the meaning of a word is discovered by the context in which it is used, and the context here is definitely sexual, as is indicated by the reference to the wickedness of the city (18:20) and the virgins offered to appease their passions (19:8). Fourth, *know* cannot mean simply to get acquainted with because it is equated with wickedness (19:7).

Genesis 22:2—*Did God intend for Abraham to kill his son?*

The context of Genesis 22 makes it clear that God never intended for this command to be executed. God restrained Abraham's hand just in the nick of time: " 'Do not lay a hand on the boy,' he said. 'Do not do anything to him. Now I know that you fear God, because you have not withheld from me your son, your only son'" (Genesis 22:12). Scholars agree that God was only testing Abraham's faith. The test served to show that Abraham loved God more than he loved his own son.

Genesis 32:30—*How can this verse affirm that Jacob saw God when John 1:18 asserts that no one has seen God?*

John 1:18 affirms that no one has ever seen God in His full glory, for if that were to occur, the human being beholding God would die instantly. In Genesis 32:30, Jacob merely interacted with a *theophany*—an appearance of God that shielded His intrinsic overpowering glory. God never appeared to human beings either in the Old Testament or the New Testament in His full glory, for He is aware of our finite limitations as creatures.

Exodus

Exodus 1:20-21—*How could God render kindness to the midwives after they blatantly lied to Pharaoh?*

Scripture forbids lying (Exodus 20:16). Lying is viewed as a sin (Psalm 59:12) and is an abomination to God (Proverbs 12:22 KJV). God never lies (Numbers 23:19). Righteous men hate lying (Proverbs 13:5).

Yet some Scriptures indicate that under certain circumstances, lying is not condemned. The midwives found themselves in a moral dilemma. Would they obey God's higher law of saving lives or the lesser obligation of submitting to the dictates of Pharaoh? The midwives chose to obey God's higher law. The saving of innocent lives was a higher obligation than obeying and telling the truth to the government. God thus did not hold the midwives responsible for what they did. In fact, the text tells us that God blessed them "because the midwives feared God" (Exodus 1:21). Their fear of God caused them to obey the high law of saving lives.

Exodus 3:1-2—*Who is the angel of the Lord that appeared to Moses in the burning bush?*

Appearances of this "angel" in Old Testament times were apparently preincarnate appearances of Jesus Christ, the second person of the Godhead. (*Preincarnate* means before becoming a human being.)

When the word *angel* is used in reference to Christ in the Old Testament, it indicates not a created being (like other angels) but—true to its Hebrew root—a messenger, one who is sent, or an envoy. Christ as the angel of the Lord was sent by the Father as a messenger or envoy to accomplish specific tasks in Old Testament times.

How do we know the angel of the Lord (or, more literally, angel of Yahweh) was actually the preincarnate Christ?

1. The angel of Yahweh is God. He makes claims to deity. For example, He identifies Himself as God to Moses (Exodus 3:6).

2. The angel of Yahweh is distinct from Yahweh. In Zechariah 1:12 we find the angel of Yahweh interceding to another person called Yahweh on behalf of the people of Jerusalem and Judah. This is much like the Jesus of the New Testament, who regularly prays to the Father for His people (John 17; Hebrews 7:25; 1 John 2:1).

3. The angel of the Lord must be the preincarnate Christ by virtue of what we learn of the Father, Son, and Holy Spirit in Scripture:

Christ is the visible God of the New Testament, but neither the Father (John 1:18; 5:37; Colossians 1:15; 1 Timothy 1:17; 6:16) nor the Holy Spirit (John 3:8; 14:17) characteristically manifest themselves visibly. Only Jesus took on visible, bodily form (John 1:14; see also Colossians 2:9). We can reasonably assume a consistency between the Old and New Testaments, with Christ being the visible manifestation of God in both Testaments.

Both the angel and Jesus were sent by the Father—one in the Old Testament (Judges 13:8-9), the other in the New (John 3:17).

The angel of the Lord and Christ engaged in amazingly similar ministries. For example, both were involved in revealing truth (Daniel 4:13,17,23; 8:16; 9:21; John 1:1,14,18) and delivering the enslaved (Exodus 3; Galatians 1:4; 1 Thessalonians 1:10; 2 Timothy 4:18; Hebrews 2:14-15).

The angel of the Lord no longer appears after the Incarnation. It is true that Scripture says that *an* angel of the Lord (Gabriel) appeared to Joseph (Matthew 1:20), *an* angel of the Lord spoke to Philip (Acts 8:26), and *an* angel of the Lord released Peter (Acts 12:7), but not *the* angel of the Lord. *The* angel of the Lord in the Old Testament is not the same as *an* angel of the Lord in the New Testament. To be fair, I should note that the King James Version mentions *the* angel of the Lord nine times in the New Testament. In all but one of these (Matthew 1:24), however, the Greek does not include the definite article, so "*an* angel of the Lord" is a more accurate translation (and is reflected in other translations of the Bible). The reference to *the* angel of the Lord in Matthew 1:24 is the same as *an* angel of the Lord in Matthew 1:20, whom, most scholars believe, was the same angel who spoke to Mary—that is, Gabriel (compare with Luke 1:26-33).

Exodus 3:22—*How could a loving God instruct His people to plunder the Egyptians?*

For more than 400 years, the Israelites had been in bondage in Egypt, forced into slavery, forced to engage in hard labor without any pay whatsoever. The items of silver and gold could thus be considered "back pay" that was justly due to the Israelites.

Besides, God did not command the Israelites to plunder the Egyptians in the sense of taking items of value against the will of the Egyptians. Rather, God instructed the Israelites to *ask* for items of value, and God Himself gave them favor in the eyes of the Egyptians so that they would leave Egypt with many items of value. Clearly, this is not plundering as normally understood.

Exodus 4:21—*Did God harden Pharaoh's heart?*

Ten times in Scripture we are told that Pharaoh hardened his own heart (Exodus 7:13-14,22; 8:15,19,32; 9:7,34-35; 13:15), and ten times we read that God hardened Pharaoh's heart (4:21; 7:3; 9:12; 10:1,20,27; 11:10; 14:4,8,17). Pharaoh hardened his own heart seven times *before* God first hardened it, though the prediction that God would do it preceded all.

The whole of Scripture seems to indicate that God hardens on the same grounds as showing mercy. If men will accept mercy, He will give it to them. If they will not, thus hardening themselves, He is only just and righteous in judging them. Mercy is the effect of a right attitude; hardening is the effect of stubbornness or a wrong attitude toward God. For example, imagine some clay and some wax sitting in the sun. The same sunshine hardens one and softens the other. The responsibility is with the materials, not with the sun. Scholars have suggested that the danger of resisting God is that He will eventually give us over to our own choices (see Romans 1:24-28).

Exodus 4:24—*Why did God almost kill Moses?*

Moses had failed to circumcise his male child, something that was a requirement in the covenant community of Israel. How could Moses lead the covenant community of Israel if he himself was living in disobedience to God and His covenant? Moses' failure nearly led to his death. Zipporah, his wife, intervened in the nick of time and circumcised the boy.

Exodus 4:25—*Why was it necessary for male children to be circumcised in Old Testament times?*

Circumcision (Hebrew: *mula;* Greek: *peritome*) means a cutting around). The Old Testament ceremony of circumcision consisted of cutting away the foreskin of the male organ with a sharp knife or stone (Exodus 4:25; Joshua 5:2). The son's father usually performed the ritual, although any Israelite could do it (but never a Gentile).

After God made a covenant with Abraham (Genesis 15), He commanded that every male should be circumcised as a token of the covenant. Everyone not so circumcised was to be "cut off from his people" as having broken the covenant (Genesis 17:10-14).

Exodus 7:11—*How could Pharaoh's wise men and sorcerers perform the same feats of power that God told Moses to perform?*

The Bible indicates that one of Satan's tactics in his effort to deceive humankind is to employ counterfeit miracles (see 2 Thessalonians

2:9). Our passage states that the feats of Pharaoh's magicians were performed by their "secret arts."

Some commentators believe the feats of the magicians were merely tricks. Perhaps the magicians had enchanted snakes so that they became stiff and appeared to be rods. When cast down on the floor, they came out of their trance and began to move as snakes. Others say these were acts of Satan who actually turned the rods of the magicians into snakes. This, however, does not seem plausible in view of the fact that only God can create life, as even the magicians later recognized (Exodus 8:18-19).

Of course, Pharaoh's magicians sought to show that they possessed as much power as Moses and Aaron and that Pharaoh did not need to let Israel go. They were successful with the first three encounters (Aaron's rod, the plague of blood, and the plague of frogs). However, when Moses and Aaron, by the power of God, produced lice from the sand, the magicians were not able to counterfeit this miracle. They could only exclaim, "This is the finger of God" (Exodus 8:19). They knew only God could create life.

Note also that though the magicians could turn their rods into snakes, their rods were swallowed up by Aaron's rod, indicating superiority. Though the magicians could turn water to blood, they could not reverse the process. Though the magicians could bring forth frogs, they could not get rid of them. Their acts were *supernormal* but not *supernatural*.

Exodus 9:3,6; 14:9—*Did all of Egypt's horses die?*

Moses gave Pharaoh this warning: "The hand of the LORD will bring a terrible plague on your livestock in the field—on your horses and donkeys and camels and on your cattle and sheep and goats." Exodus 9:6 then tells us that "all the livestock of the Egyptians died." The problem is that according to Exodus 14:9, sometime later "the Egyptians—all Pharaoh's horses and chariots, horsemen and troops—pursued the Israelites and overtook them as they camped by the sea near Pi Hahiroth." How is the conflict to be explained?

We can make several observations. It is well-known that Scripture sometimes uses the word *all* in a less than total sense. The term could mean all in a certain area (of Egypt). Or it could mean all in a general sense—that is, the death toll was so near-complete that the term *all* is appropriate.

Another important observation is that Exodus 9:3 explicitly tells us that the plague affected the livestock that were *in the field.* Not all livestock were in the field. Some were contained in barns or military forts.

The Israelite horses were not affected by this plague, so perhaps the Egyptians stole horses from them following the plague that fell on the Egyptian livestock.

Exodus 12—*What is the significance of Passover?*

The Passover is the most significant event in Israel's religious history. This festival celebrates the escape of the Jews from Egypt under the leadership of Moses.

Passover was celebrated the evening before the fourteenth day of Nisan (see Exodus 12:3-11). Each family sacrificed a lamb to commemorate the sacrifice that took place just prior to the Israelites' exodus from Egypt. On that occasion, God literally "passed over" each Israelite house that had the blood of a lamb sprinkled on the doorpost. The lives of the firstborn children of Israel were thereby spared.

During the Passover meal and throughout the following week, Israelites ate unleavened bread (see Exodus 23:15). This type of bread was made without yeast and was prepared very quickly. It reminded those celebrating Passover of the hurried preparations that were made when Pharaoh finally allowed the Israelites to leave Egypt.

Exodus 14—*Are critical and liberal explanations of the Israelites' crossing of the Red Sea viable?*

Critical and liberal scholars have attempted to explain away the Israelites' crossing of the Red Sea. But none of their explanations are viable. Some suggest that the place at the Red Sea where they crossed was very shallow. Others suggest that a strong natural wind accounted for the dividing of the waters. Still others suggest that a volcanic eruption sent a blast of wind across the land that temporarily separated the Red Sea.

Such suggestions fail to do justice to the biblical data. First, if the Israelites crossed at a shallow part of the Red Sea, how did the Egyptian soldiers drown when they were in pursuit (Exodus 14:28; 15:4-6)? A strong natural wind couldn't have caused this phenomenon because the natural winds in this area flow north and south; the wind that separated the Red Sea blew from the east—something that is completely unnatural. It is also impossible that a natural wind could have created two walls of water that ran through the Red Sea. Moreover, a single blast from a volcano cannot explain what happened because the separation of the Red Sea had to last long enough for more than two million people to cross. (And besides, a volcano blast would have incinerated the Israelites.) Clearly, what happened at the Red Sea was a supernatural miracle.

Exodus 15:11—*If there is only one God, why did Moses refer to gods?*

Moses asked, "Who among the gods is like you, O LORD?" Moses often used this kind of rhetorical question to emphasize the absolute incomparability of God in the face of the many false gods of pagan cultures—especially Egypt, where he grew up and where he eventually took a stand against Pharaoh and the false gods of Egypt. Of course, the implied answer to the rhetorical question is that no one in all the universe is like God.

Exodus 19:16-20—*Did Moses encounter a UFO on Mount Sinai?*

In this passage we read of thunder and lightning, a thick cloud over the mountain, a very loud trumpet blast, fire, and the whole mountain trembling violently. Some misunderstand this verse to mean that Moses encountered a UFO with aliens on Mount Sinai, and he mistook the aliens for God.

Such a view is ridiculous. Exodus 19:16-20 is not a description of a spacecraft landing on Mount Sinai but a record of God Himself coming down onto the mountain. The Lord had told Moses He would come down onto Mount Sinai "on the third day" (Exodus 19:11). This was in contrast to pagan deities who supposedly dwelt on the mountains. (For example, Greek gods were believed to live on Mount Olympus.) Scripture depicts God as dwelling in heaven (1 Kings 8:30-49; John 8:23), so He would have to "come down" in order to meet the people on the mountain. As promised, on the third day God descended to Mount Sinai and gave an awesome display of His power and majesty (Exodus 19:16-19).

Exodus 20:8-11—*Are New Testament believers to worship on the Sabbath or the Lord's Day?*

The Hebrew word for *Sabbath* means cessation. The Sabbath was a holy day and a day of rest for both human beings and animals (Exodus 20:8-11). This day was to commemorate God's rest after His work of creation (Genesis 2:2). God set the pattern for living—working six days and resting on the seventh. The Sabbath thus finds its ultimate origin in the creation account.

At Mount Sinai, the Sabbath—already in existence—formally became a part of the law (it is one of the Ten Commandments) and a sign of God's covenant relationship with Israel. Keeping the Sabbath was a sign that showed submission to God, and honoring it brought great blessing (Isaiah 58:13). By contrast, to break the Sabbath law was to rebel against Him and warranted the death penalty (see Exodus 31:14-15). God provided detailed instructions for Sabbath observance in Leviticus 25, Numbers 15:32-36, and Deuteronomy 5:13-15.

Keeping the Sabbath, however, is the only one of the Ten Commandments not repeated after the Day of Pentecost (Acts 2). The early church made Sunday (the first day) the day of worship for a number of reasons:

- New Testament believers are not under the Old Testament law (Romans 6:14; 2 Corinthians 3:7-11; Galatians 3:24-25; Hebrews 7:12).

- Jesus rose from the dead and appeared to some of His followers on the first day of the week (Sunday) (Matthew 28:1).

- Jesus continued His appearances on succeeding Sundays (John 20:26).

- The descent of the Holy Spirit took place on Pentecost, which was a Sunday (Acts 2:1).

- The early church was thus given the pattern of Sunday worship, and this they continued to do regularly (Acts 20:7; 1 Corinthians 16:2).

- Jesus appeared to John on "the Lord's day" (Revelation 1:10).

- In Colossians 2:16 we read, "Therefore do not let anyone judge you by what you eat or drink, or with regard to a religious festival, a New Moon celebration or a Sabbath day." This verse indicates that the distinctive holy days of the Old Testament are no longer binding on New Testament believers.

Exodus 20:13—*In view of God's command not to murder, how can war ever be justified?*

The difference between murder and war is substantial. Scripture indicates that sometimes war is necessary.

The Bible records many accounts of fighting and warfare. The providence of God in war is exemplified by His name YHWH Sabaoth (the LORD of hosts—see Joshua 5:14 NASB). God is portrayed as the omnipotent Warrior-Leader of the Israelites. God, the LORD of hosts, raised up leaders among the Israelites called the *shophetim* (savior-deliverers). Samson, Deborah, Gideon, and others were anointed by the Spirit of God to conduct war. The New Testament commends Old Testament warriors for their military acts of faith (Hebrews 11:30-40). Moreover, neither the New Testament writers nor Jesus Himself instructed a military convert to resign from his line of work (Matthew 8:5-13; Luke 3:14).

The Bible also supports self-defense. Prior to His crucifixion, Jesus revealed to His disciples the future hostility they would face and encouraged them to sell their outer garments in order to purchase a sword (Luke 22:36-38; see also 2 Corinthians 11:26-27). This sword (Greek: *maxairan*) was a short blade that Jewish travelers used as protection against robbers and wild animals. This passage makes perfectly clear that Jesus approved of self-defense. Self-defense may actually result in one of the greatest examples of human love. Christ said, "Greater love has no one than this, that he lay down his life for his friends" (John 15:14), a verse which many scholars believe can be applied to laying down one's life while defending a friend from attackers. On a larger level, a just war is sometimes necessary when a bully nation invades a lesser nation in order to subjugate it. Defending the weaker nation in such a scenario has biblical support.

Exodus 21:23-25—*"An eye for an eye" seems a rather brutal rule to enforce in society.*

This law may seem to open the door to violence, but it was actually intended to limit brutality in society. Prior to the enforcement of this law, people had a tendency to go to extremes. Instead of an eye for an eye, people took a life for an eye. Instead of life for life, people took the life of an entire family for a person's lost life. This law served to restrict responses to personal injury.

Exodus 23:19—*Why was boiling a kid in its mother's milk forbidden?*

God gave this command probably because boiling a young goat in its mother's milk was a pagan, idolatrous practice engineered to invoke magic to bring about a more productive land. God did not want His people to be involved in any such idolatrous practices. Besides, this is a cruel practice.

Exodus 24:9-11—*How could people see God when God said in Exodus 33:20, "No man may see me and live"?*

In this passage we read, "Moses and Aaron, Nadab and Abihu, and the seventy elders of Israel went up and saw the God of Israel." This passage and other passages of Scripture (Exodus 33:19-20; Numbers 12:8) indicate that these people saw a limited and shielded visual representation of the glory of God. Recall that even when Moses asked to see God's glory (Exodus 33:18-23), he saw only a likeness of God and not His full essence. (See Numbers 12:8, where the Hebrew word *temunah,* meaning form or likeness is used.)

This is in keeping with the New Testament, where we are told that no one has seen God at any time (John 1:18 NASB). Only in heaven will believers see His face (Revelation 22:4). For "now we see but a poor reflection as in a mirror; then we shall see face to face" (1 Corinthians 13:12).

Exodus 33:11—*Since Moses spoke with God "face to face," are we actually able to see God?*

The apostle Paul tells us that God the Father is invisible (Colossians 1:15; 1 Timothy 1:17) and "lives in unapproachable light, whom no one has seen or can see" (1 Timothy 6:16). John's Gospel likewise tells us that "no one has ever seen God [the Father], but God the One and Only [Jesus Christ], who is at the Father's side, has made him known" (John 1:18). John 5:37 similarly tells us that no one has ever seen the Father's form, though people have been occasionally permitted to witness a limited and shielded visual representation of the glory of God (Exodus 33:18-23).

The phrase "face to face" (Exodus 33:11) is simply a figurative way of indicating that God communicated with Moses personally, directly, or intimately. Moses was in the direct presence of God and interacted with Him on a personal and intimate basis.

Exodus 33:21-23—*Does the fact that Moses saw God's back mean God has a physical body?*

In this passage the Lord says to Moses, "There is a place near me where you may stand on a rock. When my glory passes by, I will put you in a cleft in the rock and cover you with my hand until I have passed by. Then I will remove my hand and you will see my back; but my face must not be seen." We know from other passages that God is Spirit and formless (see Isaiah 31:3; John 4:24). Just as the word *hand* is an anthropomorphism, so are the words *back* and *face*. The Hebrew word for *back* can easily be rendered *aftereffects*. Moses did not see the glory of God directly or in its fullness, but once it had gone past, God did allow him to view the results, or the afterglow, of His glorious presence.

Leviticus

Leviticus 7:26-27—*Does this verse prohibit blood transfusions?*

In this passage we read, "Wherever you live, you must not eat the blood of any bird or animal. If anyone eats blood, that person must be cut off from his people." Some people have concluded that this verse prohibits blood transfusions, but such a view is a misinterpretation of the biblical text. Eating blood is entirely different from a blood transfusion. Eating blood involves partaking of blood as food through the mouth. A blood transfusion involves a transference of life-sustaining fluids.

The backdrop to this command is that some of the pagan nations surrounding Israel had no respect whatsoever for blood. They ate blood on a regular basis, sometimes as part of the worship of false gods and at other times because they thought it might bring them supernatural power. In any event, the prohibition against eating blood set Israel apart from such ungodly nations.

Leviticus 10:1-2—*Why were Nadab and Abihu killed by fire from God for offering "unauthorized fire before the LORD"?*

The sons of Aaron held a high and holy office, and yet they showed total disregard for God's commands. God judged them not only for their own sin but as a warning to the rest of Israel that God's priests must show respect to Him. Had God not judged them, other people would have begun showing disregard for God's commands.

Leviticus 11:5-6—*Why does the Bible contradict modern science in claiming that the hyrax and rabbit chew the cud?*

These animals do not chew the cud in the modern, technical sense, but they do engage in a chewing action that gives this appearance. Chewing the cud involves a process called *rumination*. Rabbits actually engage in a different process called *refection,* in which indigestible vegetable matter absorbs certain bacteria and is passed as droppings and then eaten again. The term *chewing the cud* in the Bible is used in a loose and inclusive sense and should not be pressed to be taken in its modern technical sense.

Leviticus 12:2-5—*Why were certain things categorized as unclean in Old Testament times?*

The ancient Jews believed that a number of things rendered a person unclean. A woman was ceremonially unclean during menstruation and following childbirth (Leviticus 12:2-5; Ezekiel 16:4). Touching a dead animal rendered one unclean (Leviticus 11:24-40), as did touching any dead body (Numbers 19:11). A person with a skin infection was considered unclean (Leviticus 13:3). Sexual discharges rendered one unclean (Leviticus 15:2). The Samaritans of New Testament times were considered unclean because they were a mixed breed, with Israelite and Assyrian ancestry (see John 4:9).

Once people were rendered unclean, they had to go through the purification rituals prescribed by the Mosaic law. For example, these rites purified people from skin diseases (Leviticus 13–14), sexual discharges (Leviticus 15), or contact with a dead body (Numbers 19:11-19).

Jesus taught that the truly unclean part of the human being is the heart, and the only possible cleansing for this condition comes by following Him (Mark 7:14-23; John 15:3) and being reborn (John 3:1-5; Titus 3:5).

Leviticus 17:11-12—*Does this passage prohibit blood transfusions?*

See comments on Leviticus 7:26-27.

Leviticus 18:22—*Have the laws against homosexuality been abolished along with other laws, such as those against eating pork?*

The laws against homosexual practices are not merely ceremonial (like the laws about eating pork). The inclusion of the Mosaic prohibition against homosexuality in Leviticus does not make it part of the ceremonial law that has passed away.

If laws against homosexuality were merely ceremonial (and therefore abolished), then laws against rape, incest, and bestiality also have passed away because these sins are found in the same chapter with homosexual sins (Leviticus 18:6-14,22-23). But the laws against rape, incest, and bestiality are still binding, so those dealing with homosexuality are as well.

Homosexual sins among Gentiles were also condemned by God (Romans 1:26), and Gentiles did not have the ceremonial law (which was for Jews alone) (Romans 2:12-15). This is the reason God brought judgment on the Canaanites (Genesis 18:1-3,25).

Furthermore, in the Jewish levitical law, the punishment for violating the ceremonial law of eating pork or shrimp (which was a few days in isolation) was different from the punishment for homosexuality (which was capital punishment) (Leviticus 18:29).

Finally, Jesus changed the dietary laws of the Old Testament (Mark 7:18; Acts 10:12), but the moral prohibitions against homosexuality are still enjoined in the New Testament (see Romans 1:26,27; 1 Corinthians 6:9; 1 Timothy 1:10; Jude 7).

Leviticus 23:27—*What is the Day of Atonement?*

The Day of Atonement was annually celebrated on the tenth day of the seventh month of the Jewish calendar—the month of Tishri (September/October). Only once a year could Aaron (or the high priest) enter into the Holy of Holies, the innermost part of the tabernacle, where the ark of the covenant was located. Before doing this, however, he had to secure forgiveness for his own sins. He did this by sacrificing a bull as a sin offering for himself and sprinkling some of the blood in front of the ark of the covenant. So insecure was the high priest, that a rope would be tied around his leg so that if he entered the Holy of Holies without taking care of all his sin and then died, the other priests could pull him out by the rope (see Leviticus 4:5; 16; 23:27).

Only after the high priest's sin had been forgiven could he then go on to offer sacrifices on behalf of the people of Israel. He would first kill a goat for the sins of the people. Then he laid his hands on a second goat and confessed Israel's sin, symbolically transferring the guilt of the people to it. Then it was driven into the desert to symbolize that the nation's sins had been carried away.

These sacrifices took place annually, reminding the Israelites year in and year out that their sin cut them off from God and that they regularly needed atonement. This makes the sacrifice of Christ all the more important, for His sacrifice was once for all, never again having to be repeated (see Hebrews 9:9,23-28).

Numbers

Numbers 4:3—*Why is the Levitical age of 30 in this verse contradicted by Numbers 8:24 (age 25) and Ezra 3:8 (age 20)?*

The type of service is different in each case. Numbers 4:3, which stipulates age 30, refers to those officially entering into the service to perform the business of the tabernacle. Numbers 8:24, which stipulates age 25, apparently refers to apprentices who engage in manual labor in the tabernacle while engaging in training, and who will later be admitted into the official business at age 30. Ezra 3:8, which stipulates age 20, refers to those who "oversee the work of the house of the LORD" (rebuilding the temple).

Numbers 11:31-34—*Why did God send a plague on the Israelites after giving them quail?*

The Israelites displayed increasing levels of disbelief and ingratitude. Numbers 11:1-3 reveals that the people engaged in complaining, which greatly displeased the Lord. This was a direct affront to God's provision for the people. Then, in verse 4, the people complained again because they wanted meat to eat instead of manna. Throughout the rest of the chapter, instead of thanking God for His provisions, the people continued to complain against God. God therefore chose to discipline His covenant community by sending a plague on them.

Let us not forget the teaching of Hebrews 12:6: "The Lord disciplines those he loves, and he punishes everyone he accepts as a son" (Proverbs 3:11-12).

Numbers 21:9—*Wasn't it idolatrous for Israel to construct a bronze serpent?*

Exodus 20:4 (NKJV), which prohibits making a carved image, has specific reference to the construction of idols. Numbers 21:9 is not about the construction of an idol but describes a symbol to which people could look in faith to be healed. It is true that the people later made this symbol into an idol, but this does not make the original symbol idolatrous, for it was not constructed for the purpose of idolatry.

Numbers 25:9—*Why are 24,000 said to have died at Baal-Peor, while 1 Corinthians 10:8 reports it as 23,000?*

Some Bible expositors believe 1 Corinthians speaks of the number of people who died in a single day, whereas Numbers 25 refers to the total number of casualties. Other Bible expositors suggest that perhaps two different events are in view. After all, 1 Corinthians refers to the casualties that resulted from God's judgment for worshipping the golden calf. Numbers 25 refers to the casualties of God's judgment for worshipping Baal at Baal-Peor.

Numbers 31—*How can the destruction of Midian be morally justified?*

The Midianites seduced the Israelites into gross fornication and idolatry (Numbers 25:1-9). The Midianites engaged in sexual orgies and ritual prostitution as a means of invoking the power of their pagan gods. Such unrelenting debauchery threatened the continued purity and even survival of God's people. God thus had no choice but to act.

God's judgment against Midian is comparable to radical surgery being performed on a cancer victim. If the cancer is not entirely excised, it will eventually kill the whole body. Likewise, had the Midian cancer not been excised, Israel's very survival was threatened.

Deuteronomy

Deuteronomy 5:6-21—*Why are the words of the Ten Commandments here not identical to those found in Exodus 20:2-17?*

Deuteronomy was never intended to be an exact repetition of the words found in Exodus, Leviticus, and Numbers. Rather, Deuteronomy was intended to be a selective paraphrase of certain relevant text found in these earlier books that would be especially helpful in preparing the chosen nation for the coming conquest and occupation of Canaan. Moses was not only reviewing important aspects of the law but also more fully explaining what all of it entailed, especially in regard to entering the promised land. As such, one ought not to be concerned about minor differences in phraseology between Deuteronomy 5:6-21 and Exodus 20:2-17, for no essential teaching in the two accounts was changed.

Deuteronomy 6:4—*Does the existence of only one God argue against the idea of the Trinity?*

No. In fact, the beginning plank of the doctrine of the Trinity is the biblical assertion that there is only one God. From Genesis to Revelation, Scripture consistently testifies to only one true God (see, for example, Isaiah 44:6; 46:9; John 5:44; 17:3; Romans 3:29-30; 16:27; 1 Corinthians 8:4; Galatians 3:20; Ephesians 4:6; James 2:19). It is like a thread that runs through every page of the Bible.

Later, as God continued to unfold further revelation about Himself in New Testament times, He made clear that within the unity of the one Godhead are three coequal and coeternal persons—the Father, the Son, and the Holy Spirit, fully equal in the divine nature but distinct in personhood (Matthew 28:19; 2 Corinthians 13:14).

Deuteronomy 7:2—*Why did God command the Israelites to utterly destroy the Canaanites?*

The Canaanites were polytheists who were intent on spreading their false religion as far as they could. Like other pagan nations, they believed that numerous gods and goddesses controlled the world of nature. El was considered the chief among the Canaanite deities. Likened to a bull in a herd of cows, the people referred to him as "father bull" and regarded him as creator. Asherah was the wife of El.

Chief among the seventy gods and goddesses that were considered offspring of El and Asherah was Hadad, more commonly known as Baal, meaning Lord. As reigning king of the gods, Baal controlled heaven and earth. As god of rain and storm, he was responsible for vegetation and fertility, so his blessing was critical if the Canaanites were to obtain good harvests.

The Canaanites often gave sacrifices to their gods—sometimes involving an animal but at other times, humans (Hosea 13:2). This of course was considered an abomination to God (Deuteronomy 12:31).

The Canaanites had to be destroyed because of their potential influence on the Israelites. As we read in Deuteronomy 7:4, "They will turn your sons away from following me to serve other gods, and the LORD's anger will burn against you and will quickly destroy you."

Deuteronomy 10:12—*How can we both fear the Lord and love Him?*

In this verse we are instructed both to fear the Lord and to love Him. To fear the Lord does not mean to have the emotional feeling of being afraid of Him. Rather, the term means to show Him reverence, or religious awe. There is no conflict in loving God and showing Him great reverence.

Deuteronomy 18:10-22—*How can false prophets be recognized?*

Deuteronomy 18:21-22 indicates that false prophets are those who give false prophecies that do not come true. Other verses in the Bible indicate that false prophets sometimes...

- cause people to follow false gods or idols (Exodus 20:3-4; Deuteronomy 13:1-3)
- deny the deity of Jesus Christ (Colossians 2:8-9)
- deny the humanity of Jesus Christ (1 John 4:1-2)
- advocate abstaining from certain foods and/or meats for spiritual reasons (1 Timothy 4:3-4)
- deprecate or deny the need for marriage (1 Timothy 4:3)
- promote immorality (Jude 4-7)
- encourage legalistic self-denial (Colossians 2:16-23)

A basic rule of thumb is that if a so-called prophet says anything that clearly contradicts any part of God's Word, his teachings should be rejected (Acts 17:11; 1 Thessalonians 5:21).

Deuteronomy 18:15-18—*Who is the greater prophet referenced in this passage?*

Jesus Christ was the fulfillment of Moses' prediction of "a prophet like me from among your own brothers," of whom God said, "I will put my words in his mouth, and he will tell them everything I command him." Consider these facts:

- Jesus was from among His Jewish brethren (Galatians 4:4).
- Jesus' words were from the Father (John 8:28; 12:49).
- Jesus called Himself a prophet (Luke 13:33).
- The people considered Him a prophet (Matthew 21:11; Luke 7:16; 24:19; John 4:19; 6:14; 7:40; 9:17). (Of course, He was also priest [Hebrews 7–10] and king [Revelation 19–20].)

How was Jesus like Moses?

- As babies both Moses and Jesus were targets of death plots and rescued by divine intervention (Exodus 1:15-16,22; 2:2-10; Matthew 2:13-15).

- Both were authenticated by signs and wonders (Exodus 7:10,19-20; 8–12; Matthew 8:14-17; 12:15-17).

- Moses liberated the Israelites from bondage in Egypt, and Christ liberated believers from the bondage of sin (Exodus 3–12; Isaiah 53; John 8:32-36; Romans 6:18-22, 8:2; Galatians 5:1).

- Moses spoke to God face-to-face, as did Christ on the Mount of Transfiguration (Exodus 33:11; Matthew 17:3).

- Moses was the mediator of the Old Covenant, whereas Christ was the mediator of the New Covenant (Exodus 19–20; Hebrews 12:24).

Deuteronomy 21:18-21—*How could parents condemn their own sons to death for being stubborn and rebellious?*

This passage is not referring to the natural rebellion we witness in young children. Rather, this is referring to fully-grown *adult* sons who have committed a religious sin—rebellion against the Lord as expressed in rebellion against parents. Because such rebellion was like a cancer that could eat away at the fabric of society and spread, God commanded that "radical surgery" be done, with the cancer being excised so it would not spread. This was especially important since Israel was a new and fragile nation.

Deuteronomy 29:29—*What are the secret things that belong to the Lord?*

God is omniscient (all-knowing), but man has finite understanding. We will never fully understand God's thoughts or know all that God knows. "'My thoughts are not your thoughts, neither are your ways my ways,' declares the LORD. 'As the heavens are higher than the earth, so are my ways higher than your ways and my thoughts than your thoughts'" (Isaiah 55:8-9). The primary emphasis in Deuteronomy 29:29 is that God has revealed to Israel precisely what Israel needed to know, and Israel was responsible to obey. Some things, however, Israel did not need to know ("secret things").

Deuteronomy 34—*How could Moses have written Deuteronomy when chapter 34 contains his obituary?*

Interpreters have considered several options. First, Moses may have written the account of his death prophetically as the Holy Spirit directed him. God could reveal the future in great detail, so perhaps the Holy Spirit gave Moses prophetic foresight regarding his death (Isaiah 44:7; 46:10).

A second possibility is that another person, likely Joshua, penned the last chapter of Deuteronomy and appended it to what Moses had already written. In biblical days, people commonly appended obituaries to the written works of great men. If this was the case, then Moses wrote most of the book (chapters 1–33), and then the last chapter was added. All of this was done under the superintendence of the Holy Spirit, who inspired all Scripture (2 Timothy 3:16).

Joshua

Joshua 1:8—*Can Christians practice meditation?*

Biblical meditation involves pondering God's Word and His faithfulness (Joshua 1:8; Psalm 48:9; 77:12; 119:148; 143:5). The Hebrew term for *meditation* can, in different contexts, mean to utter, imagine, speak, roar, mutter, meditate, and muse. The underlying idea is that of murmuring. It portrays a person who is very deep in thought, mumbling with his lips as though talking to himself. It is as if strong feelings build up in the innermost depths of his soul, and the pressure is finally released (like steam) in verbal expression. When David meditated on God's Word (as recorded in his psalms), he concentrated so intensely that he no doubt murmured with his lips as he read. Christians should engage in this kind of biblical meditation.

Joshua 1:8—*Can we gain financial prosperity by meditating on God's Word?*

The context of this verse is military, not financial. In fact, finances are nowhere in sight in this entire chapter of Joshua. In the conquest of the promised land, God promised Joshua that his military efforts would prosper if he maintained his commitment to meditate upon and obey God's Word. The prospering also no doubt included the full outworking of the land promises that were given unconditionally by God in the Abrahamic covenant (Genesis 13:14-17). Later, just before his death, Joshua urged the people to continue living in submission to the Scriptures (Joshua 23:6).

Joshua 2:4-5—*How could God commend Rahab's lie and bless her for it?*

Scripture forbids lying (Exodus 20:16). Lying is a sin (Psalm 59:12) and an abomination to God (Proverbs 12:22). God never lies (Numbers 23:19). Righteous men hate lying (Proverbs 13:5).

The Bible never says that God blessed Rahab for lying. God blessed her *despite* her lie. By protecting the Israelite spies, she demonstrated great faith in the God of Israel. She exhibited her strong trust by siding with the people of Israel instead of the wicked people of Jericho.

Rahab was faced with a moral dilemma. It would apparently have been impossible for her to both tell the truth to her king and save the lives of the spies. Saving lives was more important than truthfully revealing the spies, so God did not hold her responsible for the lie.

Joshua 6:21—*Why did God order the extermination of whole peoples?*

God commanded the Israelites to exterminate entire nations—the Canaanites being a primary example. God issued this command not because He is cruel and vindictive but because the Canaanites were so horrible, evil, oppressive, and cancerous to society that—like a human cancer—the only option was complete removal. These were people who were burning their children in honor of their false gods, engaging in sex with animals, and practicing all sorts of other loathsome activities (Leviticus 18:23-24; 20:3). They were unrepentant in all these activities. Human society itself would have been poisoned without the utter removal of the cancerous Canaanites. God would have been showing utter disregard for the righteous if He had not acted to stop this gangrenous nation from taking over all society.

One must keep in mind that the Canaanites had had plenty of time to repent. The biblical pattern is that when nations repent, God withholds judgment (Jeremiah 18:7-8). This principle is clearly illustrated for us in the case of Nineveh. God had prophesied judgment, but Nineveh repented, and God withheld that judgment (see Jonah 3). God shows mercy where repentance is evident (Exodus 32:14; 2 Samuel 24:16; Amos 7:3,7).

The Canaanites were not acting blindly. They had heard of the God of the Israelites and knew what was expected of them, but they defied Him and continued in their sinful ways. They were ripe for judgment.

Joshua 7:15,24—*Why did God punish Achan's family for Achan's sin?*

There are several interpretive options. Some Bible expositors believe that Achan's family was not punished as he was. Note, for example, that only Achan admitted guilt (Joshua 7:20). We are then told that "Israel stoned him" (verse 25). "Burning them" is said to refer not to Achan and his family, but to the items of silver and gold that Achan had taken. It is noted that an execution of Achan's family would have violated Old Testament law, for Ezekiel 18:20 says that children will not bear the punishment for something their parents did.

The problem with this view is that Joshua 7:25 says, "All Israel stoned him, and after they had stoned the rest, they burned them." It appears that the whole family was stoned and burned. (To stone items of gold and silver wouldn't make sense.)

Other Bible expositors suggest that perhaps the entire family was executed because every member of the family had participated in the crime. These expositors note that Achan could not have stored these various items of gold and silver in his family's tent without the family being fully aware of all of it. These expositors also note that no young children are mentioned in the text. All the children may have been old enough to be responsible for the crime.

In any event, we must not forget the Scriptural teaching that the same God who gives life has the right to take life if circumstances call for it (see Deuteronomy 32:39; Job 1:21).

Joshua 10:12-14—*Did the sun actually stand still?*

Scholars have two primary suggestions as to how to interpret this passage. Some believe God may have just slowed down or stopped the normal rotation of the earth so that Joshua's forces were able to complete their victory over the Amorites. Others suggest that God prolonged the daylight by some sort of unusual refraction of the sun's rays. This would have given Joshua and his men more daylight hours but not necessarily more hours in the day.

Personally, I think God stopped the earth's rotation on its axis. Such a miracle poses no problem for the Almighty God of the universe.

Performing a mighty miracle (stopping the earth's rotation) is no more difficult for Him than performing a minor miracle (such as withering a fig tree).

The Amorites worshipped the sun and the moon as deities. Evidently, then, the true God brought about the defeat of the Amorites through the agency of their own supposed deities. This showed the utter futility of their belief in false gods.

Joshua 18:6-8—*Did the Israelites just throw dice for their inheritance in the promised land?*

In this passage we read that Joshua cast lots in the presence of the Lord to determine the land to be apportioned to the tribes of Israel. The Jews cast lots (essentially pebbles) with the expectation that God would so control them as to reveal His will. Proverbs 16:33 tells us, "The lot is cast into the lap, but its every decision is from the LORD." The casting of lots in Joshua 18 was not considered a game of chance (like throwing dice in a casino), but a means of uncovering God's will on the allocation of land.

Judges

Judges 11:30-39—*Did God command Jephthah to sacrifice his daughter?*

There are a few interpretive options. One view is that Jephthah actually did offer his own daughter as a burnt sacrifice to the Lord. If this is the case, this does not in any way mean that God endorsed what Jephthah did. He certainly was not under orders from God to do what he did. God had earlier revealed that human sacrifice was absolutely forbidden (Leviticus 18:21; 20:2-5; Deuteronomy 12:31; 18:10).

Many things happen in the Bible that God does not agree with. God certainly does not agree with the words or actions of Satan, but the Bible nevertheless accurately reports them. In the present case, the author of Judges may have simply provided an objective account of the event without passing judgment.

One must also remember that the book of Judges deals with a period in human history when everyone was doing what was right in his or her own eyes. Judges 21:25 says, "In those days Israel had no king; everyone did as he saw fit." Jephthah may simply have done what was right in his own eyes, thereby victimizing his own daughter. If Jephthah actually committed this act, we can only conclude that he was acting in great folly and was going against the will of God despite his good motives and apparent desire to please the Lord.

Another way to interpret this passage is that Jephthah offered up his daughter in the sense of consecrating her for service at the tabernacle for the rest of her life and devoting her to celibacy. This would involve offering up his daughter in a spiritual way instead of physically offering her as a burnt offering. As the apostle Paul said in Romans 12:1, people can offer their bodies to God as living sacrifices.

If Jephthah's daughter was indeed offered as a living sacrifice, this necessarily would involve a life of perpetual virginity, which was a tremendous sacrifice in the Jewish context of the day. She would not be able to bring up children to continue her father's lineage.

This may explain why his daughter responded by saying, "Grant me this one request...Give me two months to roam the hills and weep with my friends, because I will never marry" (Judges 11:37). Note that she did not weep because of an impending death. She wept because she would never marry and would remain a virgin.

Judges 14:4—*Did God use Samson's lust for accomplishing Israel's deliverance?*

Samson was not entirely committed to God. His lustful lifestyle made that clear. His problem with lust shows that he was self-focused, seeking gratification of fleshly desires. Judges 14 clearly reveals that Samson had no intention of battling the Philistines out of a spiritual commitment to God. God therefore used Samson's self-interests to incite his anger against the Philistines, which ultimately resulted in Israel's deliverance. This is an example of how God can providentially bring good out of evil.

Judges 15:4—*How could Samson have possibly caught 300 foxes?*

There are several considerations. Samson was endowed with supernatural strength, so he could have easily accomplished what no other man could—including capturing 300 foxes. Moreover, Samson, as a judge, likely had workers under him. Samson could have had a number of people gather the foxes, and then, as the judge in charge of all of them, he could have taken credit for capturing them all. Others have suggested the less likely scenario that God moved the animals to be easily captured (noting that God, earlier in the Bible, moved animals to travel toward Noah and his ark so they could be saved).

Judges 16:26-27—*If suicide is a sin, why did God bless Samson for doing it?*

Suicide is unquestionably wrong. Issues of life and death lie in the sovereign hands of God alone. Job said to God, "Man's days are determined; you have decreed the number of his months and have set limits he cannot exceed" (Job 14:5). David said to God, "All the days ordained for me were written in your book before one of them came to be" (Psalm 139:16). Moreover, suicide goes against the commandments of God. In fact, the sixth commandment tells us, "You shall not murder" (Exodus 20:13). This command is based on the sanctity of human life. We must remember that man was created in the image of God (Genesis 1:26). Notice that the command "You shall not murder" has no direct object. It doesn't say, "You shall not murder someone else," or "You shall not murder your fellow man." It simply says, "You shall not murder." The prohibition thus includes not only the murder of one's fellow man but also the murder of oneself. Suicide is certainly not the "unforgivable sin," but we must never forget that God prohibits murder of any kind.

And in fact, Samson did not commit suicide. Rather, he sacrificed his life for a greater cause. Recall that Jesus Christ Himself said, "Greater love has no one than this, that he lay down his life for his friends." This is precisely what Samson did. He laid down his life for his people. As a result of what Samson did, many more Philistines (enemies of Israel) died with his death than during his life (Judges 16:30).

Judges 19:18-24—*How could a man offer his daughter to be raped so that his guest could be protected?*

This is a difficult passage. We must first note that this verse is *descriptive*, not *prescriptive*. That is, Scripture simply describes something that historically took place. Scripture does not prescribe that what took place was right or that it is okay for such a thing to happen again. Also, note that Judges 21:25 tells us that "in those days Israel had no king; everyone did as he saw fit." The man who offered his daughter to be raped did as he saw fit. But that doesn't mean Scripture condones what occurred. Obviously, the rest of Scripture condemns any kind of sexual sin (1 Corinthians 6:13,18; Ephesians 5:3). We can only conclude that this was a tragic example of the effects of sin in a man who had gone astray (Isaiah 53:6).

Ruth

Ruth 3:7—*Did Ruth have intercourse with Boaz in order to obligate him to redeem her?*

Nothing in the context indicates this. Ruth went to Boaz at night not to pursue an immoral relationship with him but to enable him to avoid public scrutiny. Ruth, a righteous woman, did not want Boaz to feel public pressure to act on her behalf.

The reference to Ruth uncovering Boaz's feet is not a euphemism for intercourse; rather, it describes a Hebrew custom indicating subjection and submission.

Ruth did lie next to Boaz, they did not *lie with* each other—the term that normally refers to sexual intercourse.

1 Samuel

1 Samuel 2:25—*Did God prevent Eli's sons from repenting?*

In this verse we read that it was the Lord's will to put Eli's sons to death. Both sons were priests, yet they sinned grossly by engaging in sexual relations with women who served in the tabernacle (1 Samuel 2:22). They themselves chose not to repent. God responded to their unrepentant sin by death. The word *for* ("for it was the Lord's will to put them to death") implies "as a result." They refused to repent of their gross sins, so they died as a result.

1 Samuel 4:3—*Why did Israel take the ark of the covenant into battle against the Philistines?*

The ark symbolized God's presence (1 Samuel 4:3-22). The Israelites came to believe that if the ark were present during a battle, that would mean Yahweh (God) was in battle with them, so they would surely win. They believed the presence of the ark would ensure victory. Such misguided thinking essentially amounted to using the ark as a magical talisman. Israel still needed to learn the lesson that having sacred objects is not the same as controlling God.

1 Samuel 6:19—*Why did God kill 70 persons for peering into the ark of the Lord?*

The ark was considered holy. The Israelites maintained a great separation between the holy and the secular. That which is holy cannot be treated as a secular, non-sacred object. Even the Levites who served in the temple had to treat holy objects with great reverence. Indeed, they "must not go in to look at the holy things, even for a moment, or they will die" (Numbers 4:20). If this is true of even the Levites, then what the men of Beth Shemesh did was true sacrilege. God gave strict regulations about handling the ark because it symbolized His presence (see Exodus 25:10-22; 26:32-34; 37:1-9). In view of such regulations, these men committed an impious act.

1 Samuel 13:5—*Did the Philistines have 3000 chariots or 30,000 chariots?*

In this verse we read, "The Philistines assembled to fight Israel, with three thousand chariots, six thousand charioteers." Older translations of the Bible, however, list 30,000 chariots.

The Hebrew manuscript lists 30,000 chariots. However, 3000 chariots seems more likely. After all, there were only 6000 charioteers. How could 6000 charioteers handle 30,000 chariots? Many scholars conclude that this must represent a textual error in the Hebrew manuscript copy of 1 Samuel at verse 13:5. The Hebrew numbers for 3000 and 30,000 look similar, so we can easily understand how a copyist could have made an error in this regard.

1 Samuel 15:11—*How could God be grieved if He is all-knowing and already knew that Saul would disobey Him?*

In His omniscience, God already knew that Saul would sin. Nevertheless, the Bible portrays God as engaging in active relationships with people. When people are obedient, God is glad, and He blesses them. When people are not obedient, God is grieved, and He disciplines or judges them. This was the case with Saul. God grieved at Saul's disobedience—a grief likely rooted in His awareness of the trouble Saul's actions would bring upon Israel. That God responds in grief to human wickedness is clear also in the New Testament (Ephesians 4:30).

1 Samuel 16:10—*This verse says Jesse had eight sons, but 1 Chronicles 2:13-15 says he had seven sons. Which is it?*

The most likely explanation is that one of Jesse's sons died at a young age. People commonly refer to the number of living people in a family. This is especially so if a family member died at a young age.

1 Samuel 16:14—*How can the Holy Spirit depart from a person as He did from Saul?*

Since New Testament times, the Holy Spirit has permanently indwelt believers (Romans 8:9; 1 Corinthians 12:13). However, in Old Testament times, the Holy Spirit came upon people on a temporary basis to enable them to accomplish special tasks (see Judges 15:14; 1 Samuel 10:5-6). In Saul's case, the Holy Spirit had formerly come upon him to enable him to accomplish his task of being a leader, but now that Saul had turned away from God, the Holy Spirit departed from him.

1 Samuel 17:50—*Who killed Goliath, David or Elhanan?*

Contrary to 1 Samuel 17:50, which says that David killed Goliath, 2 Samuel 21:19 says that Elhanan "killed Goliath the Gittite, who had a spear with a shaft like a weaver's rod." We may have an inaccuracy in our existing copies of the original Hebrew manuscripts of 2 Samuel. After all, the parallel passage of this verse in 1 Chronicles 20:5 tells us, "In another battle with the Philistines, Elhanan son of Jair killed Lahmi the brother of Goliath the Gittite, who had a spear with a shaft like a weaver's rod." Elhanan killed the brother of Goliath, not Goliath himself. First Chronicles 20:5 is apparently the correct reading, and 2 Samuel 21:19 is apparently missing "brother of."

This should not be taken to mean that you cannot trust your Bible. You can! Through the science of textual criticism, scholars have been able to examine the thousands of biblical manuscripts, each of which have minor differences between them, and come to a near certainty as to what the original text must have said. The more early biblical manuscripts we discover, the more minor discrepancies are cleared up. Second Samuel is a good example. Note that (strictly speaking) only the original manuscripts are inspired and inerrant. Manuscript copies are inspired and inerrant to the extent that they reflect the original documents.

1 Samuel 18:1-4—*Were David and Jonathan homosexuals?*

Some people infer that David and Jonathan were homosexuals because Jonathan loved David (18:3) and stripped in David's presence (18:4), and they kissed each other. Contrary to such a perverted view, David's attraction to Bathsheba (2 Samuel 11) reveals that his sexual orientation was heterosexual, not homosexual. Judging by the number of wives he had, David seemed to have too much heterosexuality!

David's love for Jonathan was not a sexual (erotic) love but a friendship (philic) love. In Eastern cultures, heterosexual men commonly express love and affection toward one another.

The text clearly reveals that Jonathan did not strip himself of all his clothes in David's presence. He only stripped off his armor and royal robe (1 Samuel 18:3) as an act of his deep respect for David and commitment to him.

Further, the kiss was a common cultural greeting for men in that day. Note also that the kiss did not occur until two and a half chapters after Jonathan gave David his clothes (1 Samuel 20:41).

1 Samuel 28—*Did the medium of Endor really call up the dead?*

The biblical account of the medium at Endor is quite controversial, and Christians have expressed different views. A minority believe the medium worked a miracle by demonic powers and actually brought Samuel back from the dead. In support of this view, certain passages seem to indicate that demons have the power to perform lying signs and wonders (Matthew 7:22; 2 Corinthians 11:14; 2 Thessalonians 2:9-10; Revelation 16:14). This view is unlikely, however, because Scripture also reveals that death is final (Hebrews 9:27), the dead cannot return (2 Samuel 12:23; Luke 16:24-27), and demons cannot usurp or overpower God's authority over life and death (Job 1:10-12).

A second view is that the medium did not really bring up Samuel from the dead. Rather, a demonic spirit simply impersonated the prophet. Those who hold to this view note that certain verses indicate that demons can deceive people who try to contact the dead (Leviticus 19:31; Deuteronomy 18:11; 1 Chronicles 10:13). This view is unlikely, however, because the passage affirms that Samuel did in fact return from the dead and that he provided a prophecy that actually came to pass. Demons would not have been likely to utter God's truth because the devil is the father of lies (John 8:44).

A third view is that God sovereignly and miraculously allowed Samuel's spirit to appear in order to rebuke Saul for his sin. Samuel's spirit appeared not as a result of the medium's powers (for indeed, no human has the power to summon dead humans—Luke 16:24-27; Hebrews 9:27), but rather because God sovereignly brought it about. This view is supported by the fact that Samuel actually returned from the dead (1 Samuel 28:14), and this caused the medium to shriek with fear (verse 12). The medium's cry of astonishment indicates that this appearance of Samuel was not the result of her usual tricks.

That God allowed Samuel's spirit to appear on this one occasion should not be taken to mean that mediums have any real power to summon the dead. God had a one-time purpose for this one-time special occasion. This passage is therefore descriptive, not prescriptive. That is, it simply describes something that happened historically. It does not prescribe something that people should expect in the future.

1 Samuel 31—*How did Saul really die?*

First Samuel 31 says Saul committed suicide by falling on a sword. Second Samuel 1:10 says Saul was killed by an Amalekite as he was about to lean on his sword.

There are a few interpretive options in resolving this apparent contradiction. Some Bible expositors say both accounts are true. In this view, Saul fell on the sword but was not yet dead, and so the Amalekite finished the job. The problem with this view is that according to 1 Samuel 31:4-5, Saul's armor bearer saw that Saul was dead after he fell on the sword.

Other Bible expositors believe that the correct account is found in 1 Samuel, and the account in 2 Samuel is an accurate record of a *fabrication* of the Amalekite who came upon Saul after he had died, and who thought he could gain favor with David by taking credit for the feat. The main problem with this view is that there is no statement in the text that the account is a fabrication.

Both of these interpretations have scholarly support.

2 Samuel

2 Samuel 8:4—*Did David capture 1700 horsemen or 7000?*

Second Samuel 8:4 says David captured 1700 horsemen, but 1 Chronicles 18:4 says he captured 7000. Scholars agree that 1 Chronicles is correct in its reference to 7000 horsemen. There is apparently a simple copyist error in 2 Samuel 8:4. Recall that only the original Old Testament and New Testament manuscripts are inspired and inerrant. The manuscript copies are inspired and inerrant only to the extent that they accurately reflect the originals.

2 Samuel 12:14—*How could God execute a baby for David's sin with Bathsheba?*

Some Bible expositors say the child died as an atonement for David's sin. Others say the ancient Hebrews had a unitary view of the family unit such that when one member of the family sinned, all the family members were viewed as responsible. This being the case, the baby was put to death. Still others say the baby's death had nothing to do with David's punishment but rather relates to the baby as a living symbol of sin. As the baby continued to grow up, he might—as a symbol—stimulate others to act sinfully as David had. To remove this possibility, God took the baby.

2 Samuel 24:1—*Did God or the devil incite David to number Israel?*

Satan was the actual instrument used to incite David to number Israel (1 Chronicles 21:1), but God permitted Satan to do this (2 Samuel 24:1). In the Hebrew mind-set, whatever God permits, God commits. By allowing this census, God is viewed as having brought about the act Himself. (Keep in mind that the Hebrews were not too concerned about "first causes" and "secondary causes.") Satan did what he did because he wanted to destroy David and the people of God. God's purpose, however, was simply to humble David and teach him and his people a valuable spiritual lesson.

2 Samuel 24:9—*Why do the census numbers in this verse contradict those in 1 Chronicles 21:5-6?*

Second Samuel 24:9 refers to 800,000 men of valor in Israel and 500,000 men of valor in Judah, but 1 Chronicles 21:5-6 refers to 1,100,000 men who drew the sword in Israel and 470,000 men who drew the sword in Judah.

The discrepancy is easy to resolve. The 800,000 figure in 2 Samuel 24:9 does not include the standing army of 288,000 mentioned in 1 Chronicles 27:1-15 or the 12,000 soldiers in Jerusalem mentioned in 2 Chronicles 1:14. Adding these figures together comes to 1,100,000. Moreover, the 470,000 figure in 1 Chronicles 21:5-6 does not include the 30,000 men in the standing army of Judah mentioned in 2 Samuel 6:1. Adding these figures together comes to 500,000.

1 Kings

1 Kings 4:26—*How should the 40,000 stalls in this verse be reconciled to the parallel reference in 2 Chronicles 9:25 to 4000 stalls?*

This involves an apparent copyist error in 1 Kings 4:26. In the Hebrew language, the number 40,000 looks very similar to 4000, so we can easily see how such an error could occur. The ratio of horses to chariots is much more reasonable in the account in 2 Chronicles 9:25.

1 Kings 11:1—*Does this verse, which speaks of Solomon and his many women, teach that polygamy is acceptable to God?*

Monogamy is clearly God's standard for the human race. This is clear from numerous scriptural facts:

- From the beginning God set a pattern by creating a monogamous marriage relationship with one man and one woman, Adam and Eve (Genesis 1:27; 2:21-25).

- This God-established example of one woman for one man guided the general practice of the human race (Genesis 4:1) until the interruption of sin (Genesis 4:23).

- The law of Moses commands against taking many wives (Deuteronomy 17:17).

- The warning against polygamy is repeated in the very passage where it numbers Solomon's many wives: "You must not intermarry with them, because they will surely turn your hearts after their gods" (1 Kings 11:2).

- Our Lord reaffirmed God's original intention by citing this passage (Matthew 19:4) and noting that God created one "male and female" for each other (Matthew 19:4).

- The New Testament stresses that "since there is so much immorality, each man should have his own wife, and each woman her own husband" (1 Corinthians 7:2).

- Likewise, Paul insisted that a church leader should be the husband of one wife (1 Timothy 3:2,12).

- Monogamous marriage prefigures the relation between Christ and His bride, the church (Ephesians 5:31-32).

1 Kings 11:1-13—*Why did Solomon have hundreds of wives and concubines?*

History reveals that Solomon was aggressive in his foreign policy. To seal an ancient treaty, a lesser king customarily gave his daughter in marriage to the greater king (in this case, Solomon). Every time a new treaty was sealed, Solomon ended up with yet another wife. These wives were considered tokens of friendship and sealed the relationship between the two kings. Solomon may not even have been personally acquainted with some of these wives even though he was married to them.

In this process, Solomon was utterly disobedient to the Lord. His obsession with power and wealth apparently overshadowed his spiritual life, and he eventually fell into apostasy. He worshipped some of the false gods of the women who became married to him. Moreover, by marrying more than one woman, Solomon disregarded God's revealed will regarding monogamy.

From the very beginning God created one woman for one man (see Genesis 1:27; 2:21-25). Deuteronomy 17:17 explicitly warns against taking many wives. So Solomon sinned in two ways: He engaged in polygamy, and he violated God's commandment against marrying pagans, which ultimately led to his own apostasy.

1 Kings 15:3—*David was an adulterer and a murderer. Why does this verse say he was fully devoted to the Lord?*

David had a sin nature like all the rest of us (Psalm 51:1). He was not perfect, but the overall orientation of his life was consistently godward. When he did fall into sin, he confessed his sin to God and was restored in his relationship with Him (see Psalms 32; 51). This is the sense in which David's heart was fully devoted to the Lord.

2 Kings

2 Kings 2:24—*Why would Elisha curse a group of youths for mocking his baldness?*

These youths were mocking Elisha not as a mere man but rather as a divinely appointed prophet of God. They were mocking the one who represented Yahweh in a culture committed to false pagan deities (like Baal). Ultimately, this jeering represented a challenge to God through God's appointed representative. The youths paid for this mockery of God and his servant by forfeiting their lives. This youthful group was akin to an irreligious street gang seeking to terrorize Elisha. The consequence suffered by this gang was no doubt intended to strike fear in the hearts of other such sacrilegious gangs.

2 Kings 14:29—*Are the dead asleep (unconscious)?*

Sleep is an appropriate figure of speech for the death of the body because death is only temporary. At the resurrection, the body will be awakened from its sleep. Further, both sleep and death have the same posture—lying down.

The Bible is very clear that the believer's soul (spirit) survives death (Luke 12:4). It is consciously present with the Lord (2 Corinthians 5:8) in a better place (Philippians 1:23), where other souls are talking (Matthew 17:3) and even praying (Revelation 6:9-10). Likewise, the unbeliever's soul is in a place of conscious torment (Matthew 25:41; Luke 16:22-26; Revelation 19:20–20:15).

1 Chronicles

1 Chronicles 21:1—*Did Satan incite David to take a census or did God?*

See comments on 2 Samuel 24:1.

1 Chronicles 22:14—*How can the reference to 100,000 talents of gold given by David be reconciled with the 3000 talents given by David in 1 Chronicles 29:4?*

Both amounts are correct. First Chronicles 22:14 records the amount given by David for the preparation of the building of the temple. First Chronicles 29:4 records the amount David gave out of his own private treasures, over and above what he raised for the building of the temple.

2 Chronicles

2 Chronicles 7:1—*What was the "glory of the Lord" that filled the temple?*

God's glory is the luminous manifestation of His person. Scripture tells us that brilliant light consistently accompanies the manifestation of His glory (Matthew 17:2-3; 1 Timothy 6:16; Revelation 1:16). Moreover, the word *glory* is often linked with verbs of seeing (Exodus 16:7; 33:18; Isaiah 40:5) and verbs of appearing (Exodus 16:10; Deuteronomy 5:24), both of which emphasize the visible nature of God's glory. God's glory includes not only brilliant light but also smoke (Isaiah 6:4) and a cloud (Numbers 16:42). This visible glory filled the temple in Old Testament times.

2 Chronicles 9:25—*How can the 4000 stalls in this verse be reconciled with the parallel reference in 1 Kings 4:26 to 40,000 stalls?*

See comments on 1 Kings 4:26.

2 Chronicles 16:12—*Did King Asa die because he sought help from physicians and not the Lord?*

Such an inference is not necessary in this context, and it is contrary to other passages of Scripture. Note that the verse does not say it is wrong to seek the aid of a physician but to do this *instead of* seeking the Lord. God wants to be put first (Matthew 6:33; Colossians 1:18). As Jeremiah put it, "Cursed is the one who trusts in man, who depends on flesh for his strength and whose heart turns away from the LORD" (Jeremiah 17:5).

Both the Old and New Testaments recommend the use of medicine. Isaiah the prophet was commanded to "prepare a poultice of figs" for a boil. This poultice was applied to the boil, and he recovered (2 Kings 20:7). Paul told Timothy, "Stop drinking only water, and use a little wine because of your stomach and your frequent illnesses" (1 Timothy 5:23).

Finally, as a number of scholars have noted, the apostle Paul may have traveled with Dr. Luke specifically because he was afflicted with an infirmity (Galatians 4:13; see also 2 Corinthians 12:7; Colossians 4:14; 2 Timothy 4:11). Nowhere does the Bible condemn going to a physician or taking medicine. Even Jesus said, "It is not the healthy who need a physician, but the sick" (Matthew 9:12). The Bible simply insists that we should seek God first to determine whether or not the sickness is sent by Him.

2 Chronicles 18:18—*What is the host of heaven?*

Angels are often called God's heavenly host in Scripture. The term *host* has a distinctive military ring to it. And indeed, the Bible often portrays the angels as God's host in military fashion. The term refers to God's heavenly army that accomplishes His will and engages in His battles. God is often called "the LORD of hosts" in the Bible ("the LORD Almighty" in the NIV). This title pictures God as the sovereign commander of the heavenly angelic army (see 1 Samuel 17:45; Psalm 89:6,8).

2 Chronicles 18:20-21—*Does God's allowance of a lying spirit indicate that God condones lying?*

No. As a backdrop, remember that Scripture forbids lying (Exodus 20:16). Lying is a sin (Psalm 59:12) and an abomination to God (Proverbs 12:22). Further, Numbers 23:19 explicitly tells us that "God is not a man, that he should lie."

In 2 Chronicles 18:20-21, God does permit the activity of a "lying spirit." However, what God *causes* and what He *allows* are not the same. For example, God allowed Adam's sin in the Garden of Eden, but He did not cause it. God allowed Lucifer's rebellion against Him, but He did not cause it. God allowed Ananias and Sapphira to lie to Peter, but

He did not cause them to do so. Likewise, God permitted the activity of a lying spirit, but He did not cause it. He does not condone lying.

Ultimately, this is not much different than when God used the evil Assyrians (1 Chronicles 5:26) and the evil Babylonians (Daniel 1:1-2) as instruments of discipline against rebellious Israel. God also permitted the ultimate evil spirit (Satan) to inflict injury upon Job to sift his character (Job 1:6–2:10) and a messenger of Satan to torment the apostle Paul to keep him humble (2 Corinthians 12:7). In all cases, God sovereignly allowed these events in order to bring about a greater good according to His plan.

In Scripture, God affirms, "My thoughts are not your thoughts, neither are your ways my ways...As the heavens are higher than the earth, so are my ways higher than your ways and my thoughts than your thoughts" (Isaiah 55:8-9). We are also told that "the secret things belong to the LORD our God" (Deuteronomy 29:29). We may wish we knew more about these difficult verses. But one thing is certain: God's sovereignty embraces all things such that even the enemies of God can be used to bring about His ultimate desired ends.

Ezra

Ezra 10:3-4,10-12—*How could Ezra demand that Israelites divorce their foreign wives and send them away along with the children born to them?*

Jewish law prohibited Israelites from intermarrying among pagan peoples (see Exodus 34:11-16; Deuteronomy 7:1-5). These pagans had not left their paganism and converted to belief in Yahweh, the true God. For this reason, they were divorced and sent away. In such situations, women returned (with their children) to their original families, who cared for them.

Esther

Esther—*This book doesn't include a single reference to God, so why is it in the Bible?*

The book of Esther never mentions God, but it shows Him working behind the scenes sovereignly and providentially all throughout the book. It describes how the evil Haman launched an insidious plot to destroy the Jews. God not only thwarted the plot but also brought the plotter's evil back on himself (Haman was executed instead of the Jews). In order to bring about this end, God had earlier providentially brought the beautiful (Jewish) Esther to become the queen of the Persian king Xerxes I, who ruled Persia from 486 to 465 BC. God apparently elevated Esther to this position of authority specifically to save the Jews from destruction (see Esther 4:14). Her cousin Mordecai was instrumental in helping Esther to understand this fact. This drama illustrates God's providential control of human history.

Esther 2:1-4—*Did Esther do the right thing by participating in a pagan beauty contest and becoming a part of Xerxes' harem?*

We may find a hint of the answer to this question in Esther 2:8: "When the king's order and edict had been proclaimed, many girls were brought to the citadel of Susa and put under the care of Hegai. Esther also was *taken* to the king's palace and entrusted to Hegai, who had charge of the harem." Esther may have been taken against her will to participate in the contest and become a part of the harem. Whether or not this is so, God was certainly providentially guiding Esther, for He apparently elevated her to a high position for the specific purpose of frustrating Haman's goal of exterminating the Jews. The text gives no indication that Esther had to do anything immoral while participating in the contest. Her character was beyond reproach throughout the book.

Job

Job 2:1-2—*Does Satan have access to heaven?*

Apparently so. The events that took place in the book of Job show that Satan has the freedom to appear before God and engage in discourse with Him (Job 1:6; 2:1). We are told in Revelation 12:10 that Satan is "the accuser of our brothers," which means he goes before God's throne and makes slanderous statements about the saints. In the future tribulation period, however, the devil will be decisively cast out of heaven (Revelation 12:9). Sometime later he will be cast into the lake of fire (Revelation 20:10). His time is definitely limited.

Job 2:3,6—*How could a loving God allow Job, an upright man, to suffer?*

We can make a number of observations. First, Satan is on a leash. God instructed Satan that he could go so far with Job but no further. Moreover, Scripture reveals that God sometimes allows His children to go through periods of suffering so they can condition and strengthen their faith muscles and increase their perseverance. James 1:2-3 tells us, "Consider it pure joy, my brothers, whenever you face trials of many kinds, because you know that the testing of your faith develops perseverance." Certainly this was true in the case of Job. We might also observe that God has the unique ability to bring long-term good out of short-term suffering. My young child might question why I allow him to suffer going to the dentist, for in his youthful ignorance he has no idea that this is for the long-term good of his dental health. Likewise, God may allow us to go through short-term sufferings to bring about long-term benefits.

Job 7:9—*Does this verse contradict the Bible's teaching about resurrection?*

This verse speaks of one who goes down to the grave and does not return. Job was not denying resurrection, for he later said: "After my skin has been destroyed, yet in my flesh I will see God" (Job 19:26). What Job meant when he spoke of someone going down to the grave and not coming up is explained in the very next verse: "He will never come to his house again; his place will know him no more." In other words, those who die do not return to their mortal lives again.

Job 25:4-6—*How can the statement that man is a maggot be reconciled with the fact that man was created in God's image (Genesis 1:26-27)?*

The statement in Job 25 is simply a hyperbole (exaggerated statement) that emphasizes the vast difference between God above and man below. God is so incredibly awesome and exalted that by comparison, man seems like a mere maggot.

Job 38:7 (KJV)—*Who are the sons of God?*

This title refers to angels (see Job 1:6; 2:1; 38:7). Theologians are practically unanimous in saying that angels are sons of God in the sense of being created directly by the hand of God. The phrase *sons of God,* when used of angels, simply denotes spirit beings who were brought into existence by a direct creative act of God. Every angel that exists was a direct creation of God.

One must keep in mind that angels do not give birth to other baby angels (Matthew 22:30). We never read of sons of angels. Every angel was directly created by the hand of God, so it is appropriate that they be called sons of God.

This is entirely different from Christ being called the Son of God. The Bible is clear that Christ is *eternally* the Son of God. Ancient Semitics and Orientals sometimes used the phrase *son of* to indicate likeness or sameness of nature and equality of being. When Jesus claimed to be the Son of God, His Jewish contemporaries fully understood that He was using the term in this way—making a claim to be God in an unqualified sense. This is why, when Jesus claimed to be the Son of God, the Jews tried to kill Him for blasphemy (John 5:18; 19:7). We might also note that Jesus, as God, created all the angels (Colossians 1:16).

Job 40:15—*What is a behemoth?*

The behemoth probably isn't an elephant or a hippopotamus, as is often claimed. After all, Scripture indicates that this beast moves its tail like a cedar tree (Job 40:17), and neither the elephant nor the hippopotamus has such a giant tail. This sounds more like a dinosaur. The behemoth may have been a brontosaurus or a tyrannosaurus.

Job 41:1—*What is a leviathan?*

Just as the behemoth is apparently a land dinosaur, the leviathan might be a marine dinosaur—or at least a very large crocodile. After all, it is far too large to capture with a fishhook. This must be a giant sea creature.

Psalms

Psalm 1:2—*Should Christians meditate?*

Yes. See comments on Joshua 1:8.

Psalm 2:7—*Does this verse indicate that Jesus came into being at a point in time?*

In this verse we read prophetic words of the Father to Jesus: "You are my Son; today I have become your Father." A basic interpretive principle is that Scripture interprets Scripture. The best way to find out what Psalm 2:7 means is to let Scripture tell us what it means. According to Acts 13:33-34, the verse deals not with Jesus coming into being at a point in time but rather His resurrection from the dead by the Father. Other Scriptures make clear that Christ never came into existence at a point in time but is rather an eternal being (John 1:1; 8:58).

Psalm 37:9,11—*In what sense do the righteous inherit the earth?*

This passage indicates that unrighteous Jewish people would be cut off from living in the promised land, but righteous people would experience blessing there. The Hebrew word for *earth* in this context has reference to land—more specifically, the land of Judea, given by God Himself as an inheritance to their fathers and their posterity forever. Though the Hebrew word *('eres)* is often translated *earth* in the Old Testament, it also often refers to land (see Deuteronomy 4:38; 8:7-9; 11:13-15; Jeremiah 2:7; Hosea 9:13). The Hebrew word *'eres* is used in Psalm 37 of the promised land.

Psalm 37:20—*Does the fact that the wicked will perish mean they will lose consciousness at the point of death?*

No. This verse does not teach annihilationism. The same word used to describe the wicked perishing in the Old Testament (*abad*) is used to describe the righteous perishing (see Isaiah 57:1; Micah 7:2). But even many annihilationists admit that the righteous are not snuffed out of existence, so we have no reason to believe the wicked will be. Moreover, the same Hebrew word is used to describe things that are merely lost but then later found (Deuteronomy 22:3). This proves that *perish* does not mean to go out of existence. Further, the Bible makes clear references to the lost being in conscious torment and punishment after their death (Luke 16:19-28; Revelation 19:20; 20:10).

Psalm 37:25—*Are the righteous never forsaken?*

In this verse David affirms, "I was young and now I am old, yet I have never seen the righteous forsaken or their children begging bread." However, the Bible contains plenty of examples of bad things happening to good people. For example, God's servants (like the apostles Paul and Peter) were sometimes thrown into jail for their service to God. In reality, Psalm 37 is classified as a wisdom psalm. As such, it contains wisdom that is generally true (much like Proverbs), but it does not contain covenant promises with absolute guarantees. (Note that David says, "I have never seen," instead of "Thus saith the Lord.")

Psalm 82:1,6—*Does the phrase "You are gods" mean human beings are really gods?*

No. First, unlike the word LORD (*Yahweh*), which always refers to God, the word *gods* (*elohim*) can be used of God (Genesis 1:1), angels (Psalm 8:4-6; Hebrews 2:7), or human beings (here in Psalm 82).

In Psalm 82 we find God's judgment against the evil Israelite judges. These judges were, of course, intended to act righteously and be His representatives on earth. They were divinely ordained to make life-and-death decisions over the people, so they are called gods with a small *g*.

These judges became corrupted and were unjust in their dealings with men. God's charge against them was that they administered justice unjustly, showing favor to the wicked instead of upholding the rights of the helpless and oppressed. Thus, Asaph indicates that even though they were called gods, they would in fact die like the men they really were. They were not truly gods.

Besides, in Isaiah 44:8, God Himself asks, "Is there any God besides me? No, there is no other Rock; I know not one." Similarly, Isaiah 43:10 portrays God as saying, "Before me no god was formed, nor will there be one after me." Clearly human beings can't become gods.

This psalm helps us to understand what Jesus was saying in John 10:34. When Jesus alluded to this psalm, He was saying that the Israelite judges were metaphorically called gods (with a small *g*) because of their God-appointed works among human beings, but Jesus Himself was rightfully called God in view of His divine works (miracles).

Psalm 97:7—*Who are the gods that worship God?*

Here we find this statement: "Worship him, all you gods!" Of course, in reality, there is only one true God, but there are many false gods. Paul in the New Testament informs us that demons are behind false gods (1 Corinthians 10:20), and one day even the demons will bow before the true and living God and confess that He is Lord (Philippians 2:10). Psalm 97:7 may be referring to this.

Other Bible expositors note that good angels are sometimes called gods (*elohim*) in the Bible (Psalm 8:5; see also Hebrews 2:7). Therefore, Psalm 97:7 could be a command for the angels to worship God, as they are so commanded in Psalm 148:2: "Praise Him, all His angels."

Psalm 105:15—*Does this verse indicate that certain contemporary leaders allegedly called by God are beyond criticism and doctrinal accountability?*

In this verse we read, "Do not touch my anointed ones; do my prophets no harm." The phrase *the Lord's anointed* is used in Old Testament Scripture to refer to Israel's kings (see 1 Samuel 12:3,5; 24:6,10; 26:9,11,16,23; 2 Samuel 1:14,16; 19:21; Psalm 20:6; Lamentations 4:20). In this context the word cannot be interpreted to refer to modern teachers in the church. Further, the word *prophets* in this context is referring to Old Testament prophets, not to modern church leaders. So neither of these designations can be interpreted with reference to teachers in the modern church.

Even if we allowed that this verse could loosely refer to modern church leaders, the warning is against physically touching or harming them. It has nothing to do with testing their teachings. In Old Testament times prophets and kings were very much in danger of physical harm—thus the warning.

Scripture itself instructs us to test all teachings by the Word of God (1 Thessalonians 5:21). Like the Bereans of old, we must make the Scriptures our measuring stick for truth (Acts 17:11). Paul affirmed, "All Scripture is God-breathed and is useful for teaching, rebuking, correcting and training in righteousness, so that the man of God may be thoroughly equipped for every good work" (2 Timothy 3:16-17). All of us are to be constantly on guard against false teachings (Romans 16:17-18; see also 1 Timothy 1:3-4; 4:16; 2 Timothy 1:13-14; Titus 1:9; 2:1).

Finally, every believer in Christ is anointed in one sense (see 1 John 2:20). In view of this, no Christian leader can lay claim to being special or above others and beyond doctrinal criticism.

Psalm 110:1—*Are there two Lords?*

In this verse we read, "The LORD says to my Lord: 'Sit at my right hand until I make your enemies a footstool for your feet.'" This verse implies Trinitarian distinctions in the Old Testament. The words "my Lord" are simply a reference to David's Messiah. This divine Messiah is invited to sit at the right hand of "the LORD" (God the Father). Here we have the first person of the Trinity speaking to the second person of the Trinity. We learn in the New Testament that following His resurrection and ascension into heaven, Jesus did indeed sit at the right hand of God the Father.

Psalm 115:16—*In what sense has the earth been given to man?*

God has given mortal human beings the earth to dwell in it and to rule over it. Genesis 1:28 tell us, "God blessed them and said to them, 'Be fruitful and increase in number; fill the earth and subdue it. Rule over the fish of the sea and the birds of the air and over every living creature that moves on the ground.' " We see this same thought reflected in Psalm 8:6-8: "You [God] made him [man] ruler over the works of your hands; you put everything under his feet: all flocks and herds, and the beasts of the field, the birds of the air, and the fish of the sea, all that swim the paths of the seas."

Psalm 137:8-9—*How can a verse about dashing infants against rocks be in the Bible?*

Though such a thing sounds horrible, the sentiments of the psalmist are rooted in Israel being held captive by the Babylonians. The psalmist is actually calling for "an eye for an eye and a tooth for a tooth." The Babylonians had taken Israelite infants and dashed them against rocks, so the psalmist is praying for justice. His desire is that the atrocities that the Babylonians visited on others might now be visited upon themselves.

Psalm 139:13—*In view of God knitting people together in the womb, is abortion to be considered murder of a human being?*

I think the answer must be yes. Numerous Scripture verses portray the baby in the womb as a human being (Exodus 21:22-24; Psalm 139:13-15; Jeremiah 1:5). The only difference between born and unborn babies is their size and location, not their essential nature as human beings. Just as it is murder to kill a baby outside the womb, so it is murder to kill a baby in the womb.

Psalm 146:3-4—*Does this verse mean we are not conscious following the moment of death?*

In the King James translation of this passage we read, "Put not your trust in princes…His breath goeth forth, he returneth to his earth; in that very day his thoughts perish." While some interpret this as meaning that people are not conscious following death, the original Hebrew indicates that peoples' plans, ambitions, and ideas for the future will cease and come to naught at the moment of death. A person's plans and ideas for the future die with him. Once a man dies, his ambitions on earth are no more, his schemes for making money vanish, his plans for building a new and bigger house disintegrate, and his plans for that vacation of a lifetime are obliterated. In view of this, people are urged by the psalmist to put their trust in the one who is infinitely more powerful than any mortal man, including princes. His plans do not fail. Putting trust in a mere mortal man can only lead to disappointment, for mortal men die.

Proverbs

Proverbs 1:1—*How can the book of Proverbs belong in the Bible in view of Solomon's sin?*

The inclusion of a book in the Bible is based not on the lives of the human authors (all of whom had a sin nature—Isaiah 53:6), but on the inspiration of the Holy Spirit (2 Timothy 3:16; 2 Peter 1:20-21). The book of Proverbs was inspired by the Holy Spirit just as all other biblical books were.

Proverbs 8:22-23—*Was Jesus brought forth as a created being?*

In this passage, we read, "The Lord brought me forth as the first of his works, before his deeds of old; I was appointed from eternity, from the beginning, before the world began."

The first nine chapters of Proverbs deal with wisdom personified. A personification is a rhetorical figure of speech in which inanimate objects or abstractions are endowed with human qualities or are represented as possessing human form. In Proverbs 1–9, wisdom is figuratively endowed with human qualities.

With this backdrop in mind, there is no indication in the text that Proverbs 8 is to be taken any differently from chapters 1 through 7 and 9. This being the case, if we take Proverbs 8:22-23 to be referring to Christ, then—to be consistent—it would seem that Christ is also a woman who cries in the streets (Proverbs 1:20-21) and who lives with someone named Prudence (Proverbs 8:12). Obviously, Proverbs 1–9 makes no sense if one tries to read Christ into the text.

Proverbs 16:4—*Does God ordain wickedness?*

In this verse, we read, "The Lord works out everything for his own ends—even the wicked for a day of disaster." This verse does not mean that God specifically created certain wicked people for the sole purpose of destroying them or sending them to hell. Scripture assures us that God is not willing that any should perish (2 Peter 3:9) and that God loves the whole world of humanity (John 3:16). God "desires all people to be saved and to come to the knowledge of the truth" (1 Timothy 2:4). The redemption that Christ purchased at the cross is made available to all people (1 John 2:2). These verses provide an important backdrop to the proper interpretation of Proverbs 16:4, for if we learn anything from such verses, it is that God cares for and loves all people.

The primary thrust of the passage is that in the end, there will be commensurate justice corresponding to human actions. God, in His sovereignty, ensures that everything in life will receive its just retribution. Actions and consequences will ultimately correspond.

Proverbs 22:6—*Is this verse a promise or a principle regarding raising our children?*

In this verse we read, "Train a child in the way he should go, and when he is old he will not turn from it." The word *train* comes from a word root for the palate or the roof of the mouth. The ancient Arabs used a form of this verb to denote the action of a midwife rubbing the palate of a newborn child with olive oil or crushed dates to give it a desire for food. The word connotes the idea of creating a desire for or creating a taste for. Proverbs 22:6 thus calls on Christian parents to develop in a child a personal desire for the things of God—a hunger for His Word and a desire for fellowship with His people.

Having said all this, we must acknowledge that this verse is not a promise but a wisdom principle. As such, the wisdom contained in the verse is generally true. But sometimes parents may have done everything right, and their children may still choose the path of disobedience. (God is certainly a perfect Father, but His children Adam and Eve disobeyed Him.)

Proverbs 29:18—*Is it true that where there is no vision for the future, the people perish?*

This verse has often been twisted to say that unless we have long-range plans and a well thought-out strategy, we will perish. Such an idea is completely foreign to the context. The NIV correctly renders this verse: "Where there is no revelation, the people cast off restraint; but blessed is he who keeps the law." This verse simply means that when God's Word is suppressed or silenced, people lose restraint and become ungovernable. Instead of doing God's will, they allow their own baser appetites to take over, and they indulge in all kinds of sinful activities. We find this illustrated in the book of Exodus. Moses had left the Israelites alone for a mere 40 days when he was on Mount Sinai receiving God's law. During that time, the people lost all restraint and ended up making an idol in the form of a golden calf (Exodus 32:25).

Proverbs 31:6—*Does this verse encourage drinking strong alcoholic beverages?*

In this verse we read, "Give beer to those who are perishing, wine to those who are in anguish." Getting drunk is condemned in Scripture (Ephesians 5:18), but using wine medicinally is not wrong. Paul encouraged Timothy to use wine medicinally for a stomach problem (1 Timothy 5:23). Likewise, giving wine to those who are dying or those who are in great pain is a mercy, helping them to deal with their situation.

Ecclesiastes

Ecclesiastes 1:2—*How can this book belong in the Bible? It seems so pessimistic.*

Ecclesiastes presents two contrasting ways of looking at man's plight in the world. One is the secular, humanistic, materialistic viewpoint. It interprets all things from a limited earthly perspective (a perspective "under the sun") that does not recognize God or His involvement in man's affairs (see Ecclesiastes 1:14; 2:11,17,26; 4:4,16; 6:9). This earthly perspective is completely unaided by divine revelation. It sees life as futile, meaningless, and without purpose. There is nothing new under the sun; rather, what is taking place now is what has already taken place many times in the past. The future will simply repeat what is happening in the present. Life is meaningless. Nothing we do can bring ultimate satisfaction because we will end up with the same doomed fate as all the humans who preceded us.

The other perspective is a godly, spiritual perspective that interprets life and its problems from a God-honoring viewpoint (see Ecclesiastes 3:1-15; 5:19; 6:1-2; 9:1). It takes divine revelation into account. This perspective recognizes God and finds meaning in life and enjoys life. God can be involved in all that we do (2:24-26; 3:13; 5:18-20; 9:7-10). Our ultimate meaning in life is not to be found in the things around us, which pass away, but in God alone (2:25). The conclusion of the writer of Ecclesiastes is that we should remember God while we are still young (12:1).

Ecclesiastes 2:24—*Is Solomon a proponent of hedonism?*

In this verse we read, "A man can do nothing better than to eat and drink and find satisfaction in his work." Solomon was not speaking of a hedonistic lifestyle divorced from God. His statement should be taken in the context of other statements he makes, such as his exhortation to live life on earth in anticipation of the afterlife: "Be happy, young man, while you are young, and let your heart give you joy in the days of your youth. Follow the ways of your heart and whatever your eyes see, but know that for all these things God will bring you to judgment" (Ecclesiastes 11:9).

Ecclesiastes 3:19—*Is humanity's fate the same as that of the animal kingdom?*

Ecclesiastes presents two contrasting ways of looking at man's plight in the world. One is the secular, humanistic, materialistic viewpoint that interprets all things from a limited earthly perspective. The other is a godly, spiritual perspective that interprets life and its problems from a God-honoring viewpoint. The statement that man's fate is like that of the animals represents the secular, humanistic, materialistic viewpoint.

The Bible highlights both similarities and differences between the death of animals and humans. In both cases, their bodies die and return to dust. Likewise, their death is certain, and both are powerless to prevent it. On the other hand, humans have immortal souls (spirits), and animals do not (Ecclesiastes 3:21; 12:7). Of no beast does the Bible say that to be absent from the body is to be present with the Lord (2 Corinthians 5:8 NKJV). Likewise, nowhere does the Bible speak of the resurrection of animals, as it does of all human beings (John 5:28-29; Revelation 20:4-6). The Scriptures show a big difference between the death of humans and animals.

Ecclesiastes 9:5—*Does this verse indicate that human beings are not conscious in the afterlife?*

In this verse we read that "the dead know nothing." There are two interpretive possibilities regarding what this verse means:

Ecclesiastes presents two contrasting ways of looking at man's plight in the world. One is the secular, humanistic, materialistic viewpoint that interprets all things from a limited earthly perspective.

The other is a godly, spiritual perspective that interprets life and its problems from a God-honoring viewpoint. Many scholars believe Ecclesiastes 9:1-10 reflects the earthly perspective that is unaided by divine revelation. That is, a strictly human perspective is that the dead are conscious of nothing at all. Since this is only a human perspective, the verse certainly does not teach God's truth. This being so, the verse cannot be used to support the contention that there is no conscious existence after death.

Other evangelical scholars interpret this verse as meaning that the dead are not conscious of events taking place in the physical realm. The dead know nothing so far as their bodily senses and worldly affairs are concerned. The dead are still conscious of things not associated with the physical, earthly realm.

Song of Solomon

Song of Solomon—*Why is this book in the Bible?*

The Song of Solomon, also known as the Song of Songs in ancient Hebrew versions, was written by Solomon shortly after 971 BC. Solomon is said to have written 1005 songs (1 Kings 4:32), so the ancient Hebrew rendering of the title of this book as Song of Songs is an indication that this is his best of the bunch.

The Song of Solomon is an extended poem, full of metaphors and imagery, that shows the richness of sexual love between husband (lover) and wife (his beloved) (see Song of Solomon 1:8–2:7). The backdrop, of course, is that God Himself created male and female (Genesis 1–2), and He created them as sexual beings (see Genesis 1:28). Therefore, sex within the boundaries of marriage is God-ordained and is to be enjoyed (see Genesis 2:24; Matthew 19:5; 1 Corinthians 6:16; Ephesians 5:31). Of course, any deep relationship includes both joy and pain, and the Song of Solomon reflects this, pointing to both the joys and heartaches of wedded love (Song of Solomon 5:2–7:9).

Some Bible expositors throughout the centuries have interpreted the Song of Solomon allegorically, suggesting that it points to the love relationship between God and Israel. Others have said it is an allegory pointing to the love relationship between Christ and the church (His bride). However, nothing in the text of the book indicates that it is to be taken in any other way than describing an amorous relationship between husband and wife as intended by God. God's choice for this book to be in the Bible points to the importance of the husband-wife relationship.

Song of Solomon 6:8—*Why does this verse say Solomon had 140 wives and concubines, and 1 Kings 11:3 says he had 1000?*

Many Bible expositors believe these verses are referring to two

different times in Solomon's life, the lower number referring to an
earlier time. Others make note of the reference in Song of Solomon
6:8 to "virgins beyond number"—which could easily equal the 1000
mentioned in 1 Kings 11:3.

Isaiah

Isaiah 7:14—*Does this verse really point to the virgin birth of Jesus Christ?*

Some have denied that this verse points to the virgin birth of Jesus Christ and say it was fulfilled in Isaiah 8:3 with the natural birth of Maher-Shalal-Hash-Baz. But we have evidence that the verse points to the virgin birth of Jesus. First, the Hebrew word *almah* in this text should definitely be translated *virgin* because it signifies a young unmarried girl every time it is used in the Old Testament. This person was to conceive and bear the child *as* a virgin, so the prediction could not be fulfilled in someone who conceived in a natural way, such as the mother of Maher-Shalal-Hash-Baz.

In support of this, the Greek translation of the Hebrew Old Testament (LXX), which predates the time of Christ, translated the Hebrew word *almah* by the unambiguous Greek word *parthenos,* which always refers to a virgin. The translators of the Greek Old Testament evidently believed this was a prediction of the virgin birth of the Messiah. Moreover, the inspired New Testament text sanctioned the LXX translation of *almah* when it quoted the LXX of Isaiah 7:14 to show that this prophecy was fulfilled in the virgin birth of Christ (see Matthew 1:23).

Isaiah 9:6—*Is Jesus the Father?*

In this verse Jesus is referred to as Everlasting Father. As we seek to interpret this title, it is critical to keep in mind what other Scriptures have to say about the distinction between the Father and the Son. For example, the New Testament calls Jesus "the Son" more than 200 times. Moreover, the Father is considered by Jesus as someone other than Himself more than 200 times in the New Testament. And more than 50 times in the New Testament the Father and Son are seen to be distinct within the same verse (for example, Romans 15:6; 2 Corinthians 1:4; Galatians 1:1-2; Philippians 2:10-11; 1 John 2:1; 2 John 3).

If the Father and the Son are distinct, then in what sense can Jesus be called Everlasting Father? *Everlasting Father* in this verse is better translated *Father of eternity*. The words *Father of* in this context carry the meaning, possessor of eternity. *Father of eternity* is here used in accordance with a Hebrew and Arabic custom in which he who possesses a thing is called the father of it. According to this common custom, *father of strength* means strong; *father of knowledge,* intelligent; *father of glory,* glorious. In like manner, the meaning of *Father of eternity* in Isaiah 9:6 is "eternal." Christ as the Father of eternity is an eternal being.

Support for this view is found in the Targums—ancient Jewish paraphrases of the Old Testament Scriptures. It is highly revealing that the Targum of Isaiah renders Isaiah 9:6, "His name has been called from of old, Wonderful Counselor, Mighty God, *He who lives forever,* the Anointed One (or Messiah), in whose days peace shall increase upon us." Clearly, the ancient Jews considered the phrase *Father of eternity* as indicating the eternality of the Messiah.

Isaiah 11:12—*Does the Bible use unscientific and thus inaccurate language?*

Does this verse use unscientific language in referring to "the four quarters of the earth"? No—such language is just a metaphorical way of referring to north, south, east, and west. Elsewhere, Isaiah acknowledges that the earth is circular (Isaiah 40:22).

Isaiah 14:12-17—*Does this verse refer to a human being or to Lucifer?*

Some Bible scholars see no reference whatsoever to Lucifer in this passage. They argue that this passage refers to a man (verse 16) and compares him to other kings on the earth (verse 18). They say the words "How you have fallen from heaven" (verse 12) refer to a fall from great political heights.

Other scholars interpret this passage as referring *only* to the fall of Lucifer, with no reference whatsoever to a human king. They point out that the description of this being is beyond humanness, so it could not refer to a mere mortal man.

A third view sees Isaiah 14:12-17 as having a dual reference. According to this interpretation, verses 4 through 11 deal with an actual king of Babylon. Verses 12 through 17 contain a dual reference that includes not only the king of Babylon but also a typological description of Lucifer.

Isaiah 18:1-17—*Does this verse refer to America?*

This passage refers to a land "divided by rivers." Some interpreters claim that the United States is the fulfillment of the passage since it is divided by the Mississippi River. The passage also makes reference to this nation being feared because of its military conquests, something believed to fit the way many people around the world view the United States. The obvious problem with this view is that the nation is explicitly identified in Isaiah 18:1-2 as ancient Cush, which is modern Sudan, not America.

Isaiah 45:7—*Does God create evil?*

God said, "I bring prosperity and create disaster; I, the LORD, do all these things." The Hebrew word for *disaster* here does not refer to moral evil. Hebrew linguists tell us that the word need not have any moral connotations at all. This word is appropriate for the plagues that God inflicted on the Egyptians through Moses. These plagues involved not moral evil but rather calamitous events engineered to bring the Egyptians to repentance. God as the Judge of the earth can rightly inflict such plagues on sinful human beings without having His character impugned with accusations of evil. Certainly the plagues seemed evil to those experiencing them, but these people were experiencing due justice. God was merely bringing just judgment on unrepentant sinners. God's good end—that is, the deliverance of the Israelites from Egyptian bondage—was the result of this judgment.

Isaiah 51:6—*In what way will the heavens vanish?*

This verse tells us that "the heavens will vanish like smoke." *The heavens* in this verse refers not to the domain of God but rather to earth's atmosphere and interstellar space. Scripture speaks of three heavens. The first heaven is earth's atmosphere (Job 35:5). The second heaven is that of the interstellar universe (Genesis 1:17; Deuteronomy 17:3). The third heaven is the ineffable and glorious dwelling place of God (2 Corinthians 12:2), elsewhere called the "heaven of heavens" and the "highest heaven" (1 Kings 8:27; 2 Chronicles 2:6). Isaiah 51:6 teaches that the first two heavens—earth's atmosphere and interstellar space—will vanish like smoke.

Jesus likewise taught that "heaven and earth will pass away, but my words will never pass away" (Matthew 24:35; Mark 13:31; Luke 21:33). The apostle Paul addresses the reason why heaven and earth will pass away: "The creation was subjected to frustration, not by its own choice, but by the will of the one who subjected it, in hope that the creation itself will be liberated from its bondage to decay and brought into the glorious freedom of the children of God. We know that the whole creation has been groaning as in the pains of childbirth right up to the present time" (Romans 8:20-22).

One day this bondage will end, and God will renew the universe. Before the eternal kingdom can be made manifest, God must deal with this cursed earth. Indeed, the earth—along with the first and second heavens (the earth's atmosphere and the stellar universe)—must be renewed. The old must make room for the new.

Thus, in the book of Revelation we read, "Then I saw a new heaven and a new earth, for the first heaven and the first earth had passed away, and there was no longer any sea...He who was seated on the throne said, 'I am making everything new!'" (Revelation 21:1-5).

Isaiah 53:4-5—*Is healing guaranteed in the atonement?*

Ultimate physical healing is guaranteed in the atonement (a healing we will enjoy in our future resurrection bodies), but the healing of our physical bodies while in the mortal state (prior to our death and resurrection) is not guaranteed in the atonement. The Hebrew word for healing (*napha*) can refer not only to physical healing but also to spiritual healing. The context of Isaiah 53:4-5 indicates that spiritual healing is in view. In verse 5 we are explicitly told, "He was pierced for our transgressions, he was crushed for our iniquities...By his wounds we are healed" (verse 5). *Transgressions* and *iniquities* set the context, so spiritual healing from the misery of man's sin is in view.

Further, numerous verses in Scripture substantiate the view that physical healing in mortal life is not guaranteed in the atonement and that it is not always God's will to heal. The apostle Paul couldn't heal Timothy's stomach problem (1 Timothy 5:23), nor could he heal Trophimus (2 Timothy 4:20) or Epaphroditus (Philippians 2:25-27). Paul spoke of a bodily illness he had (Galatians 4:13-15). He also suffered a thorn in the flesh, which God allowed him to retain (2 Corinthians 12:7-9). God certainly allowed Job to go through a time of physical suffering (Job 1–2).

Neither Paul nor any of the others acted as if they thought their healing was guaranteed in the atonement. They accepted their situations and trusted in God's grace for sustenance. On one occasion, Jesus indicated that sickness could be for the glory of God (John 11:4).

Finally, numerous verses in Scripture reveal that our physical bodies are continuously running down and suffering various ailments. Our present bodies are perishable and weak (1 Corinthians 15:42-44). Paul said that "outwardly we are wasting away" (2 Corinthians 4:16). Death and disease will be a part of the human condition until we receive resurrection bodies that are immune to such frailties (1 Corinthians 15:51-55).

Isaiah 65:17—*What is meant by the "new heavens and a new earth"?*

The phrase "new heavens and a new earth" does not refer to a cosmos that is totally other than the present cosmos. Rather, the new cosmos will stand in continuity with the present cosmos, but it will be utterly renewed and renovated. In keeping with this, Matthew 19:28 (NKJV) speaks of "the regeneration." Acts 3:21 (NKJV) speaks of the "restoration of all things." Our planet will be altered, changed, and made new, to abide forever.

The new earth, being a renewed and eternal earth, will be adapted to the vast moral and physical changes that the eternal state necessitates. Everything is new in the eternal state. Everything will be according to God's own glorious nature. The new heavens and the new earth will be brought into blessed conformity with all that God is in a state of fixed bliss and absolute perfection.

There will even be geological changes in the new earth, for there will be no more sea (Revelation 21:1). At present about three-quarters of the earth's surface is covered with water and is therefore uninhabitable. In the new earth, an immensely increased land surface will exist as a result of the disappearance of the oceans. Glorified humanity will inhabit a glorified earth recreated and adapted to eternal conditions.

An incredible thing to ponder is that in the next life, heaven and earth will no longer be separate realms, as they are now, but will be merged. Believers will thus continue to be in heaven even while they are on the new earth. The new earth will be utterly sinless, bathed and suffused in the light and splendor of God, and unobscured by evil of any kind or tarnished by evildoers of any description. Heaven will thus encompass the new heaven *and* the new earth. And the New Jerusalem—the eternal city that measures 1500 by 1500 by 1500 miles—will apparently come down and rest on the newly renovated earth (see Revelation 21:2). This city will be the eternal dwelling place of the saints of all ages.

Jeremiah

Jeremiah 1:5—*Does this verse teach reincarnation?*

In this verse we read of God's words to Jeremiah: "Before I formed you in the womb I knew you, before you were born I set you apart; I appointed you as a prophet to the nations." This verse speaks not of reincarnation but of God calling and setting apart Jeremiah for the ministry long before he was born. "I knew you" does not refer to a pre-existent soul but to the prenatal person. Jeremiah was known by God in the womb (compare Jeremiah 1:5 with Psalm 51:6 and 139:13-16). The Hebrew word for *know* (*yada*) here implies a special relationship of commitment (see Amos 3:2) and ordination that reveals that God had a special assignment for Jeremiah even before birth. *Know* in this context indicates God's act of making Jeremiah the special object of His sovereign choice.

Jeremiah 2:13—*What is the living water referenced in this verse?*

Living water literally means flowing water. This verse speaks of how Israel had forsaken God, the only true flowing source of life-giving spiritual nourishment and power. Instead they sought refuge in idolatrous pagan (man-made) religions (they "have dug their own cisterns"). What a foolish trade!

Jeremiah 31:31—*What is the New Covenant?*

The New Covenant is an unconditional covenant God made with humankind in which He promised to provide for forgiveness of sin, based entirely on the sacrificial death and resurrection of Jesus Christ (Jeremiah 31:31-34). Under the Old Covenant, worshippers never enjoyed a sense of total forgiveness. Under the New Covenant, however, Christ our High Priest made provisions for such forgiveness.

When Jesus ate the Passover meal with the disciples in the upper room, He spoke of the cup as "the new covenant in my blood" (Luke 22:20; see also 1 Corinthians 11:25). Jesus has done all that is necessary for the forgiveness of sins by His once-for-all sacrifice on the cross. This New Covenant is the basis for our relationship with God in the New Testament.

Lamentations

Lamentations 3:22—*Is God compassionate, or is He wrathful?*

In this verse we read that God's compassions never fail. How can this be reconciled with other verses that say He is wrathful (Deuteronomy 7:16; 1 Samuel 6:19)? Biblically, God is loving and compassionate, but He also responds with wrath when His holiness is violated by human sin. God is entirely separate from all evil and is absolutely righteous (Leviticus 19:2). He is pure in every way (Exodus 15:11; Psalm 71:22; Isaiah 6:3; Revelation 15:4). When man violates His holiness, He appropriately responds in wrath. As Christians, we can be thankful that Jesus on the cross took upon Himself God's wrath for our sins (Romans 5:9).

Ezekiel

Ezekiel 1:5-28—*Did Ezekiel see a UFO?*

Ezekiel speaks of living creatures whose faces were manlike and who sped "back and forth like flashes of lightning" (verse 14). They "rose from the ground," and their "wheels would rise along with them." This is not a reference to UFOs, but a vision of the glory of God. The text states clearly that "this was the appearance of the likeness of the glory of the LORD" (verse 28). Moreover, what Ezekiel witnessed was referred to as "visions of God" in the very first verse. Visions are usually in highly symbolic form (Revelation 1:9-20). So the "likeness" (verse 28) given of things should not be taken literally but symbolically.

Further, the living creatures were angels, since they had wings (verse 6) and flew in the midst of heaven (see Ezekiel 10). They compare to the angels mentioned in Isaiah 6:2 and especially the living creatures (angels) that are around God's throne (Revelation 4:6).

Still further, their message was from the Lord God of Israel to the prophet Ezekiel (see 2:1-4), not from some alleged UFO beings. The context was a message from the God of Israel through the Jewish prophet Ezekiel to His rebellious nation (2:3-4; 3:4).

Ezekiel 18:4—*Does this verse teach that man's soul (or immaterial nature) can die?*

In this verse we read that "the soul that sinneth, it shall die" (KJV). The Hebrew word for soul (*nephesh*) is here used in the sense of a living being or living person. The *person* who sins will die.

Ezekiel's intention was to combat a wrong interpretation of the doctrine of inherited guilt. Some people were arguing that children were suffering and dying because of the sins of their fathers. Sin can in fact have an accumulative effect (see Exodus 20:5-6), but Ezekiel's goal was to emphasize that each individual is accountable for his own sin. That's why he said that the soul (or person) who sins will die.

Ezekiel 28:11-19—*Does this passage refer to the fall of a mighty human ruler or to Lucifer?*

The context of Ezekiel 28 seems to indicate that the first ten verses in this chapter speak about the ruler of Tyre (who was condemned for claiming to be a god though he was just a man), and then the discussion moves to the king of Tyre starting in verse 11. The switch from *ruler* to *king,* and the allusions to the Garden of Eden, seem to imply that the individual described here was more than human. Many scholars believe that though there was a human ruler of Tyre, the real king of Tyre was Satan, for he was ultimately at work in this anti-God city, and he worked through the human ruler of the city.

Some have suggested that these verses may actually deal with a human king of Tyre who was empowered by Satan. Satan may have indwelt this human leader. In describing this human ruler, Ezekiel also gives us glimpses of Satan, who was influencing him.

In Scripture Satan is sometimes addressed through the creature he is influencing. Recall that when Jesus rebuked Peter, He said, "Get behind Me, Satan!" (Matthew 16:23). When God pronounced a curse on Satan in Genesis 3:14-15, He addressed Satan indirectly through the serpent. So even though Ezekiel 28:11-19 refers to a human king, the ultimate subject of these verses may be Satan.

Certainly some things are true of this king that—at least ultimately—cannot be true of human beings. For example, the king is portrayed as having a different nature than man (he is a cherub, considered to be in the inner circle of angels with closest access to God—verse 14). He had a different status than man (he was blameless and sinless—verse 15). He was in a different realm than man (the Holy Mount of God—verses 13-14; see also Genesis 3:1-7). He received a different judgment than man (verse 16—he was cast out of the mountain of God and thrown to the earth, which seems to parallel the description of Satan's fall in Revelation 12). Also, the superlatives used to describe him don't seem to fit with a normal human being (full of wisdom, perfect in beauty, and having the seal of perfection—verse 12).

Our text tells us that this king was a created being, that he left the creative hand of God in a perfect state, and that he was perfect in his ways until iniquity was found in him (verses 12,15). What was this iniquity? We read in verse 17, "Your heart became proud on account of your beauty, and you corrupted your wisdom because of your splendor." Lucifer apparently became so impressed with his own beauty, brilliance, intelligence, power, and position that he began to desire for himself the honor and glory that belonged to God alone. The sin that corrupted Lucifer was self-generated pride.

This mighty angelic being was rightfully judged by God: "I threw you to the earth" (verse 18). This doesn't mean that Satan had no further access to heaven, for other Scripture verses clearly indicate that he maintained this access even after his fall (for example, Job 1:6-12; Zechariah 3:1-2). However, Ezekiel 28:17 indicates that Satan was absolutely and completely cast out of God's heavenly government and his place of authority (Luke 10:18).

Ezekiel 37—*Does the vision of the valley of dry bones describe the reestablishment of Israel as a nation?*

In the vision of dry bones in Ezekiel 37, the Lord is portrayed as miraculously bringing the bones back together into a skeleton. The skeleton becomes wrapped in muscles and tendons and flesh, and God then breathes life into the body. This is clearly speaking about Israel, for we read, "Son of man, these bones are the whole house of Israel" (verse 11). So this chapter portrays Israel as becoming a living, breathing nation, brought back from the dead, as it were. To be sure, this is portrayed as being a gradual process (from bones to muscles to tendons to flesh), but the prophecy will absolutely be fulfilled.

In AD 70, Titus and his Roman warriors trampled on and destroyed Jerusalem, definitively ending Israel's existence as a political entity (see

Luke 21:20). Since then, the Jews have been dispersed worldwide. In the year 1940, no one could have guessed that within a decade Israel would be a nation again. And yet it happened. Israel achieved statehood in 1948, and Jews have been returning to their homeland ever since. The vision in Ezekiel 37 is coming to pass just as predicted.

Ezekiel 38—*Who are the nations in this chapter that will one day launch a massive invasion into Israel?*

Though there is debate on this issue, many scholars believe these are the nations referenced in Ezekiel:

- Gog is the powerful leader of the invading coalition. He is referred to as the "prince of Rosh, Meshech and Tubal" (Ezekiel 38:2).

- Magog refers to the geographical area in the southern portion of the former Soviet Union—probably including the former southern Soviet republics of Kazakhstan, Kyrgyzstan, Uzbekistan, Turkmenistan, Tajikistan, and possibly even northern parts of modern Afghanistan.

- Rosh—a much-debated term—likely refers to modern Russia, to the uttermost north of Israel.

- Meshech and Tubal refer to the territory to the south of the Black and Caspian Seas, which is modern Turkey.

- Persia refers to modern Iran. Persia became Iran in 1935 and the Islamic Republic of Iran in 1979.

- Ethiopia refers to the geographical territory to the south of Egypt on the Nile River—what is today known as Sudan.

- Put, a land to the west of Egypt, is modern-day Libya. The term may also include the modern-day countries of Algeria and Tunisia.

- Gomer apparently refers to part of modern Turkey.

- Beth-togarmah also apparently refers to modern-day Turkey, though it may also include Azerbaijan and Armenia.

These, then, are the countries that will make up the northern military coalition that will one day invade Israel.

Daniel

Daniel 4:13—*What kind of angel is a "watcher" (KJV)?*

Apparently these are angels that have been sent by God specifically to observe what is transpiring on earth. The name suggests that these angels are especially vigilant in their activity of watching the affairs of earth. The word *watcher* in the Hebrew communicates the idea of vigilantly making sleepless watch. We might consider the watchers to be God's reconnaissance agents.

Some Bible expositors have related these watchers to Scriptures that mention the many eyes of certain angels. The cherubim, for example, are described as being full of eyes (Ezekiel 1:18). The angels in Revelation 4:6 are likewise described as being "covered with eyes, in front and in back."

Daniel 4:36-37—*Did Nebuchadnezzar become a believer?*

In Daniel 4:37 we read the words of Nebuchadnezzar: "I, Nebuchadnezzar, praise and exalt and glorify the King of heaven, because everything he does is right and all his ways are just. And those who walk in pride he is able to humble." It's hard to say for sure whether Nebuchadnezzar became a true believer. Scholars debate the issue. However, the fact that he praised, exalted, and glorified God as the King of heaven lends credence to the possibility that he became a believer. (Would an unbeliever utter such words?) When we arrive in heaven, it's possible we just may see him there!

Daniel 7:10—*How many angels are there?*

The Scriptures use terminology indicating that the number of angels is vast. Scripture makes reference to "a great company of the heavenly host" (Luke 2:13), and the angels are spoken of as "tens of thousands and thousands of thousands" (Psalm 68:17). Their number is elsewhere described as "myriads of myriads" (Revelation 5:11 NASB).

Daniel 7:10 says that "ten thousand times ten thousand stood before him"—which is 100,000,000 (one hundred million) angels. This is a number almost too vast to fathom. Job 25:3 understandably asks, "Can his forces be numbered?"

Scripture does not specify just how many angels there are. But one thing is certain: However many angels there are, there is certainly no increase or decrease in their number. Angels do not die, nor do they propagate and give birth to baby angels. The number of angels remains constant at all times.

Daniel 9:25-27—*What can we conclude about the timing of Daniel's 70 weeks?*

In Daniel 9 God provided a prophetic timetable for the nation of Israel. The prophetic clock began ticking when the command went out to restore and rebuild Jerusalem following its destruction by Babylon (verse 25). According to this verse, Israel's timetable was divided into 70 groups of 7 years, totaling 490 years. The first 69 groups of 7 years—or 483 years—counted the years "from the issuing of the decree to restore and rebuild Jerusalem until the Anointed One, the ruler, comes" (verse 25).

The Anointed One, of course, is Jesus Christ. *Anointed One* means Messiah. The day that Jesus rode into Jerusalem to proclaim Himself Israel's Messiah was 483 years to the day after the command to restore and rebuild Jerusalem had been given. At that point God's prophetic clock paused. Daniel describes a gap between these 483 years and the final 7 years of Israel's prophetic timetable. Several events were to take place during this gap, according to Daniel 9:26:

1. The Messiah was to be killed.

2. The city of Jerusalem and its temple would be destroyed (which occurred in AD 70).

3. The Jews would encounter difficulty and hardship from that time on.

The final "week" of seven years will begin for Israel when the Antichrist will confirm a covenant for seven years (Daniel 9:27). When this peace pact is signed, the tribulation period will begin. That signature marks the beginning of the seven-year countdown to the second coming of Christ (which follows the tribulation period).

Daniel 11:31—*What is the abomination that causes desolation?*

The abomination of desolation will take place in the future tribulation period when the Antichrist sets up an image of himself inside the Jewish temple (see Matthew 24:15). This will desecrate the temple. Such an abomination took place once before when Antiochus Epiphanies in 168 BC erected an altar to Zeus in the temple at Jerusalem and sacrificed a pig (an unclean animal) on it.

Daniel 12:2—*Will the resurrection involve all human beings or just some human beings?*

In this verse we read, "Multitudes who sleep in the dust of the earth will awake: some to everlasting life, others to shame and everlasting contempt." There are actually two resurrections—the resurrection of Christians and the resurrection of unbelievers (John 5:28-29; Acts 24:15). These resurrections will be separated by 1000 years (see Revelation 20:6). This means that the first resurrection is partial, involving only saved people. The second resurrection, involving the unsaved who will populate the lake of fire, completes the picture.

Hosea

Hosea 1:2—*How could a holy God instruct Hosea to take to himself an adulterous wife?*

The book of Hosea presents a graphic, metaphorical picture of God's own love for the adulterous nation of Israel. Hosea committed no immorality in marrying and remaining faithful to Gomer. In fact, when God commanded Hosea to take Gomer as his wife, she may not yet have actually committed adultery. Like Hosea, God committed no immorality for loving and remaining faithful to His bride, the unfaithful Israel.

Hosea had the legal right to have Gomer executed for her crime of adultery, but he nevertheless remained faithful to her. Likewise, God had the right to utterly obliterate Israel for her adulterous unfaithfulness, but He continued to love her, even though she suffered disciplinary consequences for her actions (in the form of invasion and domination by the Assyrians).

Joel

Joel 1:15—*What is the day of the Lord?*

The day of the Lord includes a time of great divine judgment and wrath that will one day come on all the nations and on Israel (Isaiah 2:12-21; 13:9-16; 34:1-8; Joel 1:15–2:11,28-32; 3:9-12; Amos 5:18-20; Obadiah 15-17; Zephaniah 1:7-18). That day will see the overthrow of God's enemies (Isaiah 2:12) and will serve to purge the rebels from Israel. It will result in Israel's return to the Lord (Ezekiel 20:33-39). It begins with judgment to defeat the enemies of God (the tribulation period) and ushers in a time of great blessing in the millennial kingdom in which Christ will reign with the church, the body of Christ (Zephaniah 1:7-18; 3:14-17).

Joel 2:28-32—*Was this prophecy of the outpouring of God's Spirit completely fulfilled on the Day of Pentecost (Acts 2:16)?*

Most conservative scholars don't think so. What we see in Acts 2 is simply an example of prophetic foreshadowing. Peter, who cited Joel 2:28-32, never said this prophecy was *completely* fulfilled on that day. He was saying, however, that the events that occurred on Pentecost in association with the Holy Spirit were not a result of intoxication but rather were in harmony with Old Testament revelation and prophecy. It is common in prophetic literature to witness foreshadowing. The ultimate fulfillment of Joel's prophecy is yet future.

Amos

Amos 5:21—*Why did God say, "I despise your religious feasts"?*

God hated them because His people, the Israelites, were merely engaging in external rituals with no heartfelt obedience. While they were engaging in religious feasts, they were at the same time trampling on the poor, taking and giving bribes, and depriving people of justice. The religious establishment had become utterly corrupt.

Amos 8:14—*Does this verse deny that a resurrection will occur?*

This verse speaks of those who "will fall, never to rise again." It refers not to resurrection but to the fact that this enemy of God will never rise in power again.

Jonah

Jonah 1:17—*How could Jonah have been swallowed by a great fish?*

Some fish are certainly big enough to swallow human beings, so such a thing is definitely possible. As for Jonah surviving inside the fish for three days, this was unquestionably a miracle of the Lord. God providentially guided things from beginning to end.

Jonah 3:4-10; 4:1-2—*Did the prophets utter erroneous prophecies?*

Jonah prophesied that in 40 days, Nineveh would be overthrown and destroyed because of its sin. Nineveh did not get overthrown or destroyed, so was Jonah wrong?

No, Jonah did not make a mistake. He told the Ninevites exactly what God told him to say (see Jonah 3:1). Jonah's prophecy to the Ninevites apparently included a repentance clause (this clause is stated in Jeremiah 18:7-8). The Ninevites thus understood the final outcome of things to be dependent on how they responded. They understood Jonah's prophecy to mean that Nineveh would be toppled in 40 days *unless* they repented (Jonah 3:5-9). The Ninevites responded to Jonah's prophecy with national repentance, so God withdrew the threatened punishment in keeping with His promise in Jeremiah 18:7-8.

Micah

Micah 3:4—*Does God sometimes withhold blessing to those who cry out for it?*

God does not withhold blessing to the righteous or to the repentant or to the sincere of heart. But God does withhold blessing from the wicked, the unrepentant, and the insincere of heart. God may also withhold blessing for a lack of faith (James 1:6), for asking selfishly (James 4:3), or for asking for things outside of God's will (see 2 Corinthians 12:8-9).

Micah 5:2—*Did Jesus come into being at a point in time?*

In this verse we read that Christ's "origins are from of old, from ancient times." Some misunderstand the phrase *from of old* as meaning that Christ must have come into being at a point in time.

Contrary to such a view, the same Hebrew word is used by the prophet Habakkuk to refer to God's eternal nature (Habakkuk 1:12). Certainly this doesn't mean that God is a created being. We may conclude that Micah's use of the phrase points to Christ's eternal nature, just as the term points to God's eternal nature in Habakkuk. Moreover, the phrase "from ancient times" is literally "days of immeasurable time." Taken together, the terms place Christ beyond time altogether. He is, along with the Father and the Holy Spirit, the eternal one—and His rule reaches back into eternity.

Nahum

Nahum 1:2-3—*How can we reconcile the statement that the Lord is a jealous and avenging God with what we learn elsewhere about God's love?*

All these things are true of God at the same time. On the one hand, God most certainly is a God of love, seeking the highest good of all His creatures. On the other hand, God is a jealous God, not in the sense of the negative emotion, but in the sense that He desires His people to be utterly faithful and obedient to Him. He is an avenging God in the sense that there are consequences for how people treat Him—especially if they spurn Him. The plagues against pharaoh and the Egyptians reveal how God can be an avenging God. Certainly all this is in keeping with what we learn of God in the New Testament. For example, Paul wrote, "The Lord is the avenger" (1 Thessalonians 4:6). Scripture is clear that God is "slow to anger" (Nehemiah 9:17), so when God does get angry, there is very good reason for it.

Let us note that even Jesus, who was God and who might be described as love incarnate, showed righteous anger at the hypocritical Jewish leaders and dealt harshly with them (Matthew 23:15-36).

Habakkuk

Habakkuk 3:3—*If God is omnipresent, how could He come from Teman?*

This verse states that "God came from Teman, the Holy One from Mount Paran." Other verses indicate that God is omnipresent (Psalm 139:7-8; Jeremiah 23:23-24; Acts 17:27-28). Actually, though, these verses do not contradict. God in His essence is omnipresent. Habakkuk 3:3 is referring to a theophany, or special appearance of God to His people. A special appearance of God came from Teman, though God at the same time was omnipresent in His essential nature.

Haggai

Haggai 2:6-7—*What is meant by "the desired of all nations" that will come?*

Most Bible expositors take this as a reference to the coming Messiah. The verse carries the idea that people of all nations ultimately yearn for peace and for a ruler who can bring it about. Jesus is the only one who can.

Malachi

Malachi 2:11—*What is meant by "the daughter of a foreign god"?*

This is a reference to a pagan woman. She is a daughter of a foreign god in the sense that she worshipped a pagan god and not the true God of Israel. Old Testament law forbade Israelite men from marrying such women because of the likelihood that it would lead to apostasy.

Malachi 3:8-10—*Is a 10 percent tithe required for New Testament believers?*

In Old Testament times, tithing was commanded by God on the basis that "the earth is the LORD's and all it contains, the world, and those who dwell in it" (Psalm 24:1 NASB). The tithe was a means whereby the people of God acknowledged that God owned all things and was sovereign over them. It was an acknowledgment that all the good things we have in life ultimately come from Him. God's people were commanded to tithe various things, including the land and its produce (Leviticus 27:30), the animals (Leviticus 27:32), and new wine, oil, and honey (2 Chronicles 31:5). Withholding tithes and offerings from God amounted to robbing God (Malachi 3:8-10).

Despite the heavy emphasis on tithing in the Old Testament, many Bible expositors today do not believe tithing is intended for the New Testament church—at least as a commandment from the law. In fact, the New Testament never specifies that believers should give 10 percent of their income to the church. This should not be taken to mean, however, that church members should not support the church financially. The New Testament emphasis seems to be on what might be called *grace giving*. We are to freely give as we have freely received.

And we are to give as we are able (2 Corinthians 8:12). For some, this will mean less than 10 percent. For others whom God has materially blessed, this will mean much more than 10 percent.

The starting point for a right attitude toward giving to the church is that we must first give ourselves to the Lord. The early church is our example: "They gave themselves first to the Lord and then to us in keeping with God's will" (2 Corinthians 8:5). Only when we have given ourselves to the Lord will we have a proper perspective on money.

We also read in Romans 12:1, "Offer your bodies as living sacrifices, holy and pleasing to God—this is your spiritual act of worship." The first sacrifice we make to God is not financial. Our first sacrifice is that of our own lives. As we give ourselves unconditionally to the Lord for His service, our attitude toward money will be what it should be. God is not interested in our money until He first has our hearts.

The
NEW TESTAMENT

Matthew

Matthew 1:1-19; Luke 3:23-38—*How are we to explain the differences in these two genealogies of Christ?*

Up to David, the two genealogies are practically the same. In fact, they share some 18 or 19 common names, depending on whether Matthan and Matthat are the same person. From David on, they are very different. Almost none of the names from David to Joseph coincide. (In fact, only two of the names—Shealtiel and Zerubbabel—coincide.) However, the genealogies are not irreconcilable.

Matthew's genealogy traces Joseph's line of descendants to show the passing of the legal title to the throne of David. As Joseph's adopted Son, Jesus became his legal heir so far as his inheritance was concerned. The "of whom was born Jesus" (Matthew 1:16) includes a feminine relative pronoun, clearly indicating that Jesus was the physical child of Mary and that Joseph was not His physical father.

Matthew traced the line from Abraham and David in 41 links to Joseph. (Matthew obviously did not list every individual in the genealogy. Jewish reckoning did not require every name in order to satisfy a genealogy.) Abraham and David were those with whom God enacted unconditional covenants pertaining to the Messiah. Matthew's Gospel was written to Jews, so Matthew wanted to prove to Jews that Jesus was the promised Messiah. This would demand a fulfillment of the Abrahamic covenant (Genesis 12:1-3) and the Davidic covenant (2 Samuel 7:12-14). Matthew was calling attention to the fact that Jesus came to fulfill the covenants made with Israel's forefathers.

Luke's genealogy, by contrast, traces Mary's lineage and carries all the way back beyond the time of Abraham to Adam and the commencement of the human race. Whereas Matthew's genealogy pointed to Jesus as the Jewish Messiah, Luke's genealogy pointed to Jesus as the Son of Man, a name often used of Jesus in Luke's Gospel. Matthew's genealogy was concerned with the Messiah as related to the Jews, and Luke's genealogy was concerned with the Messiah as related to the entire human race.

Matthew 2:1-12—*Does the star the Magi followed imply that astrology is helpful?*

The star was to announce the birth of Christ, not to foretell this event. God gave the star to the Magi to proclaim to them that the divine child had already been born. We know the child was already born because Herod gave a command to kill all the boys in Bethlehem and vicinity who were two years old or younger in accordance with "the time he had learned from the Magi" (Matthew 2:16).

The only sense in which the stars give revelation is that they reveal the existence of God in a general way. Psalm 19:1-6 affirms that the heavens declare God's glory, and Romans 1:18-20 teaches that creation reveals God's existence. Further, in relation to the end times, Christ indicates there will be cosmic disturbances in connection with His second coming (Matthew 24:29-30).

Matthew 4:7—*Could Jesus have succumbed to the temptations He experienced?*

Some theologians believe that since Jesus became a man, He must have been temptable with the possibility of sinning. Other theologians believe it would have been impossible for Jesus to sin by virtue of the fact that He was also God.

I believe Christ, the God-man, could not have sinned. Here's why:

1. In His divine nature, He is immutable and does not change.

2. In His divine nature, He is omniscient (all-knowing) and is therefore fully aware of all the consequences of sin.

3. In His divine nature, He is omnipotent (all-powerful) in His ability to resist sin.

4. Hebrews 4:15 tells us that He was tempted and yet was without sin.

5. Christ had no sin nature as do all other human beings, and He was perfectly holy from birth (Luke 1:35).

6. There is an analogy between the written Word of God (the Bible) and the living Word of God (Christ). Just as the authorship of the Bible involved humans (Matthew, Mark, Luke, and John, for example) and God (the Holy Spirit) and is completely without error, so Christ is fully divine and fully human and is completely without (and unable to) sin.

Does this mean that Christ's temptations were unreal? No. I believe that Christ was genuinely tempted, but the temptations stood no chance of luring Him to sin. It is much like a canoe attempting to launch an attack against a United States battleship, banging against the hull of the ship with all its might. The attack is genuine, but it stands no chance of success.

Matthew 5:8—*Did Jesus teach that only those who are sinless (pure of heart) will ultimately end up in heaven and see God?*

No one is pure enough in oneself—that is, holy enough—to earn heaven. But one who has trusted in Christ has been made pure because he has had the very righteousness of Christ imputed to him. These individuals are *accounted* as "pure of heart" before God (Romans 4:5; 5:1; Hebrews 10:14). God's declaration of righteousness is given to believers "freely by his grace" (Romans 3:24). The word *grace* literally means unmerited favor. It is thus because of God's unmerited favor that believers can freely be declared righteous before God and enjoy a destiny in heaven.

Matthew 5:13—*What does Jesus mean when He says, "You are the salt of the earth"?*

The people of Jesus' day were well acquainted with the fact that salt is effective as a preservative. Christ was saying that His followers are to have a preserving effect on the world by influencing it on His behalf. Salt that loses its flavor—probably a reference to salt that gets mixed with soil and thereby deteriorates—loses its preserving abilities. By analogy, Christ was saying that He desires that His followers serve as a preservative in society, but they will be effective in doing so only so long as they retain their commitment to Him and refuse contamination by the world system.

Matthew 5:17-18—*Are Christians still under the law of Moses?*

Christians today are no more under the Ten Commandments as given by Moses to Israel than we are under the Mosaic law's requirement to be circumcised (see Acts 15; Galatians 3) or to bring a lamb to the temple in Jerusalem for sacrifice. Hebrews 7 declares that "when there is a change of the priesthood, there must also be a change of the law" (verse 12). Today Jesus Himself is our High Priest, so the old priesthood (and old law) passed away—"the former regulation is set aside because it was weak and useless" (verse 18). The law was only a shadow, and the substance is found in Christ (Colossians 2:17 NASB).

Certainly Jesus' disciples rejected much of the Old Testament law, including circumcision (Acts 15; Galatians 5:6; 6:15). Indeed, Paul declared that "you are not under law but under grace" (Romans 6:14) and that the Ten Commandments engraved in stone have been "taken away in Christ" (2 Corinthians 3:14 NKJV).

Still, the moral principles embodied in the commandments reflect the very nature of an unchanging God and are still binding on believers today. Indeed, every one of the principles in the Ten Commandments is restated in another context in the New Testament except the command to rest and worship on Saturday. So even though the Old Testament law has passed away, similar New Testament moral requirements are still binding on the Christian.

Matthew 5:22—*Are we in danger of the fire of hell for saying "You fool!" to someone?*

Jesus' statement on this matter is found in a broader discourse in which He was teaching about the law against murder (Matthew 5:22-26). The Pharisees taught that murder involved the external act of taking someone else's life. They were concerned only with the physical act of murder. They interpreted the law to mean that so long as one did not take another man's life, one was innocent of breaking God's law. But Jesus challenged the Pharisees' understanding by pointing out that guilt comes not only from the external act but also from the internal attitude that leads up to the act. Yes, murder is wrong, but so is the anger that leads up to that murder. Seen in this light, the Pharisees certainly fell under condemnation because their inner attitudes were brimming with sin.

Jesus taught that the person who says to another, "Raca" (empty-head, shallow-brains) or "You fool" is demonstrating within his own heart the anger that can lead to murder, and this inner sinful attitude alone is sufficient to bring condemnation before God. The sin has already taken place in the heart before any kind of external act of murder has occurred. A person with this kind of inner attitude is obviously a sinner and is on a path that leads to hell (and will actually end up in hell if he does not trust in Christ).

Matthew 5:29—*Did Jesus advocate maiming our bodies—like gouging out a right eye—in order to become saved?*

Jesus is not actually teaching self-mutilation, for even a blind man can lust in his heart, and a man with no hands can yearn to steal. Remember, sin begins in the heart (Jeremiah 17:9). Jesus is purposefully using strong and graphic language to stress how utterly dangerous sin is and how it can lead to eternal condemnation. Many scholars believe Jesus is using a hyperbole in this verse. A hyperbole is a figure of speech that purposefully exaggerates to make a powerful point. In the present case, the hyperbole emphasizes the need for drastic action in dealing with sin. To keep from offending God by sin, radical changes are often necessary. Every occasion that may lead to sin is to be cut off.

Matthew 5:37—*Is it wrong to take oaths?*

Some legitimate oaths are mentioned throughout both the Old Testament (Exodus 20:7; Leviticus 5:1; 19:12; Numbers 30:2-15; Deuteronomy 23:21-23) and the New Testament (Acts 2:30; Hebrews 6:16-18; 7:20-22). Even the apostle Paul said, "I call God as my witness" (2 Corinthians 1:23), just as he also said, "I assure you before God that what I am writing to you is no lie" (Galatians 1:20). So oaths can be made in some cases.

The problem Jesus was addressing was that oaths became so common in biblical times that people started to assume that when one did not take an oath, perhaps one was not being truthful. To counter such an idea, Jesus tells His followers that they should have no duplicity in their words, that their yes should be yes and their no should be no.

Matthew 5:38-42—*Are we to turn the other cheek in virtually all circumstances?*

Probably not. Even Christ did not literally turn the other cheek when smitten by a member of the Sanhedrin (John 18:22-23).

The backdrop to this teaching is that the Jews considered it an insult to be hit in the face, much in the same way that we would interpret someone spitting in our face. The principle taught in the Sermon on the Mount would seem to be that Christians should not retaliate when insulted or slandered (see Romans 12:17-21). Such insults do not threaten a Christian's personal safety. They are a far cry from self-defense (Luke 22:36).

Matthew 5:44—*How is it possible to truly love our enemies and pray for those who persecute us?*

The Jewish leaders of Jesus' day taught that we should love those near and dear to us (Leviticus 19:18) but hate our enemies. The Pharisees believed that the very act of hating their enemies constituted a form of God's judgment against them. Jesus refuted this idea, instructing His followers to love even their enemies. After all, God the Father loves all people, and we as Christians are to take on the family likeness, imitating God in our love for all people (see Matthew 5:48).

In our own strength, loving our enemies is an impossibility. But as we walk in the power of the Holy Spirit, living in dependence on Him and His mighty power, such love—a part of the fruit of the Spirit—becomes a reality in our lives (see Galatians 5:22-23; Colossians 3:12-15).

Matthew 5:48—*In what sense can we follow Christ's command, "Be perfect...as your heavenly Father is perfect"?*

Matthew 5:48 is not communicating the idea that human beings can attain sinless perfection. Such an idea is foreign not only to the immediate context of Matthew's Gospel but also to the broader context of all of Scripture.

Contrary to the idea of sinless perfection, Jesus taught that people without exception are utterly sinful. Indeed, He taught that human beings have a grave sin problem that is altogether beyond their means to solve. He taught that human beings are evil (Matthew 12:34) and that man is capable of great wickedness (Mark 7:20-23). Moreover, He said that man is utterly lost (Luke 19:10), that he is a sinner (Luke 15:10), that he is in need of repentance before a holy God (Mark 1:15), and that he needs to be born again (John 3:3,5,7).

In view of all this, how can we make sense of Matthew 5:48? This verse is found in a section of Scripture dealing with the law of love. The Jewish leaders of Jesus' day had taught that we should love those who were near and dear to us (Leviticus 19:18) but hate those who are enemies. Jesus refutes this idea, instructing us to love even our enemies. After all, Jesus said, God's love extends to all people (Matthew 5:45). And since God is our righteous standard, we should seek to be as He is in this regard. We are to aim to be perfect in loving as He is perfect.

Matthew 6:3-4—*Why did Jesus say we should not let our left hand know what our right hand is doing when we give to others?*

Jesus was aiming His comments primarily at the Pharisees. The Pharisees used opportunities to give as ways of openly demonstrating their piety before people. They made a real show of it. They constantly tried to impress others with their liberality. The Pharisees were so well-known for doing this that beggars soon caught on and positioned themselves at the entrance of the temple so they might be the recipients of the giving of the Pharisees.

Christ, in contrast to the Pharisees, said we should give quietly and with no fanfare to impress men. We should give in such a way that our left hand does not know what the right hand is doing—that is, it should be done privately and in secret. The one who gives with a righteous motive will receive a rich reward from the Father. Even if the giving takes place in secret, the Father sees it and will reward it accordingly.

Matthew 6:7—*Did Jesus teach that we should recite only short prayers?*

In Jesus' instructions about prayer, He said, "When you pray, do not keep on babbling like pagans, for they think they will be heard because of their many words" (Matthew 6:7). These words of Jesus were aimed at the Pharisees who always made a public show of their prayers. They often prayed in public places—perhaps on crowded street corners—to impress people with their piety. They also made their prayers excessively long, a practice picked up from pagans who engaged in endless repetition and incantation (see 1 Kings 18:26). They believed that endless repetition of specific requests endeared the petitioner to God and obligated God to answer.

The point of Jesus' instruction is not that we should necessarily utter short prayers before God (although short prayers are just fine if that is all you have time for or if that meets your particular need at the moment). The point of Jesus' instruction is that we should not engage in endless babbling, repeating the same request over and over again within the confines of a single prayer, as if that would force God's hand to answer. God answers prayer not because He can be moved to do so by endless babbling but rather because He desires to do so as your heavenly Father.

Matthew 6:9—*Is belief in a heavenly Father a sexist concept?*

God equally values both men and women, for both were created in the image of God (Genesis 1:26), and both are positionally equal before God (Galatians 3:28). The four Gospels indicate that Jesus defended and exalted women in a very patriarchal Jewish culture (see John 4). So Christianity cannot be said to be sexist; rather, Jesus, the founder of Christianity, vigorously fought the sexism of His day.

Interestingly, even though God is referred to in the Bible as Father (and never Mother), some of His actions are occasionally described in feminine terms. For example, Jesus likened God to a mother hen who gathers her chicks under her wings (Matthew 23:37-39). God is also said to have given birth to Israel (Deuteronomy 32:18).

Of course, God is not a gender being as humans are. He is not of the male sex, per se. The primary emphasis in God being called Father is that He is personal and He is a strong, divine Father figure to His children. Unlike the dead and impersonal idols of paganism, the true God is a personal being with whom we can relate. In fact, we can even call Him Abba (an Aramaic word that loosely means Daddy). That's how intimate a relationship we can have with Him.

Matthew 6:13—*Does Jesus imply that God could lead us into temptation?*

No, for James 1:13 tells us, "When tempted, no one should say, 'God is tempting me.' For God cannot be tempted by evil, nor does he tempt anyone." God is not the source of our temptations. James 1:14 teaches that we are tempted when, by our own evil desire, we are dragged away and enticed. Our temptations are rooted in our own sinful nature.

With this backdrop in mind, scholars suggest two possible

explanations of Jesus' words "lead us not into temptation" in the Lord's Prayer. Some believe that all Jesus was saying is that we should ask God to so order our lives and guide our steps that we are not brought into situations in which we will find ourselves tempted to do evil. We should ask God to keep our spiritual "radar screens" active so we can steer ourselves away from tempting circumstances.

Other scholars believe Jesus may be instructing us to pray, "Let us not succumb to temptation." Seen in this light, this part of the Lord's Prayer constitutes a request of God that whenever we encounter temptations in the course of daily living, God will deliver us (see 1 Corinthians 10:13).

Matthew 6:14-15—*Will the Lord refuse to forgive us if we do not forgive others when they sin against us?*

A number of key passages indicate the absoluteness of the forgiveness God bestows on us in terms of our eternal salvation. For example, in Hebrews 10:17 God said, "Their sins and lawless acts I will remember no more." In Psalm 103:11-12 we are told, "For as high as the heavens are above the earth, so great is his love for those who fear him; as far as the east is from the west, so far has he removed our transgressions from us."

This being the case, how are we to interpret Matthew 6:14-15, where Jesus said, "If you forgive men when they sin against you, your heavenly Father will also forgive you. But if you do not forgive men their sins, your Father will not forgive your sins"?

Theologians suggest that there is one sense of forgiveness that relates to our eternal salvation and another sense that relates to our daily fellowship with God. They indicate that in Matthew 6:14-15 the latter sense is in view. The meaning of our passage would thus be this: If we do not forgive others in the body of Christ, our fellowship with God is broken because our fellowship with Him hinges on our forgiveness of others. God still views us as saved in terms of our eternal destiny, but from a temporal perspective our fellowship with God is broken until we repent and forgive others.

Matthew 7:6—*Why did Jesus say, "Do not give dogs what is sacred; do not throw your pearls to pigs"?*

Jesus was communicating to His followers that in their relationships with enemies of the gospel, they were to be very cautious, recognizing that these enemies may turn on them and even kill them. The teaching that is given to others should always be in accordance with their spiritual capacity.

For those who have little or no spiritual capacity (enemies of the gospel), we must be cautious in what we say and not throw our pearls to pigs. We must be cautious not to pass on the sacred to that which is profane. We should be careful not to pass on holy things to unholy people who will have nothing but disdain for the things of Christ.

Matthew 7:7-8—*Despite Jesus' prayer promise—"Ask and it will be given to you"—prayers don't always get answered. Why not?*

There could be a number of scriptural answers. Even this passage indicates that we must be persistent in our prayers. The tenses in the Greek for this passage carry the idea, "Keep on asking and it will be given." We must also remember that our prayers are subject to the sovereign will of God. If we ask for something God doesn't want us to have, He will sovereignly deny that request (1 John 5:14). Sin can also be a hindrance to prayer being answered (Psalm 66:18) just as living righteously is a great benefit to prayer being answered (Proverbs 15:29).

Matthew 7:21-23—*Does Jesus teach that we must successfully and consistently obey God's will to be saved?*

In Matthew 7:21 Jesus said, "Not everyone who says to me, 'Lord, Lord,' will enter the kingdom of heaven, but only he who does the will of my Father who is in heaven." Jesus was dealing with the Pharisees, whom He categorized as false prophets (Matthew 7:15). These individuals may have claimed to be God's representatives with God's message, but in fact they were not at all what they appeared to be. They were ferocious wolves who had come to destroy God's flock (see

Matthew 23:1-36). They were full of hypocrisy and unrighteousness. Despite all their righteous claims, Christ in Matthew 7:21-23 indicated that mere lip service is not enough.

Matthew 8:11-12—*What future feast is Jesus referring to?*

In Matthew 8:11-12 Jesus said that "many will come from the east and the west, and will take their places at the feast with Abraham, Isaac and Jacob in the kingdom of heaven." Participating in God's future kingdom is often pictured in the Bible as eating at a banquet (see Isaiah 25:6; Matthew 22:1-14). Many Jews thought they would enter God's kingdom and be at this banquet solely because of their blood relationship to Abraham. However, Jesus indicated in Matthew 8:11-12 that many who thought they would be at this banquet because of ties to Abraham would in fact be denied entrance altogether, and many who do not even have such blood ties (Gentiles) would be granted entrance (by faith in Christ).

Matthew 8:12—*Is hell a place of darkness, or is there light (from flames of fire)?*

Both *fire* and *darkness* are powerful figures of speech that appropriately describe the unthinkable reality of hell. It is like fire because it is a place of torment. Hell is a lake of burning sulfur (Revelation 19:20; 20:14-15), an eternal fire (Matthew 25:41), and a fiery furnace (Matthew 13:42). It is like an outer darkness because the light of God is entirely absent. Only people with darkened (sinful) souls dwell there, along with the prince of darkness, Satan himself (Matthew 8:12; 25:41).

Matthew 8:20—*If Jesus was the Son of God, why did He call Himself the Son of Man?*

Jesus was not denying His deity by referring to Himself as the Son of Man. The term *Son of Man* is used to describe Christ's deity as well. The Bible says that only God can forgive sins (Isaiah 43:25; Mark 2:7). But as the Son of Man, Jesus had the power to forgive sins (Mark 2:10). Likewise, Christ will return to earth as the Son of Man in clouds of glory to reign on earth (Matthew 26:63-64). This indicated that Jesus Himself used the phrase *Son of Man* to indicate His deity as the Son of God. Clearly, the term *Son of Man* was a messianic title.

Matthew 9:33—*Does the devil cause all illnesses?*

The devil and demons can cause dumbness (Matthew 9:33), blindness (Matthew 12:22), and epilepsy (Matthew 17:15-18). Further, they afflict people with mental disorders (Mark 5:4-5; Luke 8:27-29; 9:37-42), cause people to be self-destructive (Mark 5:5; Luke 9:42), and are even responsible for the deaths of some people (Revelation 9:14-19). However, we must be careful to note that even though demons can cause physical illnesses, Scripture distinguishes natural illnesses from demon-caused illnesses (Matthew 4:24; Mark 1:32; Luke 7:21; 9:1; Acts 5:16). Scripture mentions a number of illnesses without referring to demons (see Matthew 8:5-13; 9:19-20,27-30; 12:9-14; 14:35-36).

Matthew 10:5-6—*Why did Jesus first tell His disciples not to go among the Gentiles? Does He not love them too?*

Jesus sent out the disciples with the following instructions: "Do not go among the Gentiles or enter any town of the Samaritans. Go rather to the lost sheep of Israel" (Matthew 10:5-6). In the outworking of God's plan of salvation, the good news of the kingdom was apparently to be preached first to the Jews—God's covenant people (2 Samuel 7:12-14). But the Gentiles would certainly not be excluded. God's offer was ultimately for all humankind, as is clear in the Abrahamic covenant in Genesis 12:3 (where we are told that all the people of the earth would be blessed through the Messiah) and in Christ's Great Commission to share the good news with all people everywhere (Matthew 28:19-20).

Matthew 10:16—*Why did Jesus instruct the disciples to be as shrewd as snakes and as innocent as doves?*

This instruction must be understood as part of a larger discourse in which Jesus warned the disciples about possible dangers they might face in coming days as they ministered in His name (Matthew 10:16-23). He spoke about how they would be persecuted by religious and civil authorities (verses 17-18) and even be rejected by their own families (verses 21-22). Understandably, He began His discourse by telling them they should be as shrewd as serpents and innocent as doves.

In the ancient Near East the serpent was considered a cunning creature. So when Jesus said His followers should be as shrewd as serpents, He was speaking in a way they would have readily understood. In the original Greek, the word *shrewd* carries the idea of prudence. The disciples were to be circumspect, discreet, judicious, and sensible in the way they handled themselves before others.

The disciples were also to be innocent as doves. The Greek word for *innocent* means without any mixture of deceit, without falsity, unadulterated, harmless, and pure. Such words were to characterize Christ's disciples.

Matthew 10:21-22—*What is it in allegiance to Jesus that causes family breakups?*

We find Jesus' words about family breakups in a broader discourse in which Jesus warned the 12 disciples about possible dangers they would face in their work of ministry (Matthew 10:16-23). He first warned them that they would be persecuted and would have to answer to religious and civil authorities (verses 16-18). He then warned that they would even be hated by their own families for following Him (verses 21-22). He taught that commitment to following Him would be tested by all the significant relationships in life—civil, religious, and family.

Matthew 10:32-33—*Do we lose our salvation if we fail to tell others about Jesus?*

The broader context of this passage relates to the Pharisees, who had continuously disowned Jesus, while the disciples followed Him and spoke about Him in every city they visited. Seen against this backdrop, Jesus' words take on great significance. We might paraphrase

His teaching this way: "Whoever acknowledges me before men [such as you disciples have done], I will also acknowledge him before my Father in heaven. But whoever disowns me before men [as these Pharisees do on every occasion they get], I will disown him before my Father in heaven."

We derive a significant lexical insight from the original Greek text of this verse. The word for *disown* is in the aorist tense. This points to the fact that Jesus is not talking about a single instance of denial or disowning (as was the case with Peter, who actually denied Christ three times—Luke 22:34), but is rather referring to life in its entirety. The aorist tense views a person's life globally, or as a lifetime. The person who throughout his life denies or disowns Christ (as was typically the case with the Pharisees) will be disowned by Christ before the Father.

Matthew 11:12—*Why did Jesus say the kingdom of heaven had been forcefully advancing, and forceful men lay hold of it?*

Scholars are divided as to what this means. Some believe Jesus is indicating that opposition had constantly risen against John the Baptist and Himself. The kingdom of heaven had been assaulted, and violent men—particularly the religious leaders of Israel—continued to assault it. Yet the kingdom also continued to advance.

Other scholars believe that perhaps Jesus is referring to His own disciples. If this view is correct, the disciples are here portrayed as forceful men—that is, men full of vigor, courage, and power, committed to spreading the good news of the kingdom of God despite any persecution they might face.

Still other scholars suggest that the dynamic preaching of John the Baptist led to a great popular uprising, a virtual storming of people into the kingdom of God. People rushed with great eagerness to get into the kingdom—an eagerness that might even be called a violent zeal.

And still other scholars suggest that the forceful advancing of the kingdom of heaven may refer to the tremendous miracles that accompanied the spread of the kingdom of God through the ministry of

Jesus Christ. In this interpretation, Christ's miracles in spreading the kingdom are viewed as pushing back the forces of darkness, so His kingdom has been forcefully advancing.

Matthew 11:14—*When Jesus said John the Baptist was the Elijah who was to come, was He teaching reincarnation?*

Luke 1:17 clarifies any possible confusion on the proper interpretation of Matthew 11:14 by pointing out that the ministry of John the Baptist was carried out "in the spirit and power of Elijah." Nowhere does Scripture say that John the Baptist was a reincarnation of Elijah. Reincarnationists forget that John the Baptist, when asked if he was Elijah, flatly answered no (John 1:21). And besides, Elijah does not fit the reincarnation model because he did not die. He was taken directly to heaven like Enoch, who did not see death (2 Kings 2:11; see also Hebrews 11:5). According to traditional reincarnation, one must first die before he can be reincarnated into another body.

Matthew 12:32—*Does this verse speak of the unforgivable sin?*

In this verse we read, "Anyone who speaks a word against the Son of Man will be forgiven, but anyone who speaks against the Holy Spirit will not be forgiven, either in this age or in the age to come." The parallel account in Mark 3:29 (NASB) says, "Whoever blasphemes against the Holy Spirit never has forgiveness, but is guilty of an eternal sin."

The broader backdrop to understanding Matthew 12:32 is that the Jewish leaders who had just witnessed a mighty miracle of Christ should have recognized that Jesus performed this miracle in the power of the Holy Spirit. After all, the Hebrew Scriptures, of which the Jews were well familiar, prophesied that when the Messiah came He would perform specific mighty miracles in the power of the Spirit—like giving sight to the blind, opening deaf ears, and enabling the lame to walk (see Isaiah 35:5-6). Instead, these Jewish leaders claimed that Christ did these miracles in the power of the devil, the *un*holy spirit. This was a sin against the Holy Spirit. This shows that these Jewish leaders had completely hardened themselves against the things of God.

Bible expositors point out that "blaspheming the Spirit" involves opposing Jesus' messiahship so firmly and definitively that one resorts to accusations of sorcery to avoid the impact of the Holy Spirit's miraculous signs that confirm Christ's messianic identity. This is truly a damning sin, for the only provision for man's sin is the work of the one true Messiah, as attested by the Holy Spirit.

Moreover, the Holy Spirit brings conviction upon people and leads their hearts to repentance, making people open and receptive to salvation in Jesus Christ. So the one who blasphemes the Holy Spirit effectively separates himself from the only one who can lead him on the path to salvation in Jesus Christ. This is precisely what happened to the Jewish leaders.

Matthew 12:40—*How can it be said that Jesus was in the tomb three days and three nights?*

The Gospel accounts are clear that Jesus was crucified and buried on Friday, sometime before sundown. This means Jesus was in the grave for part of Friday, the entire Sabbath (Saturday), and part of Sunday. In other words, He was in the tomb for two full nights, one full day, and part of two days. How do we reconcile this with Jesus' words in Matthew 12:40 that He would be three days and three nights in the heart of the earth?

In the Jewish mind-set, any part of a day was reckoned as a complete day. The Babylonian Talmud (a set of Jewish commentaries) tells us that "the portion of a day is as the whole of it." Though Jesus was really in the tomb for part of Friday, all of Saturday, and part of Sunday, in Jewish reckoning He was in the tomb for "three days and three nights."

Matthew 12:43-45—*What was Jesus' point in saying that seven evil spirits might return to possess a man who had been delivered from one demon?*

Jesus was speaking with Pharisees who were seeking a sign from Him (Matthew 12:38). Jesus answered by charging that they were seeking a sign for all the wrong reasons (verses 39-45). He then zeroed in on the real problem of the Pharisees: They were seeking to externally reform themselves but were without inner spiritual conversion and lacked the power of God in their lives.

Jesus compared the Pharisees to a man who had been delivered of a demon. Following this deliverance, the man did everything he could by natural means to clean up his life. But the man did not truly convert to God and believe in Him; he merely engaged in practicing religion. Then seven other spirits returned and possessed the man, and the man was in a much worse condition than he initially was.

The lesson Jesus was teaching the Pharisees was that they were in danger of the same type of thing happening to them. Their human attempts at reformation—without personal conversion, without trusting in Christ, without experiencing the true power of God—would ultimately lead them to a worse condition than they were presently in.

Matthew 13:10-11—*Why does Jesus teach the secrets of the kingdom only to some?*

In Matthew 13, Jesus is portrayed as being in front of a mixed multitude comprised of both believers and unbelievers. He did not attempt to separate the believers from the unbelievers and then instruct only the believers. Rather, He constructed His teaching so that believers would understand what He said but unbelievers would not, and He did this by using parables.

After teaching one such parable, a disciple asked Jesus, "Why do you speak to the people in parables?" (Matthew 13:10). Jesus answered: "The knowledge of the secrets of the kingdom of heaven has been given to you [believers], but not to them [unbelievers]" (verse 11).

The Greek word for *secret* in this passage simply means a mystery. A mystery in the biblical sense is a truth that cannot be discerned simply by human investigation, but requires special revelation from God. Generally, this word refers to a truth that was unknown to people living in Old Testament times but is now revealed to humankind by God (Matthew 13:17; Colossians 1:26). In Matthew 13, Jesus provides information to believers about the kingdom of heaven that has never been revealed before.

As to why Jesus engineered His parabolic teaching so that believers could understand His teaching but unbelievers could not, the backdrop is that the disciples, having responded favorably to Jesus' teaching and having placed their faith in Him, already knew much truth about the Messiah. Careful reflection on Jesus' parables would enlighten them even further.

However, hardened unbelievers who had willfully and persistently refused Jesus' previous teachings were prevented from understanding the parables. Jesus was apparently following an injunction He provided earlier in the Sermon on the Mount: "Do not give dogs what is sacred; do not throw your pearls to pigs" (Matthew 7:6). Yet there is grace even here. For Jesus may have prevented unbelievers from understanding the parables because He did not want to add more responsibility to them by imparting new truth for which they would be held responsible.

Matthew 13:31-32—*What was Jesus teaching about the kingdom of heaven by comparing it to a mustard seed?*

Jesus taught that the kingdom of heaven would have an almost imperceptible beginning—hardly even noticeable. But just as a small mustard seed can produce a large plant—it can grow more than 15 feet high—so the kingdom would start small but grow to be very large.

Matthew 13:33—*Yeast is often representative of evil in Scripture, so why does Jesus say the kingdom of heaven is like yeast?*

Scholars have different opinions about what Jesus is saying here. Some argue that since yeast represents evil elsewhere in Scripture (Matthew 16:12; Mark 8:15; Luke 12:1; 1 Corinthians 5:6-8; Galatians 5:9), Jesus must be saying that evil will be present in some form within Christendom until Christ comes again (see 1 Timothy 4:1-5). Perhaps it refers to those who profess faith without having genuine faith.

Other scholars believe it would be wrong to assume that simply because yeast represents evil in other verses of Scripture that it must represent evil in Matthew 13. Perhaps yeast is used in a good sense in this context, simply representing the dynamic growth of the kingdom of God as a result of the penetrating power of the gospel of Christ and the supernatural work of the Holy Spirit.

Matthew 13:44-46—*What was Jesus teaching about the kingdom of heaven when He compared it to a hidden treasure and a pearl?*

Jesus was pointing to the incredible value of the kingdom of heaven. Those who truly see its importance will do anything within their power to possess it. They will allow nothing to stand in their way.

Of course, these parables should not be taken to mean that people could buy their way into the kingdom of heaven by material wealth. Such a conclusion violates the intent of the parables. These parables simply point to the incalculable value of the kingdom and remind us that we should be willing to give up everything to attain it.

Matthew 13:47-50—*Does Jesus' parable of a net that catches good fish and bad fish indicate that unbelievers are presently part of the kingdom of heaven?*

Jesus was teaching that until His second coming, when judgment will take place, genuine Christians and phony (professing) Christians will coexist within the kingdom. At the end of the age, there will be a separation of the righteous from the unrighteous. The righteous (that is, true believers) will be invited into Christ's kingdom, while the unrighteous (professing believers who are really unbelievers) will be excluded from His kingdom and sent to a place of suffering.

Fishermen can tell you that when you pull up a net, you've got all kinds of fish—some that are good and worth keeping but others that are utterly useless. The fishermen separate the good from the bad, keeping the good and throwing away the bad. At the end of the age, Christ will separate the good from the bad, the true Christians from the professing Christians, the righteous from the unrighteous.

Matthew 15:22-28—*Does Jesus teach that God shows favoritism in terms of whose prayers He answers?*

In this passage, Jesus indicates that He had specifically come to offer the nation of Israel the kingdom that had been promised in the Davidic covenant many centuries earlier (2 Samuel 7:12-14). It would not be appropriate for Him to pour out blessings on a Gentile woman—delivering her daughter from demon possession—before such blessings were bestowed on Israel. But the woman continued in her plea. Jesus responded, "It is not right to take the children's bread and toss it to their dogs" (Matthew 15:26). It is well-known that the Jews of Jesus' day looked upon all Gentiles as being dogs. It is also well-known that the Jews considered themselves to be God's children.

The picture Jesus was painting was that of a family sitting around a table at dinnertime. In the analogy, the Jews are the children seated at the table, eating the food provided by the head of the household. The Gentile woman recognized herself in the story as the household dog. The choicest morsels of food were for the children at the table, but as a dog, the Gentile woman saw herself as eligible for the crumbs that might fall from the table.

The woman was not seeking to interfere with God's blessing of Israel but rather was hoping that a little bit of the overflow of such blessing might be extended to her in her time of need. Saying this to Jesus required great faith, and because of this faith, Jesus granted her request. How ironic that the Gentile woman's faith was in great contrast to the lack of faith of Israel's hypocritical leaders.

I must confess that after studying this passage for some time, I began to wonder whether Jesus might have been exhibiting a sense of humor in His comments to the woman. Surely Jesus, who is the creator of all humanity (John 1:3; Colossians 1:16; Hebrews 1:2), does not actually look upon any person as being a dog. Could it be, then, that Jesus had a twinkle in His eye when He alluded to current Jewish sentiments and said to the woman, "It is not right to take the children's bread and toss it to their dogs"? A number of scholars have concluded that this indeed was the case.

Matthew 15:24—*Who are the lost sheep of Israel?*

This term refers to the Israelites to whom Jesus was preaching in Judah and Galilee who God saw as lost. Earlier in the book of Matthew, we read of Jesus' instructions to the disciples regarding this very same group: "Go rather to the lost sheep of Israel. As you go, preach this message: 'The kingdom of heaven is near'" (Matthew 10:6-7). Here the clear contrast is between Gentiles and the lost sheep of the house of Israel (that is, between Gentiles and Jews). The disciples were initially sent forth to minister to Jews.

In the outworking of God's plan of salvation, then, the good news of the kingdom of God was apparently to be preached first to the Jews—God's covenant people. But the Gentiles would not be excluded. God's offer was ultimately for all humankind, as is clear in Christ's great commission to share the good news with all people everywhere (Matthew 28:19-20).

Matthew 16:18—*Is Peter the rock upon which the church is built?*

In this verse we read the words of Jesus to Peter: "I tell you that you are Peter, and on this rock I will build my church, and the gates of Hades will not overcome it." A number of factors in the Greek text argue against the interpretation that Peter is the rock. First, whenever Peter is referred to in this passage (Matthew 16), it is in the second person (*you*), but *this rock* is in the third person (verse 18). Moreover, *Peter* (Greek: *petros*) is a masculine singular term, and *rock* (*petra*) is a feminine singular term. Therefore they do not have the same referent. It would seem that in context, *petra* here refers to Peter's confession of faith that Jesus is the Christ.

It is critical to note that the entire context of Matthew 16:13-20 is all about Jesus, not Peter. Indeed, the key issue of discussion is Jesus' identity. Jesus asked the disciples about who the people say He is (verse 13). Peter then declared correctly that Jesus is the Christ (verse 16). Then in verse 20, to prevent a premature disclosure of His identity, Jesus warned them not to tell anyone that He was the Christ. Throughout this entire passage Jesus is the theme, not Peter (see Romans 9:33; 1 Corinthians 3:11; 10:4; Ephesians 2:20; Colossians 1:17-18; 1 Peter 2:7).

Matthew 16:19—*Does the fact that Peter was given the keys of the kingdom indicate his primacy?*

No. Elsewhere in New Testament Scripture, the term *key* implies the authority to open a door and give entrance to a place or realm (for example, Luke 11:52; Revelation 1:18; 3:7; 9:1; 20:1). The keys of the kingdom of heaven therefore represent the authority to preach the gospel of Christ and thus to open the door of the kingdom of heaven and allow people to enter. Peter first used this authority by preaching the gospel at Pentecost (Acts 2:14-42). But the other apostles also were given this authority in a primary sense (they wrote the gospel in permanent form in the New Testament). And all believers have this key in a secondary sense, for they can all share the gospel with others and thereby open the kingdom of heaven to those who will enter it.

Matthew 16:20—*Why did Jesus warn the disciples not to tell anyone He was the Christ?*

Jesus' words were rooted in the popular misunderstandings that were floating around during that time about the Messiah (or Christ). There was a very high messianic expectation to the effect that when the Messiah came, He would deliver the Jews from Roman domination. The people were expecting a political Messiah-deliverer. Circulating news that He was the Messiah at this early juncture in His ministry would immediately excite people's preconceived imaginations about what this Messiah figure was supposed to do. The Romans may very well have subsequently marked Him as a rebel leader. Seeking to avoid an erroneous popular response to His words and deeds, Jesus issued instructions to not tell anyone He was the Christ. He did not want anyone prematurely speaking of His actual identity until He had had sufficient opportunity to make the character of His mission clear to the masses. As time passed, Christ's identity became increasingly clear to those who came into contact with Him.

Matthew 16:25-26—*Do we have to actually lose our lives to be saved?*

Jesus' point was that following Him as a disciple involves a cost. Every disciple who follows Christ will know suffering and sacrifice. But by losing one's life—by saying no to self, denying a life of self-centeredness, and placing Christ on the throne of one's heart—one will in fact find life. No one is more spiritually alive and vibrant in his relationship to God than one who has completely "sold out" to Jesus Christ.

We must draw a distinction between becoming saved and following Christ as a disciple. Scripture is clear that we become saved solely by placing faith in Jesus Christ (John 3:16; 5:24; 11:25; 12:46). But the life of discipleship goes beyond the initial conversion experience and calls for a continuous life of sacrifice and commitment. The disciple is to deny himself and turn his back on selfish interests. Christ must reign supreme.

Matthew 16:28—*How could Jesus tell some of His followers that some of them would not taste death before seeing Him come in His kingdom?*

There indeed was a sense in which Christ's contemporaries saw the Son of Man coming in his kingdom. Jesus likely was referring to the transfiguration, which happened precisely one week later. In fact, in Matthew's account the transfiguration (Matthew 17:1-13) immediately follows the prediction itself. If this interpretation is correct, as the context seems to indicate, the transfiguration served as a preview or foretaste of the kingdom, in which the divine Messiah would appear in a state of glory. More specifically, in the transfiguration, the power and the glory within Jesus broke through the veil of His flesh and shone out until His very clothing kindled to the dazzling brightness of the light. This very same glory will be revealed to the world when Christ comes to this earth again to set up His kingdom (see Matthew 24:30; 25:31).

Matthew 18:18—*Can Christians bind the devil?*

God has given us all we need to have victory over the devil (see Ephesians 6:11-18). However, the New Testament verses that speak of binding and loosing have nothing whatsoever to do with spiritual warfare. The terms *bind* and *loose* were Jewish idioms indicating that what is announced on earth has already been determined in heaven. To bind meant to forbid, refuse, or prohibit; to loose meant to permit or allow. We can announce the prohibition or allowance of certain things on earth because heaven (or God) has already made an announcement on these matters.

In the context of Matthew 18, Jesus was speaking only about church discipline. He was indicating that members of the church who sin but then repent are to be "loosed" (that is, they are to be restored to fellowship), while those who are unrepentant are to be "bound" (that is, they are to be removed from fellowship). These statements can be declared on earth because heaven (God) has already declared them.

Matthew 18:21-22—*What did Jesus mean when He said we should forgive up to 77 times?*

The Pharisees taught that righteousness demanded that a person be forgiven two times. The Jewish rabbis taught that if one wanted to be magnanimous, one should forgive up to three times. When Peter asked Jesus about forgiving someone seven times, he no doubt thought he was being quite generous. Jesus went far beyond what Peter had in mind by saying we should forgive 77 times—or, in other words, there should be no limitations on our forgiveness. (To the Jews, "77 times" meant times without number.) This should especially be the case in view of how much God has forgiven us of our sins (see Matthew 18:23-35).

Matthew 18:32-35—*Will the Lord treat us harshly if we refuse to forgive others?*

In Matthew 18:23-34 Jesus told a parable about forgiveness in answer to Peter's question, "How many times shall I forgive my brother when he sins against me?" (verse 21). Jesus spoke of a king who commanded a servant to be sold along with his family to pay for the debt that he owed (10,000 talents, which would amount to several million dollars). But the king forgave the servant and cancelled the debt when the servant begged him to (verses 23-27).

The forgiven servant then found another servant who owed him a much smaller amount of money (100 denarii, or about $16) and would not forgive him, but rather threw him into prison (Matthew 18:28-30). When the other servants witnessed what happened, they reported it to the master (verse 31). The master then ordered the wicked slave to be tortured until he repaid all that was owed to him (verses 32-34).

This is the context in which Jesus said, "This is how my heavenly Father will treat each of you unless you forgive your brother from your heart" (Matthew 18:35). Jesus is making an important and serious point to Peter. Peter needed to realize that as a human being, he was completely incapable of paying the debt he owed to God. (Peter, like all of us, was morally indebted to God because of sin.) Peter was represented by the man who had an insurmountable debt. But God had freely forgiven Peter all of His indebtedness. The story thus communicates that Peter was obligated to forgive others who may have wronged him because their wrongs were a mere pittance in comparison with the wrong Peter had done to God and for which he had received forgiveness. To not forgive others in such circumstances invites God's discipline and judgment.

Matthew 19:12—*Was Jesus in favor of people becoming eunuchs for the sake of the kingdom of God?*

This verse is found in a discourse in which Jesus taught about marriage and divorce (Matthew 19:3-12). Some Pharisees had questioned Jesus concerning the grounds for divorce (verse 3), and Jesus answered that marriage was intended by God to be a permanent relationship (verses 4-6). The Pharisees then asked Jesus why Moses commanded that a man get a certificate of divorce (verse 7). Jesus responded that God did not intend it to be this way, but He permitted divorce because of the hardness of men's hearts (verse 8). Jesus then stated that divorce and remarriage constituted adultery unless the divorce was brought about by immorality (verse 9).

The disciples responded to Jesus' strict words about divorce by commenting that perhaps a person should not even get married (Matthew 19:10). Jesus then taught that each person should accept the lot that God has given him—including that of eunuchs (verses 11-12). Jesus indicated that the "eunuch solution" is possible for some people—but only some. Indeed, those who were born eunuchs (that is—without sexual desire, or perhaps with a congenital physical deformity) could certainly adopt that solution. Others who became eunuchs as a result of surgery (such as house slaves or bondservants) could accept that solution. Others who had renounced marriage because of the kingdom of God could accept that solution. Jesus said that one who can accept this solution should accept it. But He certainly knew that most people could not accept such a solution.

Matthew 19:28—*What is meant by "the renewal of all things"?*

Many scholars relate this to God's creation of a new heaven and a new earth (Revelation 21:1-5). In keeping with this, Acts 3:21 (NASB) speaks of the "restoration of all things." The new earth, being a renewed and an eternal earth, will be adapted to the vast moral and physical changes that the eternal state necessitates. Everything is new in the eternal state. Everything will be according to God's own glorious nature. The new heaven and the new earth will be brought into blessed conformity with all that God is—in a state of fixed bliss and absolute perfection. No more decay. No more deterioration. No more disorder.

Matthew 20:18—*If Jesus is the Son of God, why is He sometimes called the Son of man?*

Jesus was both the Son of God and the Son of Man. Jesus was not denying He was God when He referred to Himself as the Son of Man. In fact, the term *Son of Man* is used of Christ in contexts where His deity is quite evident. For example, the Bible indicates that only God has the prerogative of forgiving sins (Isaiah 43:25), but Jesus as the Son of Man exercised this prerogative (Mark 2:7-10). Likewise, at the second coming, Christ will return to earth as the Son of Man in clouds of glory to reign on earth (Matthew 26:63-64). The term *Son of Man* is a messianic title. Jesus, as the Son of Man, is the divine Messiah.

Matthew 20:29-34—*How do we reconcile this passage, which says Jesus healed two blind men as He left Jericho, with Mark 10:46-52 and Luke 18:35-43, which say Jesus healed one man as He entered Jericho?*

Several explanations are possible. One is that the healing took place as Jesus was leaving old Jericho and was nearing new Jericho (there were two Jerichos in those days). If Jesus were at a place between the two Jerichos, then depending on one's perspective, He could be viewed as leaving one Jericho or entering the other Jericho. Now, there were apparently two blind men in need of healing, but Bartimaeus was the more aggressive of the two, so two of the gospel accounts (Mark and Luke) mention only him. If the blind men were healed between the two Jerichos, this would clear up the apparent contradiction between the gospel accounts.

Another possible explanation is that the blind men pled with Jesus as He entered (either the old or new) Jericho, but they did not receive their actual healings until Jesus was leaving Jericho. It is also possible that Jesus healed one blind man as He was entering Jericho, and healed two other blind men as he was leaving Jericho.

Matthew 21:19—*Why did Jesus curse the fig tree and miraculously cause it to wither?*

Jesus may appear to be responding in anger to the tree, cursing it in tantrum-like behavior. But this is not the case. Jesus' teaching methodology often involved parables and word pictures. Scholars agree that with the fig tree, Jesus was performing a living parable—an acted-out parable—to teach His disciples an important truth. His cursing of the fig tree was a dramatic visual aid.

Some scholars suggest Jesus was illustrating the principle of faith to the disciples. If the disciples had such faith, they too could do miracles, such as withering fig trees and moving mountains (see Matthew 17:20). They would need this faith in the hard days to come.

Other scholars believe that since the fig tree had leaves on it (Matthew 21:19), from a distance it gave the appearance of being fruitful. But upon closer examination it became clear that there was no fruit on it at all. So perhaps Jesus' cursing of the fig tree was an acted-out parable that taught the disciples that God will judge those who give an outer appearance of fruitfulness but in fact are not fruitful at all (like the Pharisees).

Still other scholars suggest the fig tree is representative of faithless Israel. Israel professed to be faithful to God and fruitful as a nation, but in fact it was faithless and fruitless. Indeed, Israel had rejected Jesus the Messiah and was thus ripe for judgment. Perhaps the withering of the fig tree foreshadowed the withering (or destruction) of Israel in AD 70, when Titus and his Roman warriors trampled on and destroyed Jerusalem, ending Israel's existence as a political entity (see Luke 21:20).

And still other scholars see significance in the fact that the account of Jesus' cleansing of the temple in Mark's Gospel (Mark 11:15-19) is sandwiched between the two sections of Scripture dealing with the fig tree (verses 12-14 and 20-25). It is suggested that perhaps Jesus was teaching that at a distance the temple and its sacrificial activities looked fine. But on closer inspection, the religious system was found to be without substance, full of hypocrisy, bearing no spiritual fruit, ripe for judgment.

Matthew 22:14—*What did Jesus mean when He said, "Many are invited, but few are chosen"?*

In Matthew 22:1-14 Jesus is teaching His followers the parable of the feast. The parable teaches that the King (Jesus) and His kingdom had been offered to the nation of Israel, but the Jews were virtually indifferent to the offer. The Jews even murdered those who delivered the message (the prophets). The invitation was then broadened to include any who would come, including the Gentiles. Ultimately, this parable teaches that the invitation to salvation is sent out to many people, Jews and Gentiles, but comparatively few accept the invitation.

Theologians point out that the phrase "many are invited, but few are chosen" (Matthew 22:14) indicates that God issues two calls to sinners inviting them to receive His salvation: a general call to all and a specific call (or election) to some. At the same time, this parable makes clear that human beings are responsible for their decision to receive or reject Christ, whether it is the result of indifference (verse 5), rebellion (verse 6), or self-righteousness (verse 12).

Matthew 22:30—*Did Jesus teach that in the afterlife, resurrected human beings will no longer be married?*

Matthew 22:30 indicates that once believers receive their glorified resurrection bodies, the need for procreation—one of the fundamental purposes for marriage (Malachi 2:15)—will no longer exist. We will be like the angels in the sense that we will not be married and will not procreate any longer. (We know that angels do not procreate and reproduce, for all the angels in the universe were created at the same time—see Colossians 1:16.)

We should not think of the heavenly dissolution of marriage as a deprivation. It is important to understand that the pleasures of heaven will far exceed anything that human beings have ever known on earth. Indeed, heaven is often described as *paradise,* a word that literally means a garden of pleasure or garden of delight (2 Corinthians 12:4). We are told in 1 Corinthians 2:9, "No eye has seen, no ear has heard, no mind has conceived what God has prepared for those who love him."

Matthew 23:9—*Are we not to use the title* father *for our earthly fathers?*

In Matthew 23:9 Jesus said, "Do not call anyone on earth 'father,' for you have one Father, and he is in heaven." This is definitely a puzzling saying, but it would seem from the context (which deals with the Pharisees) that Jesus was not talking about biological fathers. Nor was He apparently talking about spiritual fathers, for in the New Testament the apostle Paul was a spiritual father to the Corinthians (1 Corinthians 4:15-17) and referred to Timothy and Onesimus as his sons (2 Timothy 1:2; Philemon 10).

Among the ancient Jews, particularly the Pharisees, the rabbis of the time were often respectfully referred to as Abba or Papa. It was a title of great honor. The rabbis who had died were often collectively referred to as the fathers. They were considered the source of wisdom among the Jews. The rabbis in turn addressed their disciples as their children. The word *father* among the ancient Jews came to denote a person with authority, eminence, superiority, and a right to command. A father was worthy of respect.

Jesus' point in Matthew 23:9, then, would seem to be that only God should be in the place of reverence and unquestioned obedience. Only God truly deserves the title of *Father* in this exalted sense. Only God is truly the wise one who cares for us as His beloved children, in contrast to the Pharisees, who often led their followers into spiritual bondage.

Matthew 23:13-33—*Why did Jesus speak in such harsh, unloving terms about the Pharisees?*

In Matthew 23:1-36, Jesus pronounces woes on the nation of Israel, lamenting the abysmal spiritual state of the people. In verses 1-12, Jesus charged the multitudes and the disciples to obey the law but not to follow the example and the deeds of the Pharisees. Then in verses 13-36, Jesus pronounced specific woes against the religious leaders of the nation because...

- They kept others from entering the kingdom of heaven (verse 13).

- Their actions did not match their pious-sounding words (verse 14).

- They bound people up in mere religiosity (verse 15).

- They were more interested in material wealth than in true worship of the living God (verses 16-22).

- They were picky about the minute matters of the law while allowing the major matters of the law to go unaddressed (verses 23-24).

- They were ceremonially clean in an external sense but were totally filthy on the inside (verses 25-26).

- They gave the appearance of righteousness while being full of hypocrisy on the inside (verses 27-28).

- They self-righteously boasted that they would have stood with the martyred prophets but at the same time they themselves were trying to kill holy men (verse 29-36).

Matthew 24:34—*What generation will not pass away before "all these things have happened"?*

Evangelical Christians have generally held to one of two interpretations of this verse. One interpretation is that Christ is simply saying that those people who witness the signs stated earlier in Matthew 24—the abomination of desolation (verse 15), the great tribulation such as has never been seen before (verse 21), and the sign of the Son of Man in heaven (verse 30)—will see the coming of Jesus Christ within that very generation. Since it was common knowledge among the Jews that the future tribulation period would last only seven years (Daniel 9:24-27), it is obvious that those living at the beginning of this time would likely live to see the second coming seven years later (except for those who lose their lives during this tumultuous time).

Other evangelicals hold that the word *generation* is to be taken in its basic usage of a race, kindred, family, stock, or breed. If this is what is meant, then Jesus is here promising that the nation of Israel will be preserved—despite terrible persecution during the tribulation—until the consummation of God's program for Israel at the second coming.

Many divine promises have been made to Israel—including land promises (Genesis 12; 14–15; 17) and a future Davidic kingdom (2 Samuel 7). Jesus could thus be referring to God's preservation of Israel in order to fulfill the divine promises to them (see Romans 11:11-26).

Matthew 25:1-13—*What was Jesus teaching about the kingdom of heaven in the parable of the ten virgins?*

The main point of the parable seems to be that only those who are watchful for the kingdom of God and alert for the coming of the Son of Man (that is, believers) will be able to enter it (Matthew 25:13). Contextually, this refers to true believers who are living during the future tribulation period, prior to the second coming of Christ. His coming will be sudden and unexpected. Believers ("wise virgins") are those who anticipate Jesus' coming and seek to be prepared for it, living their lives accordingly. Jesus' return will terminate the opportunity for people to prepare themselves (trust in Jesus) to enter His kingdom. Only those who are previously prepared (saved, by trusting in Christ) will be permitted to enter. No unsaved people (foolish virgins) will be permitted to enter.

Matthew 25:35-40—*How are we to understand these verses about feeding and clothing Christ's brothers?*

After His second coming, Christ will gather all people and separate the sheep from the goats based on how they treated the brothers. These brothers may well be the 144,000 Jews mentioned in Revelation 7 and 14 who will apparently be engaged in evangelism all over the earth during the future tribulation period. The sheep are believers, who give evidence of their faith by treating the 144,000 brothers kindly by giving them drink, and food, clothing, and such. Only believers will be aware of God's teaching from the Bible regarding these 144,000 Jewish evangelists, and they show the reality of their faith by the way they treat these brothers. The goats, by contrast, show that they are not believers because they give no evidence of faith in their lives.

Matthew 25:46—*Does this verse really teach eternal and conscious torment of the unsaved?*

We must soberly concede that the verse precisely teaches this. The punishment spoken of in Matthew 25:46 cannot be defined as a non-suffering extinction of consciousness (annihilation). Indeed, if actual suffering is lacking, then so is punishment. Punishment entails suffering. And suffering necessarily entails consciousness.

Consider that there are no degrees of annihilation. One is either annihilated or not. Scripture, however, teaches that there will be degrees of punishment assigned on the day of judgment (Matthew 10:15; 11:21-24; 16:27; Luke 12:47-48; John 15:22; Hebrews 10:29; Revelation 20:11-15; 22:12). The fact that people will suffer varying degrees of punishment in hell shows that annihilation or the extinction of consciousness is not taught in Matthew 25:46 or anywhere else in Scripture. These are incompatible concepts. By definition, torment cannot be anything but *conscious* torment. One cannot torment a tree, a rock, or a house. By its very nature, being tormented requires consciousness.

Note that Matthew 25:46 shows that this punishment is eternal. Annihilationism, or an extinction of consciousness, cannot be forced into this passage. Indeed, the Greek adjective *aionion* in this verse means everlasting, or without end. This same adjective is predicated of God (the eternal God) in Romans 16:26; 1 Timothy 1:7; Hebrews 9:14; 13:8; and Revelation 4:9. The punishment of the wicked is just as eternal as our eternal God.

Matthew 27:5—*How can this verse, which says Judas died by hanging himself, be reconciled with Acts 1:18, which says Judas died by falling headlong in a field and bursting open?*

Both accounts are true. Apparently Judas first hanged himself. Then, at some point, the rope either broke or loosened so that his body slipped from it and fell to the rocks below and burst open. (Some have suggested that Judas didn't do a very good job of tying the noose.) Neither account alone is complete. Taken together, we have a full picture of what happened to Judas.

Matthew 27:52–53—*Did some people receive their permanent resurrection bodies before all others?*

In this passage we read that following Jesus' resurrection, "the tombs broke open and the bodies of many holy people who had died were raised to life. They came out of the tombs, and after Jesus' resurrection they went into the holy city and appeared to many people." These individuals did not at this time receive their permanent resurrection bodies but rather were resuscitated from the dead in much the same way Lazarus was in John 11. These individuals undoubtedly eventually died again and went back to the grave. The reception of their permanent resurrection bodies is yet future (1 Corinthians 15:50-52; 1 Thessalonians 4:13-17).

Mark

Mark 1:15—*What is the distinction between the kingdom of God and the kingdom of heaven?*

The terms *kingdom of God* and *kingdom of heaven* are essentially interchangeable in the Bible. The Gospels of Mark, Luke, and John use the term *kingdom of God* (for example, Mark 1:15; Luke 9:2). Matthew, however, uses *kingdom of heaven* some thirty-two times but *kingdom of God* only four times. The apparent reason Matthew predominantly used *kingdom of heaven* is that he was a Jew writing to Jews and was showing sensitivity to the Jewish preference of avoiding using God's name when possible to make sure one was not using this name in vain (since the third of the Ten Commandments prohibits this—Exodus 20:7). The other Gospel writers were not writing to a Jewish audience, so they used the term *kingdom of God*.

Mark 1:34—*Why would Jesus not let the demons reveal who He was?*

There are probably several reasons for this. First, Satan is called the father of lies (John 8:44; see also Genesis 3:4), and the demons who follow Satan no doubt reflect the character of their diabolical leader. Certainly Jesus would not want any testimony regarding His identity from a sinister, lying source. Moreover, one must keep in mind that some of the Jewish leaders associated Jesus with Beelzebub, the prince of the demons (Mark 3:22). Allowing testimony from lying spirits might add fuel to the fire regarding that claim.

A second possible reason for Jesus silencing the demons is that He was demonstrating that He has authority over them. This would be in keeping with other verses in the Gospels where this authority is openly demonstrated (Mark 8:33; 9:38; Luke 10:17).

A third possible reason for silencing the demons may relate to the popular misconceptions of the Messiah held by many in first-century Judaism. The Jews were expecting the coming of a glorious conquering Messiah who would deliver the Jews from Roman domination. If a demon prematurely blurted out that Jesus was the Messiah, the Jews who were present might interpret the term *Messiah* in this mistaken sense. Jesus may have silenced the demons from revealing His identity at this early juncture so that He could, in His own time, demonstrate by word and deed that He was the true biblical Messiah.

Mark 1:44—*Why did Jesus instruct the miraculously healed leper not to tell anyone but instead to go to the priest to offer sacrifices?*

There are two issues we must deal with here: Why did Jesus instruct the man not to tell anyone, and why did Jesus send him to the priest to offer sacrifices?

Jesus probably instructed the man not to tell anyone because of the popular misunderstandings that were floating around during that time about the Messiah. There was a very high messianic expectation to the effect that when the Messiah came, He would deliver the Jews from Roman domination. The people were expecting a political Messiah-deliverer. News that He was the Messiah would immediately excite people's preconceived imaginations about what this Messiah figure was supposed to do. The Romans may very well subsequently mark Him as a rebel leader.

Seeking to avoid an erroneous popular response to His words and deeds, Jesus told the leper to keep quiet about the miracle. He did not want anyone prematurely speaking of His actual identity until He had had sufficient opportunity to make the character of His mission clear to the masses. As time passed, Christ's identity became increasingly clear to those who came into contact with Him.

As to why Jesus instructed the man to go to the priest to offer sacrifices, He probably had in mind the Old Testament ritual requirements. Among the Jews, leprosy was viewed as one of the worst forms of uncleanness. According to the Mosaic law, anyone who had leprosy or who was even thought to have it was required to undergo a ritual of cleansing to be accepted back into society. If this man had remained in Galilee, walking around telling everyone how Christ had healed him, he would have been quickly categorized as unclean by all the Jews in the city, and his witness would have thus been nullified.

Mark 2:1-12—*What is the significance of Jesus pronouncing the paralytic's sins forgiven before physically healing him?*

Upon first reading, such words may seem out of place. But further investigation indicates that Jesus was making an important statement. Jesus knew that all those present were aware that only God could pronounce someone's sins as being forgiven. (In Isaiah 43:25, for example, God said, "I, even I, am he who blots out your transgressions, for my own sake, and remembers your sins no more.") When Jesus said "your sins are forgiven," He was clearly placing Himself in the position of God.

The scribes who were present understood Jesus' words this way, for they reasoned, "Why does this man speak that way? He is blaspheming; who can forgive sins but God alone?" (Mark 2:7 NASB). Of course, Jesus' subsequent healing of the paralytic served to substantiate His claim to be God (verses 10-11).

Pronouncing the man's sins forgiven first before healing him was Jesus' way of indicating that the man's highest need was not physical healing but spiritual healing. The spiritual healing was the more important of the two. Once that was taken care of, Jesus proceeded to heal the man physically as well.

Mark 2:17—*Did Jesus teach that some people are righteous enough not to need a Savior?*

In Mark 2:17 Jesus said, "I have not come to call the righteous, but sinners." By the word *righteous,* Jesus was referring not to those who were actually righteous in God's sight, but rather to those who were righteous in their own esteem, such as the scribes and Pharisees (see Luke 16:14-15). He came to minister to people who humbly acknowledged that they were sinners and needed a Savior. Jesus had no ministry to the self-righteous except to announce their condemnation before God.

Mark 2:21-22—*What was Jesus teaching about Christianity and Judaism in His comments about new wine in old wineskins?*

In ancient times a wineskin was made from the skin of goats or other animals and was used as a bag for holding and dispensing wine. Such wineskins stretched over time and eventually lost their elasticity. Wineskins that had already been stretched to capacity by the previous fermenting wine would burst if filled with new unfermented wine.

Jesus in this analogy was illustrating the fact that the Old Testament law—taken to legalistic extremes by the Pharisees of Jesus' time—was inflexible and outdated. The old wineskin of Judaism could not contain the dynamic new faith of Christianity. The grace teachings of Christ could not be contained within the legalistic wineskin of Judaism.

What Jesus was offering to the masses was not something that could simply be superimposed onto Judaism—like trying to sew new cloth onto a tattered garment. Jesus was not offering to bring about a reformation of Judaism; what He was offering was something entirely new—Christianity. The living faith He spoke of could not be patched onto a dead religious system.

Mark 2:27-28—*Did Jesus teach that breaking the Sabbath was okay?*

Jesus and His disciples had been passing through a grainfield on a Sabbath day. The disciples were hungry, so they took a few heads of grain and ate them. The Pharisees then claimed the disciples violated the law because they did this on the Sabbath (to do any type of work on the Sabbath was unlawful).

Jesus responded by pointing to the original purpose of the Sabbath: "The Sabbath was made for man, not man for the Sabbath" (Mark 2:27). Jesus' point was that man is more important than any institution, and the institution of the Sabbath was for the benefit of man. The Pharisees had twisted the teaching of the Sabbath into a legalistic burden, multiplying Sabbath requirements until they became intolerable. Jesus thus corrected the Pharisees by saying that the Sabbath was made for man and was intended to bring him spiritual, mental, and physical refreshment and restoration. The Sabbath was not to be a joyless ritual, as the Pharisees made it, but rather a time of rest in which one joyfully remembers the greatness and wonder of God.

Mark 4:25—*What did Jesus mean when He said, "Whoever has will be given more; whoever does not have, even what he has will be taken from him"?*

Jesus' intended meaning seems to be that those who respond positively to the truth they hear will receive more. Those who do not respond positively to the truth they hear will lose what they had. This principle is illustrated in the life of Cornelius. This Gentile was obedient to the limited amount of truth he had heard—that is, he had been obedient to Old Testament revelation (Acts 10:2). But he did not have enough revelation to believe in Jesus Christ as the Savior, so God sent Peter to Cornelius's house to explain the gospel. Cornelius then believed in Jesus and was saved (verses 44-48).

Mark 4:26-29—*What was Jesus teaching about the kingdom of God by comparing it to a growing seed?*

Jesus taught that the fruit that results from sowing a seed (in this case, the seed of the Word of God) depends not on the one doing the sowing but on the life that is in the seed itself (God's supernatural Word). Because the 11 disciples would soon be commissioned to proclaim Christ's message to the ends of the earth (Matthew 28:19-20), they might fall into the trap of feeling that the harvest of souls depended entirely on their efforts. Christ used this parable to clearly show that any harvest produced would be the result of sowing the seed and then allowing the life in that seed to manifest itself by growth and fruit at the time of the harvest.

Mark 6:4-5—*Why couldn't Jesus do miracles in His own hometown?*

At first glance, one might get the impression that Jesus' miraculous power depended entirely upon people's faith. That is not the meaning of this passage, however. It is not that Jesus was unable to perform a miracle in Nazareth. Rather, Jesus "could not" do miracles there in the sense that He *would not* do so in view of the pervasive unbelief in that city.

Miracles serve a far greater purpose, from the divine perspective, than just providing a raw display of power. Indeed, Jesus' miraculous deeds are called *signs* in the New Testament because they serve to signify His identity as the Messiah. The people of Nazareth had already made up their minds against Jesus and had provided more than ample evidence of their lack of faith in Him, so Jesus chose not to engage in miraculous acts there except for healing a few sick people. He refused to bestow miraculous deeds on a city that had rejected the miraculous Messiah. Unbelief excluded the people of Nazareth from the dynamic disclosure of God's grace that others had experienced.

Mark 8:15—*What did Jesus mean when He referred to the "yeast of the Pharisees"?*

In both Jewish and Hellenistic circles, yeast was often a symbol of evil or corruption. Among the Jews, yeast often represented an invisible, pervasive influence. In the present context, the yeast of the Pharisees was unbelief and the spirit of hypocrisy that their teaching encouraged. Even a tiny amount of yeast has the ability of fermenting a large piece of dough. Pharisaic unbelief and hypocrisy—once it was introduced and admitted into the heart of Jewish society—spread so pervasively that it rendered true spirituality impossible. The yeast of the Pharisees had infected the whole nation so that Israel's spiritual state was abysmal.

Mark 8:33—*Did Jesus indicate that Peter was possessed by the devil when He said to him, "Get behind me, Satan"?*

Jesus had just taught His disciples that He was to be killed but that He would rise again three days later (see Mark 8:31-38). Peter then rebuked Jesus for saying He must die. Peter may have been holding on to the popular misconception of the Messiah that involved a conquering king who would deliver Israel from Roman domination. That conception of the Messiah would be impossible if the Messiah had to die. Jesus then turned to Peter and said, "Get behind me, Satan! You do not have in mind the things of God, but the things of men" (verse 33).

Jesus recognized that Satan was behind these words of Peter. Aware of God's plan, Satan was bent on doing anything he could to prevent Jesus from going to the cross. Satan thus attempted to divert Jesus through one of His closest associates, His friend and disciple Peter.

The fact that Satan spoke through Peter does not mean Peter became possessed of the devil. Peter became an unwitting spokesman for the devil because he had set his mind on the things of men rather than the things of God. Because his mind was set on the things of men, his mind was easily swayed by the master tempter, Satan, who has had thousands of years of experience in leading human beings astray. Jesus' public rebuke of Peter was not just a warning to Peter but also a warning to the other disciples as well. All of them were to beware of the activity of the adversary.

Mark 8:34—*What does it mean to take up our crosses and follow Jesus?*

When a man had been condemned to die and the time of execution had arrived, the man would be required by the Roman executioners to carry his own cross to the place of execution. This is much as it was with Jesus when the time of His execution came (John 19:17).

What does it mean to take up our crosses and follow Jesus? Jesus' primary point seems to be related to living a life of self-denial and submitting to Him in all things. Jesus is quite obviously calling for a total commitment. The idea is this: If you really want to follow Me, do not do so in word only, but put your life on the line and follow Me on the path of the cross—a path that will involve sacrifice, self-denial, and possibly even suffering and death for My sake.

We must not miss the fact that Jesus' words about taking up one's cross and following Him are addressed to His (already-saved) disciples, as Matthew 16:24 makes clear. We would be wrong, then, to conclude that Jesus was saying that a life of self-denial and taking up one's cross is a condition of final salvation. Following a person is an ongoing process—a progression—but entrance into God's family is a singular event that begins at the new birth, which hinges on faith in Christ (Acts 16:31). Salvation is free, but discipleship is costly. In salvation, Christ pays the price (on the cross); in discipleship, the believer pays the price (by taking up his cross and following Jesus). Salvation involves a new birth; discipleship involves a lifetime of growth following the new birth.

Notice the three key verbs in Mark 8:34—*deny, take up,* and *follow.* The first two verbs are aorist imperatives, which indicate a decisive action. We must decisively deny ourselves and take up our crosses! The word *follow,* however, is a present imperative. The present tense indicates continuous action. We are to perpetually and unceasingly follow Jesus, day in and day out. (It is not just a Sunday thing.) Following Jesus is a process, not a single event. The imperative indicates it is a command. It is not a mere option. Those who seek to be Jesus' disciples must take up their crosses and follow Jesus daily. Those who do so can count on Jesus' perpetual presence in their lives, even in life's worst storms.

Mark 9:39-40—*What did Jesus mean when He said, "Whoever is not against us is for us"?*

In this passage the disciples had encountered an exorcist who did not do things the way they thought he should, so they forbade him to continue. "Do not stop him," Jesus chastened them. "No one who does a miracle in my name can in the next moment say anything bad about me, for whoever is not against us is for us" (Mark 9:39-40).

This verse indicates that though many people follow Jesus Christ, not all follow Him in exactly the same way. Although this man did not follow Jesus in the same way the disciples did, he nevertheless did stand against Satan and had obviously crossed the line so that He was on Jesus' side.

It is interesting that Jesus said, "Whoever is not against us is for us," in Mark 9:39-40, and He said, "He who is not with me is against me," in Matthew 12:30. In both verses Jesus' point was that to remain in the "neutral zone" is not possible when it comes to Him. Either you are on the rejection side of the line or you have crossed the line in allegiance to Jesus. There is no middle ground. The exorcist had crossed the line in allegiance to Jesus.

Mark 10:17-18—*Did Jesus deny that He is good?*

Jesus in this passage was not claiming that He didn't have God's good character. Nor was He denying that He was God to the young ruler asking the question. Rather, Jesus was asking the man to examine the implications of what he was saying. In effect, Jesus said, "Do you realize what you are saying when you verbalize that I am good? Are you saying I am God?" Jesus was not denying His deity. Rather, He was making a veiled claim to deity.

Mark 10:30—*Did Jesus promise a hundredfold return for our financial and material gifts?*

No. This verse has nothing to do with money or riches. It is speaking specifically of those who forsake home and loved ones for the sake of Jesus and the gospel. These individuals will receive a hundredfold return in the sense that they become a part of a community of believers. In this new community, they find a multiplication of relationships—many of which are ultimately closer and more spiritually meaningful than blood relationships (Mark 3:31-35; Acts 2:41-47; 1 Timothy 5:1-2).

Mark 11:23-24—*Did Jesus promise we can obtain whatever we ask for?*

No. This verse must be interpreted in the light of other clear Scripture verses. These other verses place limitations on what God will give us. We must abide in Him and let His Word abide in us (John 15:7). We cannot ask out of our own selfishness (James 4:3). We must submit our requests to the sovereign will of God. We are told that "this is the confidence which we have before Him, that, if we ask anything according to His will, He hears us. And if we know that He hears us in whatever we ask, we know that we have the requests which we have asked from Him" (1 John 5:14-15 NASB).

Mark 13:32—*Did Jesus indicate He was not omniscient because He does not know the day or hour of His return?*

Jesus was here speaking from the vantage point of His humanity. In His humanity, Jesus was not omniscient but was limited in understanding, just as all human beings are. If Jesus had been speaking from the perspective of His divinity, He wouldn't have said the same thing. Scripture is abundantly clear that in His divine nature, Jesus is omniscient—just as omniscient as the Father is (Matthew 10:15; 11:27; 17:25,27; 21:2-4; Luke 5:4,6; John 2:25; 11:11,14; 16:30; 18:4; 21:6-11,17). Philippians 2:5-11 indicates that in order to become a man, Jesus (as God) submitted to a voluntary nonuse of some of His divine attributes on some occasions. Mark 13:32 is an example of this.

Mark 15:34—*Why did Jesus on the cross ask the Father why He had forsaken Him?*

The word *forsaken* here carries the idea of abandonment. Jesus' statement reflects the fact that His greatest suffering on the cross was not physical, but spiritual. He bore the guilt of the entire world on Himself. Christ became sin for us (2 Corinthians 5:21). And that moment brought an agony of the soul that was unparalleled. Christ had become the object of the Father's displeasure, for He became the sinner's substitute.

The sense of abandonment that Jesus sensed was judicial, not relational. Jesus sensed a separation from the Father He had never known before, for when Jesus became sin for us, the Father had to turn judicially from His beloved Son (Romans 3:25-26). Jesus the Savior experienced the utter bitterness of the desolation of the cross.

Mark 16:9-20—*Do these verses belong in the Bible?*

The verses in Mark 16:9-20 are absent from the two oldest Greek manuscripts in our possession—Codex Alexandrinus and Codex Sinaiticus. They are also absent from the Old Latin manuscripts, the Sinaitic Syriac manuscript, about 100 Armenian manuscripts, and the two oldest Georgian manuscripts. Further, Clement of Alexandria and Origen show no knowledge of the existence of these verses. Eusebius and Jerome attest that the passage was absent from almost all the Greek copies of Mark known to them. Understandably, then, many scholars believe that Mark 16:9-20 does not belong in the Bible. Fortunately, Mark 16:9-20 does not affect a single major doctrine of Christianity.

Mark 16:12—*Did Jesus appear in different bodies after His resurrection?*

In this verse we read, "Afterward Jesus appeared in a different form to two of them while they were walking in the country." We can make a number of observations about this text. First, there are serious questions about the authenticity of the text involved. Mark 16:9-20 is not found in some of the oldest and best manuscripts. Also, this verse summarizes Luke 24:13-32, which simply says "they were kept from recognizing him." The miraculous element was clearly not in Jesus' body, but in the eyes of the disciples (Luke 24:16,31). Recognition of Jesus was kept from them until their eyes were opened.

Whatever "another form" means, it certainly does not mean a form other than His real, physical, material body. On this very occasion Jesus ate physical food (Luke 24:30), which He later gave as a proof that He was flesh and bones and not an immaterial spirit (verses 38-43).

Mark 16:16—*Does this verse teach that baptism is necessary for salvation?*

In this verse we read, "Whoever believes and is baptized will be saved, but whoever does not believe will be condemned." This verse is clear that unbelief is what brings damnation, not a lack of being baptized. When one rejects the gospel, refusing to believe it, that person is damned.

Note the words of the apostle Paul in 1 Corinthians 1:17: "For Christ did not send me to baptize, but to preach the gospel." Paul here draws a clear distinction between baptism and the gospel. And since it is the gospel that saves (1 Corinthians 15:1-2), clearly baptism is not necessary to attain salvation.

Mark 16:17-18—*Did Jesus promise that all who believe will be accompanied by miracles like healing others, speaking in tongues, driving out demons, and not being harmed by snakes and deadly poison?*

The construction of verse 18 in the original Greek utilizes conditional clauses. The verse could read like this: "And *if* they be compelled to pick up snakes with their hands, and *if* they should be compelled to drink deadly poison, it shall by no means harm them." What this means is that if some pagan or non-Christian authority or persecutor forced a Christian to engage in such activities (a real possibility in the early church), God would supernaturally protect them.

Understood in context, this verse certainly gives no justification for Christians to voluntarily drink poison or handle snakes in church services. We see no such activity in the early church. Note that Paul's encounter with the snake at Malta was completely unintentional (Acts 28:3-5).

Christians today are divided over whether such phenomena as speaking in tongues and the gift of healing occur today; charismatics say yes, cessationists say no. The cessationists argue that the gifts of healing and tongues passed away in the first century after the Bible had been delivered and verified by miraculous phenomena. Charismatics say nothing in Scripture sustains such a conclusion.

Whichever side one ends up on, it is very important for both sides to understand that Mark 16:17-18 is most certainly not teaching that if you do not experience such phenomena, you are not a true Christian. That is an unwarranted conclusion that violates the broader context of Scripture.

Luke

Luke 3:23-38—*How are we to explain the differences in the two genealogies of Christ?*

See comments on Matthew 1:1-19.

Luke 6:24—*Did Jesus teach that a rich person cannot be saved?*

The backdrop to this verse is that the disciples had given up everything to follow Jesus. In contrast to them were those who were loaded with money and wealth and who did not sense the gravity of their true situation (that is, they were blind to their need of redemption in view of the sin problem). Their basic mind-set was that personal wealth could solve most problems. Wealth predisposed them to think they had need of nothing. They relied on riches, not on God.

These blinded, self-exalted individuals are the ones Jesus spoke of in Luke 6:24. These individuals—who have not trusted in Him but instead trust in their riches and the comfort that wealth brings—will one day experience a reversal and find themselves engulfed in eternal punishment. They will realize too late that their comfort now caused them to be shortsighted regarding their eternal future.

Extreme wealth can blind one to the need for God, but the Bible includes the stories of godly, wealthy men, such as Abraham and Job. These individuals were materially rich, but they were nevertheless committed to God. So being rich in itself does not in any way bar one from heaven. Jesus' warning was against the love of riches and making money a god.

Luke 6:29-30—*Does Jesus teach that we should turn the other cheek in every circumstance in the course of daily living?*

See comments on Matthew 5:38-42.

Luke 6:37—*Does our status before God hinge on not judging others, not condemning others, and forgiving others?*

The Pharisees had a habit of setting themselves up as the judges of all human beings. They measured other people against themselves—and of course, they considered themselves to be the very epitome of righteousness. The Pharisees not only judged people's external behavior but also self-righteously claimed to know their motives. In view of this, Jesus said, "Do not judge, and you will not be judged. Do not condemn, and you will not be condemned. Forgive, and you will be forgiven." The Pharisees judged, they condemned, and they did not truly forgive. Jesus' statement was thus aimed at the inner attitude of the Pharisees. He was saying His followers should avoid such self-righteous and hypocritical judgment.

Jesus was not saying, however, that Christians should avoid making proper judgments about various issues. The apostle Paul said, "The spiritual man makes judgments about all things" (1 Corinthians 2:15). Christians are to judge between right and wrong, between true and false prophets, and between true and false doctrine (see 1 Corinthians 5:9; 2 Corinthians 11:14; Philippians 3:2; 1 Thessalonians 5:21; 1 John 4:1).

Luke 6:38—*What lesson is Jesus teaching about giving?*

In Luke 6:38 Jesus said, "Give, and it will be given to you. A good measure, pressed down, shaken together and running over, will be poured into your lap. For with the measure you use, it will be measured to you."

Jesus here used imagery that His first-century hearers would have been well familiar with. The picture is that of a large container of grain that is filled to the brim and overflowing the edge. In the same way that grain overflows the container, so we should overflow in our giving to others.

Jesus is pointing to reciprocity in the affairs of life—"With the measure you use, it will be measured to you." Jesus' meaning is that we get back what we put into life. Human generosity will be rewarded by divine superabundance.

Of course, this does not mean that God will make us financially rich if we give money away. This verse is not a get-rich formula. It simply communicates that we are to be liberal in our giving to others. God smiles on such giving and pours out blessing as a result. But remember, God Himself determines what form that blessing will take.

Luke 7:22—*Why did Jesus respond to John the Baptist's inquiry about His identity by pointing to His miraculous acts?*

The Jews of that time commonly believed that when the Messiah came, He would set up His glorious kingdom. Messianic expectations ran high in the first century, and John himself probably expected the soon emergence of the kingdom that he had been preaching about.

But now something unexpected happened—John was imprisoned. Instead of the kingdom, which (it was commonly thought) would be characterized by such things as liberty and freedom, John now found himself locked up in jail and in danger of execution. What was John to make of this development? John may have expected that Jesus would use more coercive powers as the Messiah-deliverer of Israel. He thus decided to send messengers to Jesus to ask, "Are you the one who was to come, or should we expect someone else?" (Luke 7:20).

Instead of merely giving verbal assurance that He was the Messiah, Jesus pointed to His miraculous acts, including giving sight to the blind, enabling the lame to walk, and opening deaf ears (Luke 7:22). These were the precise miracles Isaiah prophesied the Messiah would perform when He came (see Isaiah 29:18-21; 35:5-6; 61:1-2). The miraculous deeds alone were more than enough proof that Jesus was the promised Messiah. The miracles were Jesus' divine credentials.

Luke 7:23—*What did Jesus mean when He said, "Blessed is the man who does not fall away on account of me"?*

The main point of the verse is this: Christ fulfilled all the messianic prophesies of the Old Testament—such as bringing sight to the blind, hearing to the deaf, and the ability to walk for the lame—so Jesus clearly was the promised Messiah. But He was not the political deliverer-Messiah expected by the general populace. So Jesus' words amount to saying, "Blessed is the man who recognizes me as the promised Messiah and does not fall away from believing in me simply because I do not fulfill his personal preconceived expectations of what the Messiah would do. Blessed is the man who maintains faith in me as the Messiah even though I am not the political deliverer he expected."

Luke 7:28—*Why did Jesus say that the least person in the kingdom of God is greater than John the Baptist?*

Jesus was not saying here that John has virtually no part in God's kingdom, for surely He does. Jesus was simply saying that John belonged to the age of the Old Covenant—the dispensation of the law. As great as John was in the age of the Old Covenant, even the least person in the age of the New Covenant is greater than John by virtue of the high position ("in Christ") that becomes ours since the time of Jesus' resurrection and the descent of the Holy Spirit.

The New Testament church is the very bride of Christ (Ephesians 5:25-32), but John the Baptist is only a "friend of the bridegroom" (John 3:29 NASB). New Testament believers are participants of the realities John prophesied; John was only a forerunner and predictor of those realities.

Luke 8:46—*When Jesus said, "Someone touched me; I know that power has gone out from me," did His intrinsic divine power cause a miracle without Him purposing it?*

At first glance, Jesus might seem to have been unaware of the identity of the woman. Also, divine healing energy might appear to have sapped out of His body and healed the woman without Him intending it to. This is not the case, however.

Scripture portrays Jesus as always being in complete control of His divine miraculous power (see John 2:1-11; 4:50-52; 5:8-9; 11:40-44). People could not just walk up to Jesus, touch Him, and activate His miracle-working power without His consent. The reason the woman

was healed when she touched Jesus' garment was that He willed her
to be healed as a result of her faith.

The context indicates that Jesus wanted this woman to publicly
acknowledge her faith, which had led to her healing. Her desire to
approach Jesus in stealth is understandable because her hemorrhage
rendered her ceremonially unclean (Leviticus 15:25-30). As well,
anyone who came into contact with her was also rendered unclean,
according to the Jews. But Jesus forced her to "go public" and acknowledge that she was the one who touched Him. Jesus wanted the woman
to understand that it was actually her faith that led to her healing
(Luke 8:48). Jesus' cloak had no mysterious magical properties, but
her touching of that cloak was an expression of her faith, which subsequently moved Jesus to heal her with His divine power. The woman's
faith indeed did become public when she fell at Jesus' feet (verse 47).

Luke 8:51-52—*Why did Jesus say the dead child was not dead but just
asleep?*

We know the girl was physically dead because verse 55 tells us
that after Jesus healed her, "her spirit returned." (Death involves the
departure of the soul or spirit from the body.) Jesus, in saying she was
asleep, was simply saying that the girl's present condition of death was
only temporary. He used the term *sleep* to indicate that her condition was not permanent. He may have been saying that when He is
involved in the picture, death really is as sleep, for it is temporary. As
effortlessly as a parent awakens a child from sleep, so Jesus miraculously awakened the young girl from her temporary state of death
(compare with John 11:11-14). We might paraphrase Jesus' words this
way: "The girl is not permanently dead but only temporarily so. She
is, metaphorically speaking, just asleep and soon to be supernaturally
awakened in life."

Luke 9:31—*What is the meaning of Christ's "departure"?*

The Greek word translated *departure* literally means an exodus. This
casts an interesting light on Jesus' attitude toward His approaching

death. In the Old Testament Exodus, God's people were liberated from bondage and brought into freedom. Christ viewed His death as an act that would liberate Him from this period of bondage (on earth) to which He had subjected Himself by the Incarnation (Philippians 2:5-8). He anticipated the glorious liberty from bondage into which He would be brought by the resurrection.

Luke 9:60—*Why did Jesus tell a man to "let the dead bury their own dead"?*

This may seem a strange comment for Jesus to make, but the context of the verse helps us to understand what He was really saying. Jesus encountered a man to whom He had said, "Follow me" (Luke 9:59). This was an invitation not for a quick week of service but for a continuous and ongoing relationship of serving Jesus Christ in spreading the news about the kingdom of God. The man immediately gave an excuse: "Lord, first let me go and bury my father" (Luke 9:59).

Certainly the burial of the dead—especially the burial of a father—is an important thing. But the demands of the kingdom were even more important in Jesus' view. Jesus thus said, "Let the dead bury their own dead, but you go and proclaim the kingdom of God" (Luke 9:60). Jesus' words were not intended to be cruel. His meaning might be paraphrased in this way: "Let the spiritually dead bury the physically dead. You, however, have a higher priority, for I have now called you to the greater work of proclaiming the kingdom of God to other people."

Another observation brings things into clearer perspective here. Some scholars have suggested that if the father had actually already died, the man would be presently involved in burying his father. The context may suggest that the father had not yet died. He may have been just an old man but still alive. If this is correct, the man's son to whom Jesus was speaking was essentially saying that he wanted to wait to serve the kingdom until that future time—possibly years away—when his father died and was subsequently buried.

Whichever of the above interpretive options is correct, Jesus is calling for a radical commitment. It is not so much that burying one's father is unimportant. It is that the kingdom of God is so much more important.

Luke 9:62—*Did Jesus indicate that anyone who has second thoughts about being a Christian is not worthy of the kingdom of God?*

In Luke 9:62 Jesus said, "No one who puts his hand to the plow and looks back is fit for service in the kingdom of God." Admittedly, this is a strong statement. But Jesus is actually painting a picture that would have been well familiar to His first-century hearers. The plows used in that day were quite primitive, constituting a mere piece of wood with a handle at one end and a metal tip at the other end to break up soil. If a man engaged in handling the plow took his eyes off his work and looked backward, the furrow he was plowing became crooked, which was unacceptable. He could do more damage than good. Holding the metal tip in such a way that it produced the desired results while plowing required constant attention.

The point Jesus was making here was that anyone who wishes to engage in service to Him must give his whole heart to the matter and not be double minded, with one foot in service to the kingdom and one foot in the affairs of this world. There should be no divided interests. If someone wants to serve both the world and Christ at the same time, that person is not fit for service of the kingdom of God. The one who would follow Jesus and engage in kingdom work needs a firm hand and a steady eye on the forward-moving plow.

Luke 10:18—*What did Jesus mean when He said to the disciples, "I saw Satan fall like lightning from heaven?"*

It is hard to say just what Jesus was referring to here. Some scholars have surmised that perhaps this is a reference to Satan being cast out of heaven following his initial fall (Isaiah 14:12; Ezekiel 28:11-15). Other scholars suggest that as the 70 disciples went from town to town ministering, they witnessed the defeat of their great adversary, the devil. This defeat, to the disciples, was as sudden and unexpected as a flash of lightning. In this view, the phrase *from heaven* is connected not to Satan but to lightning (lightning often has the appearance of falling from the sky or the heavens). This word picture, then, would indicate that through the preaching of the gospel, Satan had suffered a great defeat, and this defeat was sudden and unexpected, just like a lightning bolt from heaven. The kingdom of God was thus making tremendous inroads as it pushed back the kingdom of darkness.

Luke 11:4—*Does Jesus imply that God could lead us into temptation?*
See comments on Matthew 6:13.

Luke 11:5-10—*Did Jesus teach that God is resistant to answering our prayers?*

Luke 11:5-10 records Jesus' parable about prayer in which a person knocked on a friend's door at midnight in need of three loaves of bread. The one inside answered, "Don't bother me. The door is already locked, and my children are with me in bed. I can't get up and give you anything" (verse 7). (This was likely a one-room house, which means that if he got up in the night, he would probably wake the children.) The parable concludes by pointing out that even though friendship was not enough to cause the person in the house to get up and provide bread, the boldness expressed in knocking on the door at midnight and his persistence in doing so (verse 8) was enough to yield results.

This is a parable about prayer, so Jesus may seem at first glance to be implying that God is resistant to answering our prayers. But that is not the intent of His words.

The whole of Scripture affirms that the Father readily responds to the needs of His children every bit as much as an earthly father responds to the needs of his children (Matthew 7:9-11). The heavenly Father is not resistant to answering our prayers. In fact, not only does the parable *not* teach that God is resistant to prayer, it gives us an assurance that God *does* answer prayer. The primary purpose of the parable was to teach Christ's followers that they need to be persistent in prayer precisely because God longs to give good gifts to them.

We see this persistence stressed in verses 9 and 10, which follow the parable. Here Jesus said, "Ask and it will be given to you; seek and you will find; knock and the door will be opened to you. For everyone who asks receives; he who seeks finds; and to him who knocks, the door will be opened." In these verses, the words *ask, seek,* and *knock* are in the present tense, which indicates continuous activity. We are to keep on asking, keep on seeking, and keep on knocking. If we do so, we will obtain our desired result, assuming our request is in keeping with God's will for our lives.

Luke 11:29-30—*What did Jesus mean when He said His wicked generation would be given only the sign of Jonah?*

As a backdrop, the Jewish Pharisees had witnessed firsthand that Jesus was acting and speaking from a position of authority. They asked Him to provide a sign to show His authority came from God.

The sinfulness of the Pharisees quickly becomes evident. Jesus had already performed many mighty miracles that were signs of His true identity. Jesus responded to the Pharisees' request for a sign as an indication of wickedness. The real issue in Jesus' mind was obedience to the Word of God and the one God had sent. Jesus thus informed them that they would be given only the sign of Jonah.

Though scholars have made a number of suggestions as to what the sign of Jonah is, the context would seem to point to the resurrection of Jesus Christ. Jonah had been in the great fish for three days (Jonah 1:17) before, as it were, coming to life again by being regurgitated out of its mouth. After his reappearance, he spoke his message of repentance, and the Ninevites quickly responded. The sign to be given to Jesus' generation would be the reappearance of the Son of man on the third day after His death.

In what way was Jesus' resurrection a sign? Among other things, Romans 1:4 indicates that the resurrection showed that Jesus was the Son of God. As well, Jesus' resurrection guarantees the approaching judgment of all humankind (Acts 17:31). So repentance is in order, every bit as much as repentance was in order among the Ninevites of Jonah's day.

Luke 12:47-48—*Are there degrees of punishment in hell?*

Yes. For those eternally consigned to hell, the degree of their punishment will be commensurate with the light they received and the degree of their sinfulness. This is the primary teaching of Luke 12:47-48 (see also Matthew 10:15; 16:27; Revelation 20:12-13; 22:12).

Luke 12:49—*Why did Jesus say He came to bring fire on the earth?*

Scholars have interpreted Jesus' words differently, and all agree that it is hard to know precisely what He had in mind here. Some scholars point out that in Old Testament times, fire often symbolized judgment. This has led some to conclude that when Jesus said, "I have come to bring fire on the earth," He was saying He would bring judgment to the earth. This would fit with John 9:39, where Jesus said, "For judgment I have come into this world."

Other scholars relate the fire to the Holy Spirit. Recall that John the Baptist had prophesied that when Jesus came He would baptize "with the Holy Spirit and with fire" (Luke 3:16). Later, when the baptism of the Holy Spirit first occurred on the Day of Pentecost, the people saw "what seemed to be tongues of fire" that came on those filled with the Spirit (Acts 2:1-4).

Other scholars say that *fire* is probably a reference to the tremendous power of God wrought on the earth through Jesus' miraculous ministry and continued in the book of Acts through the Holy Spirit, which Jesus sent to earth following His ascension into heaven (John 15:26).

Luke 12:50—*What baptism did Jesus have to undergo that He so dreaded?*

Scholars agree that the baptism Jesus faced was His suffering and death on the cross for the sins of humanity. We find a similar reference in Mark 10:38, where Jesus asked the disciples, "Can you drink the cup I drink or be baptized with the baptism I am baptized with?" Again, Jesus was referring to His suffering and death on the cross.

Luke 14:26—*Does Jesus advocate hating one's mother, father, spouse, and children for His sake?*

In this verse, Jesus may initially appear to be saying that we should have the emotion of hate for our families for His sake. But I do not think that is what He was intending with His words. The beginning point for properly understanding this statement is that Jesus' teaching leaves no room for truly hating anyone. We are to love even our enemies (Luke 6:27). As well, the fifth commandment instructs us, "Honor your father and your mother" (Exodus 20:12), a commandment repeated in the New Testament (Ephesians 6:1-3; Colossians 3:20).

Jesus in this verse is apparently using a vivid hyperbole (an exaggeration or extravagant statement used as a figure of speech). In understanding Jesus' point, one must keep in mind that in the Hebrew mind-set, to hate means to love less (see Genesis 29:31-33; Deuteronomy 21:15). Jesus is communicating that our supreme love must be for Him alone. Everything else (and everyone else) must take second place.

This is in keeping with what Jesus said in Matthew 10:37: "Anyone who loves his father or mother more than me is not worthy of me; anyone who loves his son or daughter more than me is not worthy of me." Measuring our supreme love for Christ against other lesser loves may make these lesser loves seem like hate by comparison.

Luke 16:1-8—*Did Jesus speak approvingly of dishonesty?*

At first glance, Christ might seem to be approving of dishonesty in this passage, but that is not the case. Jesus commended the manager not for his dishonesty but for taking shrewd, resolute action in the midst of a crisis. Let's consider the details.

The dishonest manager worked things for his own benefit while cheating his master. And by giving a financial break to the debtors, charging them far less than what they actually owed, they would be obligated to him after he lost his job. He was making friends with them now so they would hire him later. The manager was planning for the future and in so doing was acting shrewdly.

When the rich man heard what the manager had done, he commended him because he had handled himself shrewdly. The manager had not been honest, but that is not why the rich man commended him. The manager did act shrewdly in planning ahead, and this alone is why the manager was commended.

Luke 16:9—*Why did Jesus teach His followers to use worldly wealth to gain friends?*

In Luke 16:9 Jesus said, "I tell you, use worldly wealth to gain friends for yourselves, so that when it is gone, you will be welcomed into eternal dwellings." Jesus seemed to be teaching that if worldly wealth is good for anything at all, it should be used for some kind of eternal benefit. Money and wealth should be used shrewdly with a view to the future, not in a selfish way that focuses only on the present.

Jesus indicates we should be ready to make use of any wealth God has given us by helping other people. Those we are able to help while on earth may one day welcome us as we enter the gates of heaven at the moment of our deaths. Using money wisely will gain us friends, and it will stand us in good stead when money fails, that is, when we die and money is of no more use.

Luke 16:22-28—*Is Jesus' description of Lazarus and the rich man in Abraham's bosom just a story, or is its picture of the afterlife (involving conscious existence) true?*

When Jesus taught people using parables or stories, He always cited real-life situations. For example, Jesus spoke of a prodigal son who returned home after squandering his money (Luke 15:11-32), a man who found a buried treasure in a field (Matthew 13:44), a king who put on a wedding feast for his son (Matthew 22:1-14), a slave owner who traveled abroad and then returned home to his slaves (Matthew 25:14-30), a man who constructed a vineyard (Matthew 20:1-16), and so on. All of these were common occurrences in biblical days. Jesus never illustrated His teaching with a fairy tale. This being the case, we must conclude that Luke 16 is true to life and should be taken as a solid evidence for conscious existence after death. Any other interpretation makes an absurdity of the text.

Luke 17:34-37—*Was Jesus referring to the rapture or to judgment?*

Jesus, speaking of the time of the second coming, said: "I tell you, on that night two people will be in one bed; one will be taken and the other left. Two women will be grinding grain together; one will be taken and the other left."

"Where, Lord?" His disciples asked.

He replied, "Where there is a dead body, there the vultures will gather."

Certainly many Christians through the years have interpreted this passage as referring to the rapture. Several points rule against this interpretation, however. To begin, if you believe that the rapture happens prior to the time of the tribulation (as I do—see 1 Thessalonians 1:10; 5:9), then Luke 17:34-37 could not be referring to the rapture because the events in Luke 17 happen after the tribulation and at the time of the second coming of Christ.

Beyond this, the immediate context of Luke 17 seems to argue against the possibility that the rapture is in view. The disciples asked Jesus where these individuals would be taken. Jesus replied, "Where there is a dead body, there the vultures will gather." Jesus' answer clearly points to judgment.

In the Old Testament, God's enemies become food for vultures (Ezekiel 32:4-6), which the Jewish people considered a horrible fate (Deuteronomy 28:26; 1 Samuel 17:44; Psalm 79:2). This is the fate of those who are taken in Luke 17. Those who are left behind will be Christians who enter into Christ's millennial kingdom—a period of 1000 years, during which Christ will rule on the earth (Revelation 20:1-6; see also Matthew 25:31-46).

Luke 18:8—*Will any Christians be on earth at the second coming of Christ?*

Most scholars believe that Jesus did not doubt that some Christians would be on earth when He returned again. After all, in Matthew 25:31-46 Jesus said He would separate His sheep (Christians) from the goats (unbelievers) following His second coming. Nevertheless, Jesus indicated in Luke 18:8 that the primary characteristic of people on earth at the time of His return would be unbelief.

Jesus probably asked the question about finding faith on earth to spur His own disciples on to faithfulness. Ancient Jewish writers made predictions that in the end times, many would fall away from the faith (compare with 2 Thessalonians 2:3-4). But Jesus did not want this to happen to His followers, so He asked the question to motivate them. Jesus continued urging them on to faithfulness throughout the rest of this Gospel (Luke 21:8-19,34-36; 22:31-32,40,46).

Luke 18:18-27—*Did Jesus teach that people can merit eternal life?*

The rich young ruler asked Jesus how to inherit eternal life. Jesus then responded by telling him he must follow the commandments of God (verses 19-20). The ruler responded that he had kept the commandments (verse 21). So Jesus informed him he must do one thing more—sell all that he had and give the money to the poor (verse 22). At hearing this, the man became very sad, for he was a man of great wealth.

At first glance, Jesus might seem to be teaching salvation by works to the rich young ruler. But this was not the case. Scripture is clear that the law does not save (Romans 3:28), but it does condemn (3:19). Jesus was demonstrating to the young man that he stood condemned before the law. The fact that he was unwilling to give his money to the poor was a sure indication that he had not even kept the first great commandment to love God more than anything else (see Matthew 22:36-37).

Furthermore, the rich young ruler's question was confused. A person cannot do anything to receive an inheritance of any kind—including eternal life. An inheritance by its very nature is a gift. Eternal life is presented throughout Scripture as a gift (John 3:36; 5:24; 20:31; Romans 6:23; 1 John 5:13), so no one can do anything to earn it. The apostle Paul said, "Now when a man works, his wages are not credited to him as a gift, but as an obligation. However, to the man who does not work but trusts God who justifies the wicked, his faith is credited as righteousness" (Romans 4:4-5).

The only work by which a person can be saved is faith. Recall that when Jesus was asked, "What can we do to accomplish the works of God?" He answered, "The work of God is this: to believe in the one he has sent" (John 6:29).

Luke 18:24-25—*A camel cannot go through the eye of a needle, so was Jesus saying a rich person cannot be saved?*

Jesus was using a hyperbole—a purposefully exaggerated statement. The main point Jesus was making is that it is hard for a rich person to turn to God in the midst of his wealth, for he has little sense of need. He has so many earthly things to rely on that he senses little if any need for God. One must note, however, that many rich persons have become Christians throughout church history and have used their wealth for great good.

Luke 19:11—*Did the disciples have wrong expectations?*

In this verse we read that the disciples wrongly expected that the kingdom of God was going to appear immediately. Evangelical Christians concede that Christ's disciples occasionally held false notions as human beings. However, neither Luke 19:11 nor any other text of Scripture indicates that the disciples or prophets ever taught such false notions as part of God's revelation to humankind.

Whenever the prophets or apostles were speaking as God's mouthpieces to humanity, they never communicated any false notions. No true prophet of God ever made a mistake while uttering a prophecy because he was delivering God's words to humankind, not his own words. Note the following passages:

- "The Spirit of the LORD spoke through me; his word was on my tongue" (2 Samuel 23:2).

- "You spoke by the Holy Spirit through the mouth of your servant, our father David" (Acts 4:24-25).

- "This is what we speak, not in words taught us by human wisdom but in words taught by the Spirit, expressing spiritual truths in spiritual words" (1 Corinthians 2:13).

When interpreting Luke 19:11, one must keep in mind that Jesus had earlier told the disciples that the kingdom of God had arrived in some sense and was present in His ministry (Luke 11:20). Jesus and the disciples were near Jerusalem (the capital city), so some thought that the completion of God's kingdom purposes was near at hand—despite Jesus' continued teachings of the coming cross. For this reason, to deal with the disciples' wrong expectation, Jesus told them a parable (19:12-27) to show them that an interval of time would elapse before the kingdom was consummated. Jesus used the parable to correct their thinking and to dispel their overeager hopes.

Luke 20:38—*Does the fact that God is not a "God of the dead" prove conscious existence in the afterlife?*

Yes. The Sadducees taught that the soul dies with the body. Jesus thus directly contradicts this teaching of the Sadducees. In effect, Jesus is saying, "Abraham, Isaac, and Jacob, though they died many years ago, are actually living today. For God, who calls Himself the God of Abraham, Isaac, and Jacob, is not the God of the dead but of the living." Jesus' words to the Sadducees clearly indicate that these Old Testament patriarchs are living at the present moment even though they physically died many years ago.

Luke 22:36-38—*Did Jesus advocate the use of a sword for self-defense purposes?*

Jesus advised the disciples to buy a sword (Luke 22:36). Here the sword (Greek: *maxairan*) is a dagger or short sword that belonged to the Jewish traveler's equipment as protection against robbers and wild animals. A plain reading of the passage would seem to indicate that Jesus approved of self-defense.

Luke 22:44—*Did Jesus really sweat blood?*

Yes. Medical history includes cases in which severe mental suffering has led to the actual sweating of blood, resulting from the breakdown of blood vessels. In Jesus' case, His mental suffering was no doubt due to the fact that He knew that He—an intrinsically pure and holy being—was about to take the sins of humanity on Himself in sacrifice on a cross and experience a sense of judicial separation from the Father as a result (2 Corinthians 5:21).

Luke 23:28-31—*What catastrophic event is Jesus referring to?*

Jesus was shortly to be crucified when He turned to a group of women who were following Him and said, "Daughters of Jerusalem, do not weep for me; weep for yourselves and for your children. For the time will come when you will say, 'Blessed are the barren women, the wombs that never bore and the breasts that never nursed!' "

Jesus' words were pointing forward to Jerusalem's destruction in AD 70 at the hands of Titus and his Roman warriors. The temple in Jerusalem—the heart of Jewish worship—would be utterly destroyed. Barren women living during that time would be considered blessed, for it would be better for women not to have any children than for them to have children experience such suffering as would come in AD 70. Jesus thus sadly told these women, "Mourn for yourselves." The Jewish historian Flavius Josephus documented that some Jewish mothers were reduced to eating their own children during the famine that followed Rome's siege against Jerusalem.

Luke 24:23—*Were Jesus' resurrection appearances physical appearances or mere visions?*

In this verse we read of a "vision of angels, who said he was alive."

This verse does not say that Jesus' resurrection appearances were mere visions. Rather, it refers to a vision of angels, and these angels said Christ was alive. The postresurrection encounters with Christ are described by Paul as literal appearances (1 Corinthians 15:5-8), not as visions. Christ's resurrection appearances were accompanied by physical manifestations, including His audible voice, His physical body and crucifixion scars, physical sensations (like touch), and eating on three separate occasions. These phenomena are not purely subjective or internal—they involve a physical, external reality.

Luke 24:31—*Did Jesus dematerialize when He suddenly disappeared from the disciples after an appearance?*

In answering this, we might note that a sudden disappearance does not even require a resurrection body. Philip, for example, was immediately transported from the presence of the Ethiopian eunuch in his physical pre-resurrection body. The text says that after Philip baptized the eunuch, "the Spirit of the Lord suddenly took Philip away, and the eunuch did not see him again, but went on his way rejoicing" (Acts 8:39). One moment Philip was with the eunuch; the next he suddenly and miraculously disappeared and later appeared in another city (Acts 8:40). Such a phenomenon does not necessitate an immaterial body. Therefore, sudden appearances and disappearances are not proofs of the immaterial, but of the supernatural. Likewise, the fact that Jesus' resurrection body could suddenly disappear did not mean it was immaterial. Jesus physically rose from the dead!

Luke 24:31—*If Jesus had the same physical body after His resurrection, why did His disciples not recognize Him?*

There are a number of possible reasons:

- dullness—Luke 24:25-26
- disbelief—John 20:24-25
- disappointment—John 20:11-15

- dread—Luke 24:36-37
- dimness—John 20:1,14-15
- distance—John 21:4
- different clothes—John 19:23-24; 20:6-8

Two points are crucial: The problem was only temporary, and before the appearance was over they were absolutely convinced that it was the same Jesus in the same physical body of flesh, bones, and scars He had before the resurrection! And they went out of His presence to turn the world upside down, fearlessly facing death because they had not the slightest doubt that He had conquered death in the same physical body in which He had experienced it.

John

John 1:1—*In what sense is Jesus the Word?*

For John, the Word is a divine person who has come into the world to reveal another person (the Father). John chose the term *Word* (Greek: *Logos*) because both Greeks and Jews would be somewhat familiar with the term, but he invested it with an entirely new meaning. When John used *Logos* of Jesus Christ, he did so with the intention of presenting Christ not as a divine principle (as the Greeks held), but as a living being who was the source of all life; not as a mere personification (as some Jews held), but as a person who was nothing less than God Himself: "The Word was with God, and the Word was God" (John 1:1).

John 1:1—*Is Jesus God or just a god?*

In this verse we read, "In the beginning was the Word, and the Word was with God, and the Word was God." Some cultists have tried to argue that this verse is mistranslated, and should be translated to read that "the Word was a god," thereby indicating that Jesus is a lesser deity than God the Father. Such groups argue that in the Greek, a noun (such as *God*) with a definite article (*the*) points to an identity or a personality. The first occurrence of *God* (Greek: *theos*) in John 1:1 has the definite article *the* (Greek: *ho*) and points to God the Father. They then argue that in the Greek, when a singular predicate noun (such as the second occurrence of *God* in John 1:1) has no definite article and occurs before the verb (as is true in the Greek text of John 1:1), this points to a quality about someone—in this case a divine quality. Thus, the Word was godlike, divine—a god.

Several points can be made in response to this cultic view. First, it is interesting to observe that the word *theos* without the definite article *ho* is used of God the Father in the New Testament—with the exact same Greek construction used of Jesus in John 1:1 (an example is Luke 20:38).

Further, Greek grammarians tell us that when Greek nouns have no definite article, we need not insert an indefinite article. In other words, *theos* without the definite article *ho* does not need to be translated as *a God,* as some cultists have done. In fact, Greek grammarians agree that *theos* in John 1:1 most definitely does not have an indefinite sense and thus should not be translated with an indefinite article.

This clearly shows that John 1:1 points to the deity of Christ. We can also note that *theos* with the definite article *ho* is most definitely used of Jesus Christ in the New Testament. One example of this is John 20:28, where Thomas says to Jesus, "My Lord and my God." The verse reads literally from the Greek: "The Lord of me and the God [*ho theos*] of me." Clearly, Christ is just as much God as the Father is. Other examples of Christ as *ho theos* include Matthew 1:23 and Hebrews 1:8. We see again that the same words used of the Father's deity are used in reference to Jesus' deity.

John 2:9—*When Jesus turned water into wine, was He teaching that drinking is okay?*

Drunkenness is forbidden by God throughout Scripture. It is simply not an option for the Christian. In Ephesians 5:18, the apostle Paul explicitly instructed, "Do not get drunk on wine, which leads to debauchery. Instead, be filled with the Spirit."

Drinking wine in moderation, however, does seem to be permissible in Scripture (see 1 Timothy 3:3,8). I should note, though, that in biblical times, wine was typically diluted by a ratio of twenty parts water to one part wine, essentially creating wine-flavored water. Sometimes people in the ancient world would go as strong as one part water and one part wine, and this was considered strong wine. Anyone who drank wine unmixed was looked upon by the Greeks as a Scythian, a barbarian.

Every Christian adult must decide for himself whether or not to drink. A question we must all ask ourselves is this: Drinking may be permissible, but is it beneficial? The following verses speak to this issue:

- " 'Everything is permissible for me'—but not everything is beneficial. 'Everything is permissible for me'—but I will not be mastered by anything" (1 Corinthians 6:12).

- "It is better not to eat meat or drink wine or to do anything else that will cause your brother to fall" (Romans 14:21).

- "So whether you eat or drink or whatever you do, do it all for the glory of God" (1 Corinthians 10:31).

- "Each of you should look not only to your own interests, but also to the interests of others" (Philippians 2:4).

John 3:1-5—*Is water baptism necessary for salvation?*

Some cite this passage in favor of the view that water baptism is necessary for salvation, for in it we find reference to the necessity of being "born of water." However, this is a misinterpretation.

Jesus was speaking with Nicodemus, a Pharisee who would have been trusting in his physical descent from Abraham for entrance into the Messiah's kingdom. The Jews believed that because they were physically related to Abraham, they were in a specially privileged position before God. Christ, however, denied such a possibility. Parents can transmit to their children only the nature which they themselves possess. Since each parent's nature, because of Adam's sin, is sinful, each parent transmits a sinful nature to the child. And what is sinful cannot enter the kingdom of God (verse 5). The only way one can enter God's kingdom is to experience a spiritual rebirth, and this is precisely what Jesus is emphasizing to Nicodemus.

Nicodemus did not initially comprehend Jesus' meaning. He wrongly concluded that Jesus was speaking of something related to physical birth, but he could not understand how a person could go through physical birth a second time (John 3:4). Jesus picked up on

Nicodemus's line of thought and sought to move the argument from physical birth to spiritual birth.

Notice how Jesus went about His explanation to Nicodemus. He first speaks about being "born of water and the Spirit" in John 3:5 and then explains what He means by this in verse 6. "Born of water" in verse 5 appears to be parallel to "born of the flesh" in verse 6, just as "born of...the Spirit" in verse 5 is parallel to "born of the Spirit" in verse 6 (NASB). Jesus' message, then, is that just as one has had a physical birth to live on earth, so one must also have a spiritual birth in order to enter the kingdom of God. One must be "born from above." The verse thus has nothing whatsoever to do with water baptism as a requirement for salvation.

John 3:16—*Is Jesus, as the Son of God, a lesser deity than the Father?*

Ancient Semitics and Orientals used the phrase *son of* to indicate likeness or sameness of nature and equality of being. When Jesus claimed to be the Son of God, His Jewish contemporaries fully understood that He was making a claim to be God in an unqualified sense. This is why the Jews insisted, "We have a law, and according to that law he [Jesus Christ] must die, because he claimed to be the Son of God" (John 19:7). Recognizing that Jesus was identifying Himself as God, the Jews wanted to put Him to death for committing blasphemy (see Leviticus 24:16).

Scripture indicates that Christ's sonship is an eternal sonship. Hebrews 1:2 says God created the universe through His Son—implying that Christ was the Son of God prior to the creation. Moreover, Christ as the Son is explicitly said to have existed before all things (Colossians 1:17; compare with verses 13-14). As well, Jesus, speaking as the Son of God (John 8:54-56), asserts His eternal preexistence (verse 58).

John 4:1-28—*Why was the Samaritan woman surprised that Jesus spoke with her?*

The Samaritans of New Testament times were considered half-breeds by mainstream Jews. Some Israelites from the tribes of Ephraim and Manasseh intermarried with Assyrians following the fall of Samaria in 722 BC. Mainstream Jews therefore considered the Samaritans to be racially unclean. Samaritans claimed to worship the same God as the Jews, but they constructed a rival temple on Mount Gerizim, claiming that theirs was the true Bethel (house of God). So when Jesus (a Jew) spoke to the Samaritan woman, He violated the cultural norms of the day.

John 4:23—*Are we to worship the Father only and not Jesus?*

No. Simply because Jesus urged worship of the Father does not mean Jesus is not to be worshipped. In fact, the Gospels reveal that Christ was worshipped (Greek: *proskuneo,* the same Greek word used of worshipping the Father) as God many times. And He always accepted such worship from Thomas (John 20:28), the angels (Hebrews 1:6), the wise men (Matthew 2:11), a leper (Matthew 8:2), a ruler (Matthew 9:18), a blind man (John 9:38), an anonymous woman (Matthew 15:25), Mary Magdalene (Matthew 28:9), and the disciples (Matthew 28:17).

Jesus never sought to correct His followers or set them straight when they bowed down and worshipped Him. Indeed, Jesus considered such worship as perfectly appropriate. Of course, we wouldn't expect Jesus to try to correct people (according to Exodus 34:14) in worshipping Him if He truly was God in the flesh, as Scripture clearly indicates.

John 5:19—*If Jesus is really God, why did He say He could do nothing by Himself, but only what He sees His Father doing?*

At first glance Jesus may seem to be implying that He is not fully divine. However, understanding the biblical teaching on the Trinity helps to clear things up.

Jesus is fully equal to the Father in terms of His divine nature. Nevertheless, a functional hierarchy exists between the persons of the Trinity, with the Father in authority over the Son. To illustrate, my son, David, has my identical nature (fully human), but I am functionally in authority over him. Similarly, Jesus has the same nature as the Father (a divine nature), but the Father is functionally in authority over Him.

John 5:19 indicates that Jesus does not act independently of the Father but works in perfect harmony and submission to Him. We are told earlier in John's Gospel that the Father sent Jesus into the world (John 3:16). We are now told in John 5:19 that the Father directs Him as well.

The Jewish backdrop is significant. Among the ancient Jews it was common wisdom that sons were to imitate their fathers. Of course, Jewish sons had the same nature as their Jewish fathers (both were human). Similarly, though John 5:19 portrays Jesus as imitating the Father, Jesus nevertheless has the same nature as the Father (a divine nature).

There is actually a veiled claim to deity in this verse, for it plainly tells us that "whatever the Father does the Son also does" (John 5:19). The Father is God. And who besides God can do what God does? Since Jesus does what only God can do, Jesus Himself is quite obviously God (just as the Father is).

John 5:28-29—*Is Jesus advocating salvation by works in these verses?*

No. Earlier in John's Gospel we read, "To all who received him, to those who believed in his name, he gave the right to become children of God—children born not of natural descent, nor of human decision or a husband's will, but born of God" (John 1:12-13). Jesus Himself affirmed in John 3:16-18, "For God so loved the world that he gave his one and only Son, that whoever believes in him shall not perish but have eternal life. For God did not send his Son into the world to condemn the world, but to save the world through him. Whoever believes in him is not condemned, but whoever does not believe stands condemned already because he has not believed in the name of God's one and only Son."

Jesus' reference to good works in John 5:28-29 is to that which occurs *after* saving faith. In order to be saved one needs the grace of

God (Ephesians 2:8-9), but authentic faith expresses itself in good works (verse 10).

John 6:44—*What did Jesus mean when He said that no one can come to Him unless the Father draws him?*

Some theologians suggest that perhaps the term *draw* carries the idea of enticing, wooing, or seeking to persuade. Seen in this light, the Father merely tries to persuade people to come to Christ.

Other theologians, however, note that whenever this particular word is used elsewhere in the New Testament it carries a much stronger meaning. For example, the word is used in the book of Acts where Paul and Silas were thrown into prison (Acts 16:19-24). They were not wooed into prison, but were thrown into prison rather forcefully. These scholars suggest that the Father does more than woo us to Christ, He *compels* us to Christ.

Actually, this "drawing" ministry of the Father is a merciful act of grace. Think about it. Human beings are so deeply engulfed in sin and its horrendous effects (including pervasive unbelief and hardness of heart) that none would end up coming to Christ of their own accord unless God the Father sovereignly drew them to Christ. We should be thankful for this ministry of the Father.

John 6:53—*Was Jesus referring to His physical body when He said, "Unless you eat the flesh of the Son of Man and drink his blood, you have no life in you"?*

Jesus' words need not be taken in the sense of ingesting His actual physical body and blood. Jesus often spoke in metaphors and figures of speech. For example, He called the Pharisees blind guides (Matthew 23:27) and Herod a fox (Luke 13:32). When Jesus said, "I am the true vine" in this same book (John 15:1), this is not to be taken in a physical sense! Neither should Jesus' comment "I am the gate" be taken literally (John 10:9). There is therefore no necessity to take Jesus in a literal, physical way when He referred to eating His flesh. Jesus often spoke in graphic parables and figures, as He Himself acknowledged (Matthew 13:10-11).

Notice that when Jesus said "this is my body" in reference to the bread in His hand, He was still with them in His physical body, the hands of which were holding that very bread which He said was His body (Matthew 26:26). He was obviously speaking figuratively. Otherwise, we must believe that Christ was holding His own body in His own bodily hands.

Still further, Jesus could not have been speaking physically when He said "This is my body" because since His Incarnation He has always been a human being and has always dwelt continuously in a human body (except for three days in a grave). If the bread and the wine He held in His hands at the Last Supper were actually His literal body and blood, He would have been incarnated in two different places at the same time! But one physical body cannot be in two different locations at the same time. It takes two different bodies to do that. Clearly then, Jesus was speaking figuratively when He said to eat His flesh.

John 8:3-8—*What did Jesus write on the ground when the adulterous woman was brought before Him?*

Early in the morning, while Jesus was teaching in the temple, the religious leaders brought to Jesus a woman caught in the act of adultery (John 8:1-3). When the Jewish leaders first asked Jesus whether they should stone her to death, He bent down and "started to write on the ground with his finger" (John 8:6).

It has been assumed by many that Jesus bent down and wrote in the sand. All the Hollywood motion pictures about Christ portray this scene this way. But the context indicates in John 8:2 that Jesus was inside the temple when this event occurred. The temple, of course, is made of stone. When Jesus bent down to write on the ground, He was actually writing on stone with His finger.

Some scholars have found significance in this fact. They note that when the Jewish leaders came before Jesus, they were condemning the woman based on the commandments in the law. We read in Exodus 31:18 that the law was on "the tablets of stone inscribed by the finger of God" (see also Deuteronomy 9:10). Some have thus concluded that Jesus' action was subtly communicating that the law actually had its origin in Him (as God), and yet His assessment of the matter was that the woman should go her way and sin no more instead of being stoned to death.

Of course, we cannot be sure that this was Jesus' intended meaning. Other scholars have suggested that Jesus bent down to write down the sins of the Jewish accusers. Another suggested possibility is that Jesus wrote the Old Testament law that required the conviction of both the man and the woman in such a sin (Leviticus 20:10; Deuteronomy 22:22). The Jewish leaders had brought only the woman before Christ.

All of this is mere conjecture. The fact is, we really have no clue in the text as to what Jesus wrote on the ground.

John 8:28—*If Jesus is really God, why did He say He could speak only what the Father taught Him?*

The whole reason Jesus became flesh (a human being) in the first place was to reveal God: "No one has ever seen God [the Father], but God the One and Only [Jesus Christ], who is at the Father's side, has made him known" (John 1:18). The perfect revelation of God the Father came in the person of God the Son.

John 8:28 most certainly does not point to any weakness in the Son, or deficiency of power to do anything by Himself. After all, Jesus by His own power created the entire universe (John 1:3), upholds the universe (Colossians 1:17), and raised Himself from the dead (John 2:19), among many other divine deeds. John 8:28 simply tells us that Jesus as the Son of God could never do anything contrary to the Father because they are of the same nature and therefore never act separately from one another. Jesus does and says what the Father wills, and this shows and proves their unity of nature and their perfect equality because there was nothing in the

Father's mind but what was also known to the divine Son. (See the comments on John 5:19.)

John 8:58—*Is Jesus claiming to be eternal or just preexistent?*

Jesus said to some Jews, "I tell you the truth...before Abraham was born, I am!" Some misunderstand this verse to mean that Jesus was just claiming preexistence before Abraham. The context, however, shows that Jesus was pointing not only to His preexistence before Abraham but also to His eternality. After all, the term *I am* points back to God's name in Exodus 3:14—a name that conveys the idea of eternal self-existence. Yahweh (the "I Am") never came into being at a point in time, for He has always existed. He was never born; He will never die. He does not grow older, for He is beyond the realm of time. To know Yahweh is to know the eternal one.

All of this adds tremendous significance to Jesus' encounter with the Jews. Knowing how much they venerated Abraham, Jesus in John 8:58 deliberately contrasted the created origin of Abraham with His own eternal, uncreated nature. He was not simply showing that He was preexistent and thus older than Abraham, but that His existence is of a different kind than Abraham's. In other words, Abraham's existence was created and finite, beginning at a point in time, but Christ's existence never began, is uncreated and infinite, and is therefore eternal.

John 9:1-7—*Was the man born blind because of the sin of his parents?*

The Jewish theologians of biblical times gave two reasons for birth defects: prenatal sin (before birth, but not before conception) and parental sin. They claimed that when a pregnant woman worshipped in a heathen temple, the fetus committed idolatry as well. They also believed that the sins of the parents were visited upon the children (Exodus 20:5; Psalm 109:14; Isaiah 65:6-7). When they saw this blind man, their assumption was that his parents had committed some horrendous sin, or perhaps when he was in the womb his mother visited a pagan temple. Jesus corrects this misguided thinking. The man was born blind for the glory of God.

John 10:16—*Who are the other sheep Jesus refers to?*

The other sheep are Gentile believers as opposed to Jewish believers. In the Gospels, the Jews were called "the lost sheep of Israel" (Matthew 10:6; 15:24), and those Jews who followed Christ were called His sheep (John 10). When Jesus said, "I have other sheep that are not of this sheep pen," He was clearly referring to non-Jewish, Gentile believers. Jesus indicated that the Gentile believers, along with the Jewish believers, shall be one flock with one shepherd (John 10:16).

John 10:30—*In what sense is Jesus one with the Father?*

When Jesus said, "I and my Father are one," the Jewish leaders immediately picked up stones to put Him to death. They understood Him to be claiming to be God in an unqualified sense. Indeed, according to verse 33, the Jews said they were stoning Jesus for blasphemy—"because you, a mere man, claim to be God." The penalty for blasphemy, according to Old Testament law (Leviticus 24), is death by stoning.

Jesus was claiming to be God, but He was not claiming to be the Father, as some cultists claim. We know this to be true because in the phrase, "I and the Father are one," a first person plural, "we are" (Greek: *esmen*), is used. The verse literally reads from the Greek, "I and the Father we are one." If Jesus intended to say that He and the Father were one person, He certainly would not have used the first person plural, which clearly implies two persons.

John 10:34—*Did Jesus teach that human beings can become gods?*

No. Such an interpretation is contrary to the overall context. Jesus is not speaking to pantheists (who believe that God is everything and everything is God) or polytheists (who believe in many gods). Rather, He is addressing strict Jewish monotheists who believe that only the Creator of the universe is God. His statement should not be wrenched out of this monotheistic context and given a pantheistic or polytheistic twist.

Moreover, Jesus' statement, "You are gods" (spoken initially of judges in Psalm 82:6), must be understood as part of His overall reasoning here, which is an *a fortiori* argument that takes this form: "If God even called human judges *gods* with a small *g*, based on their work of making life-and-death decisions among human beings, how much more can I call myself the Son of God, in view of my many miraculous works."

Notice also that not all human beings are called gods, but only a special class of persons—judges, "to whom the word of God came" (John 10:35). Jesus was showing that if the Old Testament Scriptures could give some limited divine status to divinely appointed judges, why should they find it incredible that He should call Himself the Son of God? Psalm 82 goes on to say that these judges were actually mere men and would die as the men they really were (verse 7).

Finally, it is possible, as many scholars believe, that when the psalmist Asaph said of the unjust judges, "You are gods," He was speaking in irony. He indicated to these judges, "I have called you gods, but in fact you will die like the men that you really are." If this is so, then when Jesus alluded to this psalm in John 10, He was saying that what the Israelite judges were called in irony and in judgment, He is in reality.

In any event, Jesus was clearly giving a defense for His own deity, not for the deification of man.

John 11:11-14—*By describing death as falling asleep, did Jesus teach that conscious existence ends at the moment of death?*

The term *sleep*, when used in contexts of death in Scripture, always refers to the body, not the soul. Sleep is an appropriate figure of speech for the death of the body because the body takes on the appearance of sleep (see Acts 7:60; 1 Corinthians 15:20; 1 Thessalonians 4:13-18).

The evidence for conscious existence following death is very strong:

- The rich man and Lazarus were conscious following death (Luke 16:19-31).

- Jesus' spirit went to the Father the day He died (Luke 23:46).

- Jesus promised that the repentant thief would be with Him in paradise the very day he died (Luke 23:43).

- Paul said it was far better to die and be with Christ (Philippians 1:23).

- Paul affirmed that when we are absent from the body, we are present with the Lord (2 Corinthians 5:8).

- The souls of those martyred during the tribulation period are conscious in heaven, singing and praying to God (Revelation 6:9).

- Jesus, in speaking about the Old Testament saints Abraham, Isaac, and Jacob, said that God "is not the God of the dead, but of the living" (Luke 20:38).

John 13:14—*Why did Jesus tell the disciples that they should wash one another's feet?*

Jesus was teaching about humility and servanthood, and He did so through a living parable—an acted-out parable. Normally when one entered someone's house in New Testament days, the servant of that household washed that person's feet. This was not the job of the master of the household. By washing the disciples' feet, Jesus placed Himself in the role of a servant. As the Son of God was a servant, so the disciples were to be servants to each other.

This was a tremendous lesson in humility and servanthood for the disciples. Instead of trying to exalt themselves over others (the normal human tendency), they were to become each other's servants. This is in line with Jesus' teaching elsewhere that he who is greatest in the kingdom of heaven is the one who becomes the servant of all (Matthew 20:26).

John 14:7-11—*Was Jesus claiming to be the Father in this passage?*

In this passage Jesus claimed, "Anyone who has seen me has seen the Father." These verses prove only that the Father and Son are one in being, not that they are one person. Notice that in verse 6, Jesus clearly distinguished Himself from the Father when He said, "No one comes to the Father, but through Me." The words *to* and *through* would not make any sense if Jesus and the Father were one and the same person. They only make sense if the Father and Jesus are distinct persons, with Jesus being the mediator between the Father and humankind. These verses indicate that Jesus is the perfect revelation of the Father (1:18). And the reason Jesus is the perfect revelation of the Father is that Jesus and the Father, along with the Holy Spirit, are one indivisible divine being (John 10:30). Jesus, the second person of the Trinity, is the perfect revelation of the Father, the first person of the Trinity.

John 14:9—*Does this verse mean that the Father has a body like the Son does?*

Some cults claim that Jesus' statement, "Anyone who has seen me has seen the Father," means that the Father has a body like the Son does. Contrary to this view, God is spirit (John 4:24), and a spirit does not have flesh and bones (Luke 24:39).

John's Gospel makes it clear that Jesus' mission was to reveal the Father to humankind: "No one has ever seen God, but God the One and Only, who is at the Father's side, has made him known" (John 1:18). That's why Jesus could say that when a man looks at Jesus, "he sees the one who sent me" (John 12:45). And that's why Jesus could affirm, "Whoever accepts me accepts the one who sent me" (John 13:20).

John 14:12—*Did Jesus promise that His followers would do greater miracles than He did?*

No. Jesus was simply saying that His many followers would do things greater in extent (all over the world) and greater in effect (multitudes being touched by the power of God). During His short ministry on earth, Jesus was confined in His influence to a comparatively small region of Palestine. Following His departure, His followers were able to work in widely scattered places and influence much larger numbers of human beings.

Jesus in this verse was thus referring to greater works in terms of the whole scope of the impact of God's people and the church on the entire world throughout all history. In other words, Jesus was speaking quantitatively, not qualitatively. The works are quantitatively greater because Christ's work is multiplied through all His followers.

John 14:18—*Is Jesus implying He is the Father, thereby disproving the doctrine of the Trinity?*

Some cultists have claimed that because Jesus said He would not leave His disciples as orphans (John 14:18), He must be their Father. This interpretation is incorrect for several reasons. First, it confuses action with identity. Christ *in action* functions as a divine parent figure who guides, nurtures, protects, and leads His disciples. But this does not mean that Christ *in identity* is the Father (the first person of the Trinity). One must not forget that it is the uniform testimony of Scripture that the Father and Son are distinct persons within the unity of the one God (John 3:16-17; 7:29; 8:55; 10:15; 11:41-42).

John 14:28—*Does Jesus indicate He is a lesser deity than the Father when He says, "The Father is greater than I"?*

No. Jesus is not speaking in this verse about His nature or His essential being (Christ had earlier said "I and the Father are one" in this regard—John 10:30), but is rather speaking of His lowly position in the Incarnation. The Athanasian Creed affirms that Christ is "equal to the Father as touching his Godhead and inferior to the Father as touching his manhood."

Thus, Christ's statement that the Father is greater simply points to the great humiliation Jesus suffered in becoming a human being. He could honestly say, from the perspective of the Incarnation, that the Father was greater than He was, for while Jesus was in a state of humiliation on earth, the Father was in a state of glory in heaven.

We find an illustration of this in the president of the United States. The president is in a higher position than the rest of us. Therefore, the president is greater than the rest of us. However, the president is still just a human being (he has the same nature as the rest of us).

John 15:2—*Do we lose our salvation if we fail to bear fruit as Christians?*

In John 15:2, Jesus—the true vine—teaches about the issue of fruitfulness: The Father "cuts off every branch in me that bears no fruit, while every branch that does bear fruit he prunes so that it will be even more fruitful." Scholars have most often interpreted the phrase *cut off* in one of four ways.

1. Some scholars see this as referring to literally lopping off the branch and throwing it away. Seen in this light, the phrase could refer to the physical death of fruitless Christians. This would be the ultimate form of divine discipline for a believer engaged in persistent and unrepentant sin (see 1 Corinthians 11:30; 1 John 5:16).

2. Other interpreters see the lopping off as a metaphorical way of describing less drastic forms of God's discipline—that is, God disciplines the lives of believers so they are led to be more fruitful. Seen in this light, God works in the life of each believer in such a way as to cut out all that is bad so that he or she bears more spiritual fruit.

3. Still other interpreters say the lopping off involves the recognition that not all who claim to be followers of Jesus Christ are in fact true believers—a reality that soon evidences itself by a complete lack of spiritual fruit. In such a case, this branch is truly dead, and can only be lopped off, much as Judas was.

4. Still others interpret the phrase *cuts off* in the sense of lifting up. In biblical times, gardeners would often lift vines off the ground, propping them up on sticks, so they would bear more fruit. Seen in this light, John 15:2 may be saying that the Father does whatever is necessary in each Christian's life to ensure maximum production of fruit. If this interpretation is correct, then the verse would not relate in any way to the possibility of losing one's salvation. But even if the verse carried the other meaning (lopping off), this would not

demand a loss of salvation. It could refer to God's discipline of the Christian, or it could relate to professing Christians as opposed to genuine Christians.

John 16:7—*Why did Jesus say the Holy Spirit would not come to His followers unless He first went into heaven?*

The implication is that the cross, resurrection, and subsequent glorification of Christ were necessary prior to the sending of the Holy Spirit. In God's plan of salvation, Calvary had to precede Pentecost. The atoning work of Christ was needed as a prelude to the work of the Holy Spirit. Sin had to be dealt with by Christ's work before holiness could be worked out in the life of the believer by the Holy Spirit. (Of course, the Holy Spirit is also involved in regeneration and many other works in the believer's life—John 3:1-5; Titus 3:5).

John 16:24—*Does this verse mean we can obtain anything we want if we ask for it in the name of Jesus?*

This verse should not be isolated from other verses that qualify Jesus' intended meaning. In John 15:7, for example, Jesus said, "If you remain in me and my words remain in you, ask whatever you wish, and it will be given you." Here, abiding in Christ is a clear condition for receiving answers to prayer. We are also told that we "receive from him anything we ask, because we obey his commands and do what pleases him" (1 John 3:22). Moreover, we read, "This is the confidence we have in approaching God: that if we ask anything according to his will, he hears us. And if we know that he hears us—whatever we ask—we know that we have what we asked of him" (1 John 5:14-15). Finally, we are told that if we ask for something with wrong motives, we won't receive what we asked for (James 4:3).

John 18:1-6—*What caused the Roman soldiers to fall down?*

Scholars have pondered why these strong Roman soldiers drew back and fell to the ground. One scholar lamely suggested that these powerful soldiers fell over each other in confusion at Jesus' calm response to being arrested. Other scholars see a manifestation of the supernatural in this event. Perhaps Christ gave them a flash of His intrinsic divine glory when in the Garden of Gethsemane, which caused them to fall back.

The soldiers' response would have been similar to that of many others who fell down due to an encounter with the divine. For example, the apostle John saw Christ in his glory, and he "fell at his feet as though dead" (Revelation 1:17). When Abraham beheld the Almighty, he "fell facedown" (Genesis 17:3). When Manoah and his wife saw the angel of the Lord, they "fell with their faces to the ground" (Judges 13:20). Ezekiel, upon seeing the glory of God, "fell facedown" (Ezekiel 3:23; 43:3; 44:4). The soldiers would therefore have been in good company if they fell back as a result of briefly glimpsing the glory of Christ.

John 20:17—*Why did the resurrected Jesus tell Mary not to hold on to Him?*

Mary was apparently so excited to see that Jesus had risen from the dead and was present with her that she grasped on to Him, not wanting to let go. But Jesus told her to stop. He indicated to her that He had not yet ascended to the Father and would in fact still be on earth for a time prior to the ascension, so she did not need to cling to Him. She would have plenty of opportunity to see Him before He went to heaven. It was more important at the present moment for Mary to go tell the disciples that He was risen.

John 20:17—*If Jesus is God, why did He refer to the Father as "my God"?*

Prior to the Incarnation, Christ, the second person of the Trinity, had only a divine nature. But in the Incarnation, Christ took on a human nature. It was thus in His humanity that Christ acknowledged the Father as "my God." The proper duties for man include worshipping, praying to, and adoring God. Moreover, as our High

Priest—"made like his brothers in every way" (Hebrews 2:17)—Jesus could rightly address the Father as "my God."

John 20:19—*How could Jesus walk through a closed door with a physical body?*

Jesus' resurrection body was essentially and continuously material. The fact that Jesus could get into a room with closed door in no way proves that He had to dematerialize in order to do it. This is clear for several reasons.

First, the text does not actually say Jesus passed through a closed door. It simply says that "with the doors locked for fear of the Jews, Jesus came and stood among them" (John 20:19). The Bible does not say how He got into the room. The disciples could have unlocked the doors quickly and allowed Jesus to enter.

Second, let us note that if Jesus wanted to, He could have performed this same miracle before His death in His pre-resurrection material body. As the Son of God, His miraculous powers were just as great before the resurrection.

Third, even before His resurrection Jesus performed miracles with His physical body that transcended natural laws, such as walking on water (John 6:16-20). But walking on water did not prove that His pre-resurrection body was immaterial or even that it could dematerialize. Otherwise, Peter's pre-resurrection walk on water (Matthew 14:29) would mean his body dematerialized for a moment and then quickly rematerialized!

Fourth, although physical, the resurrection body is by its very nature a supernatural body (see 1 Corinthians 15:44). We should expect that it can do supernatural things, such as appearing in a room with closed doors.

John 20:22—*Did the disciples receive the Holy Spirit before the Day of Pentecost?*

Following His resurrection from the dead, Jesus appeared to His disciples and breathed on them and said, "Receive the Holy Spirit"

(John 20:21-22). Some scholars have suggested that this was a prophetic utterance that would ultimately be fulfilled 50 days later on the
Day of Pentecost. However, this viewpoint doesn't seem to do justice
to the sense of immediacy that is communicated in Jesus' words. I
believe that in this passage we witness Jesus giving the disciples a
temporary empowerment from the Holy Spirit to carry on their work
of ministry until they would be fully empowered on the Day of Pentecost. Since Christ had called them to a unique work, He gave them
a unique empowerment for that work.

John 20:23—*Do human beings (such as priests) have the authority to
forgive the sins of others?*

This verse is translated literally from the Greek, "Those whose sins
you forgive have already been forgiven; those whose sins you do not
forgive have not been forgiven." The verse does not teach that we have
the power to forgive sins in ourselves, but that we are proclaiming what
heaven has already proclaimed.

There is no dispute that the disciples to whom Christ was speaking
were given the power to pronounce the forgiveness and/or retaining of
sins. But this only means that they were given the authority to declare
what God does in regard to salvation when a person either accepts
or rejects Jesus Christ as Savior. Remember, only God can actually
forgive sin (Mark 2:7; Luke 7:48-49). The disciples—and, by exten-
sion, all believers—only have the prerogative of announcing to others
that if they trust in Christ, their sins will be forgiven; if they reject
Christ as Savior, their sins will not be forgiven. We have the authority
to make that declaration because God Himself has already declared
it in heaven. As His representatives, we declare to others what He has
already declared.

John 20:30; 21:25—*Do these verses indicate that our Bible is insufficient
because it contains an incomplete record?*

In John 20:30 we read, "Jesus did many other miraculous signs
in the presence of his disciples, which are not recorded in this book."

All this verse is saying is that while Jesus' ministry was characterized by miracles from beginning to end, John did not need to record each one in order to establish that Jesus is in fact the promised Messiah. Some thirty-five different miracles are recorded in the four Gospels, but John selected only seven for special consideration so that people might come to believe that Jesus is the Christ, the promised Messiah. Including every single miracle was not necessary. John was satisfied to provide massive evidence for Jesus' identity instead of overwhelming evidence.

In John 21:25 we read, "Jesus did many other things as well. If every one of them were written down, I suppose that even the whole world would not have room for the books that would be written." John's point here is that Jesus' ministry was so wonderful, so miraculous, so beyond the ability of human words to fully capture that the Gospel account he wrote reflects only a portion of the wonder of Jesus. John's sense was that he had but dipped a cup in the ocean of wonder that is Jesus Christ.

Inasmuch as John's gospel was directly inspired by the Holy Spirit, however, we are sure that what is communicated in this Gospel is exactly what God wanted communicated. *Sola scriptura* does not claim that what is in the Bible is exhaustive; it only claims that what is in the Bible is fully sufficient. Everything that God wants us to have in terms of His revelation to man is found within the pages of Scripture. We need nothing further.

Acts

Acts 2:5—*How could "Jews from every nation under heaven" have been in Jerusalem?*

Jewish pilgrims made their way to Jerusalem for the feast of Pentecost. Luke was using hyperbolic language to indicate that Jews had come into town from all over the Mediterranean world, not from virtually every nation on earth. Verses 8-11 makes this clear, indicating that these Jews were from such places as Mesopotamia, Judea, Cappadocia, Pontus, Asia, Phrygia, Pamphylia, Egypt, parts of Libya, and Rome.

Acts 2:38—*Does baptism have to be only in the name of Jesus?*

In this verse Peter urges his hearers to be baptized "in the name of Jesus Christ for the forgiveness of your sins." In properly interpreting this verse, we must first note that the phrase *in the name of* in biblical times often meant, by the authority of. Seen in this light, the phrase in Acts 2:38 cannot be interpreted to be some kind of baptismal formula. The verse simply indicates that people are to be baptized according to the authority of Jesus Christ. The verse does not mean that the words *in the name of Jesus* must be liturgically pronounced over each person being baptized. If Acts 2:38 were intended to be a baptismal formula, why isn't this formula ever repeated in exactly the same way throughout the rest of Acts or the New Testament? (See Matthew 28:19, which speaks of a Trinitarian baptism.)

Actually, a baptism in the name of Jesus makes good sense in the context of Acts 2 because the Jews to whom Peter was preaching had rejected Christ as the Messiah. We would expect Peter to call on them to repent of their rejection of Jesus the Messiah and become publicly identified with Him through baptism. Baptism in the name of Jesus would serve to distinguish this baptism from all the other baptisms that were a part of Judaism at the time.

Acts 2:38—*Is water baptism a requirement for salvation?*

Though this verse instructs people to "repent and be baptized...for the forgiveness of your sins," properly understood it does not teach that baptism is a requirement for salvation. First, the great majority of passages dealing with salvation in the New Testament affirm that salvation is by faith alone (for example, John 3:16-17; 5:24; 7:38; 20:29). In Acts 2:38, a single word puts everything into proper perspective. The verse reads, "Peter replied, 'Repent and be baptized, every one of you, in the name of Jesus Christ *for* the forgiveness of your sins. And you will receive the gift of the Holy Spirit.'"

Students of the Greek language have often pointed out that the Greek word translated *for* (*eis*) is a preposition that can indicate causality ("in order to attain") or a result ("because of"). This is an example of using *for* in a resultant sense: "I'm taking an aspirin for my headache." Obviously this means I am taking an aspirin as a result of my headache. I am not taking an aspirin in order to attain a headache. And this is an example of using *for* in a causal sense: "I'm going to the office for my paycheck." Obviously this means I am going to the office in order to attain my paycheck.

In Acts 2:38 the word *for* is used in a resultant sense. The verse might be paraphrased, "Repent, and be baptized every one of you in the name of Jesus Christ because of (or as a result of) the remission of sins." The verse is not saying, "Repent and be baptized every one of you in the name of Jesus Christ in order to attain the remission of sins."

Acts 2:41—*Is water baptism to be by immersion or sprinkling?*

Christians are divided on this issue. Those who argue for sprinkling point out that a secondary meaning of the Greek word *baptizo* is "to bring under the influence of." This fits sprinkling better than immersion. Moreover, they say, baptism by sprinkling better pictures the coming of the Holy Spirit upon a person.

These interpreters also suggest that immersion would have been impossible in some of the baptisms portrayed in Scripture. In Acts 2:41, for example, it would have been impossible to immerse all 3000 people who were baptized. The same is said to be true in regard to Acts 8:38; 10:47; and 16:33.

Those who hold to the immersion view, as I do, respond by pointing out that the Greek word *baptizo* primarily means, to immerse. And the prepositions normally used in conjunction with *baptizo* (such as *into* and *out of* the water) clearly picture immersion and not sprinkling. The Greek language has perfectly acceptable words for *sprinkling* and *pouring,* but these words are never used in the context of baptism in the New Testament.

History reveals that the ancient Jews practiced baptism by immersion. The Jewish converts to Christianity—including the disciples, who came out of Judaism—would have been likely to follow this precedent.

Certainly baptism by immersion best pictures the significance of death to the old life and resurrection to the new life in Christ (Romans 6:1-4). And despite what sprinkling advocates say, in every instance of water baptism recorded in the New Testament, immersion was practiced. Arguments that there was not enough water to accomplish immersion are weak and unconvincing. Archaeologists have uncovered ancient pools throughout the Jerusalem area.

Acts 2:44-45—*Did the early Christians practice communism?*

The early Christians "had everything in common. Selling their possessions and goods, they gave to anyone as he had need." We have several reasons to believe this passage does not teach an abiding form of Christian communism or socialism. First, these verses are not prescriptive but are simply descriptive. Nowhere do they lay this down as normative. They simply describe what the believers were doing.

Second, the text seems to indicate that the system was only

temporary, not a permanent arrangement. They apparently stayed together in Jerusalem because that is where the Holy Spirit had descended and the first great turning to Christ had occurred. The necessities of living together away from home occasioned this sort of common arrangement.

Third, the communal arrangement was voluntary. Nothing in the text indicates that this was a compulsory arrangement. It was apparently a temporary and voluntary convenience for the furtherance of the gospel in those early and crucial days of the Christian church.

Fourth, the selling of property and giving of money was only partial. The text implies that they sold only extra land and other possessions, not that they sold their only place of residence. After all, they all eventually left Jerusalem, to which they had come for the feast of Pentecost (Acts 2:1), and went back to their homes, which were scattered all over the world (see Acts 2:5-13).

Acts 8:26—*Does God use angels in the work of evangelism?*

Apparently so, at least occasionally. After all, an angel guided the evangelist Philip to an Ethiopian treasurer to make clear the Word of God (Acts 8:26). An angel also guided the unsaved Cornelius to the apostle Peter (Acts 10:1-8).

Acts 17:16-34—*Does Paul's quote from a pagan poet mean that the poet's work belongs in the Bible?*

No. The poet's work was not divinely inspired like Paul's writings were. The fact that Paul quoted from this poet means that the poet said something that was worthy of inclusion by Paul in order for Paul to make a point to the people to whom he was writing. The quote does not mean everything in the poem is true or theologically correct.

Acts 19:12—*Can supernatural power be transmitted by handkerchiefs?*

Not normatively. Foundationally, only the apostles were given the special "signs of an apostle" (2 Corinthians 12:12). They were the unique representatives of God, and once the apostles passed off the scene, their unique sign gifts passed with them (Hebrews 2:3-4). These special signs served to confirm God's special revelation through them—revelation that was later included in the New Testament.

Acts 19:12 is thus descriptive, not prescriptive. In other words, this passage describes a unique one-of-a-kind event that took place in relation to an apostle of God. It does not prescribe something that would be repeated throughout church history. Christians should not read more into this verse than is warranted.

Acts 20:20—*Is house-to-house witnessing required of all Christians?*

In this verse we read that the apostle Paul "taught...publicly and from house to house." The word *house* in this verse refers to house-churches. The first Christians had no centralized church building where they could congregate. Rather, many small house-churches were scattered throughout the city. For example, the early Christians "broke bread in their homes" (Acts 2:46; see also 5:42) and gathered to pray in the house of Mary, the mother of Mark (Acts 12:12). Churches often met in houses (Romans 16:5; 1 Corinthians 16:19; Philippians 2; Colossians 4:15). The use of church buildings did not appear before the end of the second century.

In light of this, the apostle Paul's ministry was apparently from house-church to house-church. This interpretation seems especially likely in view of the fact that when Paul said he "taught...publicly and from house to house" (Acts 20:20), he was speaking not to people in general but to elders of the church (see verse 17).

Acts 20:28—*Does God have blood?*

God is said to have purchased the church with His own blood (Acts 20:28). Of course, God does not have blood. But Jesus—who, in the Incarnation, was both God and man—had blood, and He shed His blood at the cross. As God, Jesus had all the attributes of deity (John 1:1; 8:58; 10:30; 20:29; Colossians 2:9; Titus 2:13). As a man,

He had all the attributes of humanity (Luke 4:2; 8:23; John 1:48; 2:24; 4:6). Yet, though Christ had two natures—one human and one divine—Christ was always one person. Christ as the God-man shed His blood on the cross.

Romans

Romans 1:7—*What is a saint?*

From a biblical perspective, a saint is not a person who has been specifically canonized by a church or denomination. Rather, all Christians are saints in the sense of being set apart to God.

Romans 1:19-20—*Are those who have never heard the gospel forever lost?*

Paul affirms that the heathen are without excuse (Romans 1:20). The heathen are thus justly condemned for several reasons.

First, Romans 2:12 states, "All who sin apart from the law will also perish apart from the law, and all who sin under the law will be judged by the law." This passage teaches that the Jews are judged by the law (the Hebrew Scriptures), but the Gentiles are condemned by the law written in their hearts. "Indeed, when Gentiles, who do not have the law, do by nature things required by the law, they are a law for themselves, even though they do not have the law, since they show that the requirements of the law are written on their hearts, their consciences also bearing witness, and their thoughts now accusing, now even defending them" (Romans 2:14-15).

Second, the question assumes innocence on the part of the unsaved man who hasn't heard the gospel. But the Bible tells us that "all have sinned and fall short of the glory of God" (Romans 3:23).

Third, if a person who has not heard the gospel lives his life to the best of his ability, he simply is doing works for salvation. But salvation is by grace: "For it is by grace you have been saved, through faith—and this not from yourselves, it is the gift of God" (Ephesians 2:8). No one can do anything to help himself gain access into heaven. If there were such a way, the work of Christ on the cross would have been a futile act.

Finally, the Bible teaches, "Seek and you will find." That is, those who positively respond to the light they have through nature, which is not sufficient for salvation, will receive the additional light they need for salvation. This is illustrated in Cornelius, for he had responded to the little light he had but did not have sufficient revelation (greater light) to believe in Jesus, which is why God sent Peter to him (Acts 10). God has many ways to get the truth about salvation through Christ to those who seek Him. He can send a missionary (Acts 10) or a Bible (Psalm 119:130), give them a vision (Daniel 2; 7), or send an angel (Revelation 14). But those who turn their back on the light they have (through nature) and find themselves lost in darkness have no one to blame but themselves (John 3:19).

Romans 2:6-7—*Did Paul teach that heaven can be merited by good works?*

Paul affirmed that God "will give to each person according to what he has done." Taken in its proper context, this passage does not teach that works are a condition for salvation. In this very book of Romans, Paul emphatically stated that salvation is entirely apart from works (Romans 3:28; 4:5). Paul's words in Romans 2:6-7 cannot be understood in a way that makes them contradict these other clear statements.

In Paul's theology, works are the result of salvation, not the condition of salvation. Ephesians 2:10 makes it clear that we are saved to do good works. We are saved *by* grace but *for* works. We do not work for grace but from grace (2 Corinthians 5:14; Titus 2:11–12). Good works do not bring salvation, they simply attest to the salvation that has already been received by faith (Romans 6:23; 10:9-10; 11:6). These works are portrayed as an evidence that one has saving faith.

So, in the context of Paul's writings, Romans 2:6-8 seems to emphasize that the way a person habitually acts or conducts himself in daily life indicates the state of his heart. A person who habitually engages in good works thereby shows that his heart has been regenerated by God (verse 7). A person who habitually engages in bad deeds shows his alienation from God (verse 8).

Romans 5:18-19—*Does Paul teach universalism when he affirms that "many will be made righteous"?*

No. Even in this context Paul speaks of being justified by faith (Romans 5:1), not justified automatically by what Christ did for us. He also refers to salvation as a gift (5:16), which is something that has to be received. He also declares that salvation comes only to those "who receive…the gift of righteousness" (5:17).

The rest of the book of Romans makes it unmistakably clear that not everyone will be saved. Romans 1–2 speaks of the heathen, who are without excuse (Romans 1:19) and upon whom the wrath of God falls (1:18). It declares that "all who sin apart from the law will also perish apart from the law, and all who sin under the law will be judged by the law" (Romans 2:12).

In the very heart of his argument, Paul concludes that apart from justification by faith, the world is guilty before God (Romans 3:19). Later, speaking of the destiny of both saved and lost, Paul affirms that "the wages of sin is death, but the gift of God is eternal life in Christ Jesus our Lord" (Romans 6:23). Likewise, Paul recognized that despite his prayers, not all of his kinsmen would be saved (Romans 11:1-5) but some would be accursed (Romans 9:3). Indeed, the whole point of Romans is to show that only those who believe will be justified (Romans 1:17; see also 3:21-26).

Romans 8:14—*What does it mean to say believers become sons of God?*

One of the greatest blessings of salvation is that believers are adopted into God's forever family. Becoming a son of God makes one a member of God's family. And God adopts into His family any who believe in His Son, Jesus Christ. This is noticeably different from human adoptions, for human adults generally seek to adopt only the healthiest and best-behaved children. But all are welcome in God's family.

Being adopted into God's family is a relationship of privilege and responsibility. As sons of God, we are called to live in a manner that reflects our new family relationship. We are called to reflect the family likeness (Matthew 5:48).

Contrary to the enslavement to sin that leads to fear, the believer has received the Spirit of sonship (Romans 8:15). The word *sonship* literally means, placing as a son. This is significant, for in New Testament times an adopted son enjoyed all the rights and privileges of a natural-born son. We need not be fearful about approaching God but can boldly approach His throne and say, "Abba, Father" (Romans 8:15). *Abba* is an Aramaic term of affection and intimacy—similar to the English word *Daddy*.

Because of this new relationship with God, believers are called heirs of God and coheirs with Christ (Romans 8:17). In a typical family, each child in the family receives a share in his parent's estate. This makes each child an heir, and the children as a group are coheirs. As God's children we are heirs, and collectively we are coheirs with Christ (Galatians 4:7).

Romans 8:16-17—*What do believers inherit?*

Believers inherit all spiritual blessings in this life (Ephesians 1:3). In the life to come they will share with the Lord Jesus in all the riches of God's glorious kingdom (1 Corinthians 3:21-23).

Romans 8:20-22—*In what way was the creation subjected to frustration?*

Christians have different views on this, but the great majority believe this bondage began at the fall of man. As a result of man's sin against God, man's entire domain was judged by God (Romans 8:21-22). Other Christians believe the universe began winding down as soon as He created it—that is, the stars began burning off their mass as soon as they were created.

The good news is that this bondage will end when God renews the universe. Before the eternal kingdom can be made manifest, God must deal with this cursed earth. Indeed, the earth—along with the first and second heavens (the earth's atmosphere and the stellar universe)—must be renewed. The old must make room for the new (see Revelation 21:1-5).

Romans 8:28—*How can God work all things for good?*

God is all-powerful, sovereign, and very creative. We see many illustrations of God working all things for good in Scripture. For example, Joseph was sold into slavery by his own brothers (Genesis 38–39), a circumstance God used to eventually elevate Joseph to great authority in Egypt (Genesis 41). The apostle Paul was thrown into prison repeatedly during his work of ministry (Acts 16:23-37; Ephesians 3:1; Philippians 1:7; Colossians 4:10; Philemon 9), during which time Paul wrote Ephesians, Philippians, Colossians, and Philemon. God is a master at working all things for good.

Romans 9:13—*In what way did God hate Esau?*

Contextually, the word *hate* should not be taken to mean that God had the human emotional sense of disgust, disdain, and a desire for revenge against Esau. God did not have a negative psychological emotion that burned against Esau. Rather the word should be understood as the Hebrew idiom it is—a word that means, to love less (compare with Genesis 29:30-33).

We gain insights into this meaning of the word in Luke 14:26, where Jesus said, "If anyone comes to me and does not hate his father and mother, his wife and children, his brothers and sisters—yes, even his own life—he cannot be my disciple." This word does not communicate the emotional feeling of hate. Keep in mind that Jesus does not leave us the prerogative of actually hating anyone. We are to love even our enemies (Luke 6:27). As well, the fifth commandment instructs us, "Honor your father and your mother" (Exodus 20:12), a commandment repeated in the New Testament (Ephesians 6:1-3; Colossians

3:20). Jesus certainly was not instructing His followers to disobey God's holy law. Rather, the word *hate* clearly means, to love less. In other words, we are to love our parents less than we love Jesus.

With this same meaning in view in Romans 9:13, we might paraphrase the verse this way: "In comparison to my great love for Jacob, my feeling for Esau, whom I love less, may seem like hatred." Contextually, it is clear that God's sovereign purposes for His people related to Jacob and his descendants alone.

Romans 12:3-8—*What are the gifts of the Holy Spirit?*

See comments on 1 Corinthians 12:8-10.

Romans 14:10—*Will Christians one day stand before the judgment seat of Christ?*

Yes. The idea of a judgment seat relates to the athletic games of Paul's day. After the races and games concluded, the emperor himself often took his seat on an elevated throne, and one by one, the winning athletes came up to the throne to receive a reward. This reward was usually a wreath of leaves, a "victor's crown." In the case of Christians, each of us will stand before Christ the Judge and receive (or lose) rewards.

This judgment has nothing to do with whether or not the Christian will remain saved. Those who have placed faith in Christ are saved, and nothing threatens that. Believers are eternally secure in their salvation (Ephesians 4:30). This judgment rather has to do with the reception or loss of rewards (1 Corinthians 9:25; James 1:12; 1 Peter 5:4; Revelation 2:10).

1 Corinthians

1 Corinthians 3:11-15—*What do the building materials of gold, silver, costly stones, wood, hay, and straw refer to in regard to the future judgment of Christians?*

The materials Paul mentions are combustible in increasing degrees. Obviously the hay and straw are the most combustible. Then comes wood. Precious metals and stones are not combustible.

Some of these materials are useful for building, and others are not. If you construct a house made of hay or straw, it surely will not stand long. And it can burn to the ground very easily. But a house constructed with solid materials such as stones and metals will stand and last a long time.

What do these building materials represent? Perhaps the gold, silver, and costly stones represent Christ-honoring motives, godly obedience, and integrity. Wood, hay, and straw, by contrast, are perishable things—perhaps referring to carnal attitudes, sinful motives, pride-filled actions, and selfish ambition.

God will examine our works, and they will be tested against the fire of His holiness. If our works are built with good materials—like precious metals and stones—our works will stand. But if our works are built with less valuable materials—wood, hay, or straw—they will burn up. Perhaps the passage is intended to communicate that those works performed with a view to glorifying God are the works that will stand. Those works performed with a view to glorifying self, performed in the flesh, are those that will be burned up.

1 Corinthians 5:5—*What does it mean to hand a man over to Satan?*

Many Bible expositors believe this refers to putting the person out of the church and into the world, where Satan rules (John 14:30). The purpose is to destroy his sinful nature, ultimately leading to godly sorrow, which will move the person to repent and then be restored to the church. Other Bible expositors take this verse to mean that the person is handed over to Satan so that Satan can inflict physical suffering upon him. Still others take the verse to mean that the person is handed over to Satan so Satan can kill him—that is, kill the body, while the spirit is yet saved.

1 Corinthians 5:9—*If Paul wrote an inspired epistle, how could God allow it to be lost?*

There are a number of possibilities regarding Paul's lost epistle. Some believe that not all apostolic letters were intended to be in the canon of Scripture. Luke refers to many other Gospels (Luke 1:1). John says that Jesus did much more than John recorded (John 20:30; 21:25). Perhaps this lost letter to the Corinthians was not intended by God to be collected in the canon and preserved for the faith and practice of future generations, as were the 27 books of the New Testament (and 39 of the Old Testament).

Others believe that the letter referred to in 1 Corinthians 5:9 may not be lost at all, but is part of an existing book in the Bible. For example, it could be part of what we know as 2 Corinthians (chapters 10–13), which some believe was later put together with chapters 1–9. In support of this is the fact that chapters 1–9 have a decidedly different tone from chapters 10–13. This may indicate that it was written on a different occasion. They also note that Paul refers in 2 Corinthians 10:10 to "letters" (plural) he had written.

Still others believe Paul is referring to the present book of 1 Corinthians in 1 Corinthians 5:9—that is, to the very book which he was writing at the time. In support of this, they suggest that even though the Greek aorist tense used here ("I wrote") may refer to a past letter, it could also refer to the book at hand. This would be an illustration of what is called an "epistolary aorist" because it refers to the very book in which it is being used. Moreover, the aorist tense often implies a decisive action, in which case Paul would be saying something like this: "I am now decisively writing to you…" This certainly fits the context of this passage in which he is urging the church to take immediate action to excommunicate a wayward member. Still further, there is absolutely no indication in early church history that any such letter of Paul, other than the existing 1 and 2 Corinthians, ever existed.

1 Corinthians 7:12—*How can this verse be reconciled with the inspiration and inerrancy of Paul's writings as an apostle of God?*

In 1 Corinthians 7:12 Paul said, "To the rest I say this (I, not the Lord)…" Paul is simply saying that Jesus did not say anything about this matter during His three-year ministry on earth, and thus nothing is recorded in the Gospels about the matter. As an apostle of God, Paul's words are divinely sourced and thus divinely authoritative (they are not merely human—1 Corinthians 2:4,13), so 1 Corinthians 7:12 is a part of the Word of God.

1 Corinthians 8:5—*Does this verse indicate that there are many gods?*

In this verse we read of so-called gods, many gods, and many lords. This verse is referring to *false* gods—pagan entities of Greek and Roman mythology who are called gods and lords. There is a world of difference between being called a god and actually being God. The very next verse tells us, "There is but one God."

1 Corinthians 8:6—*Since the Father is called the "one God," are we to conclude that Jesus is not God?*

Though the Father is called "one God" and Jesus Christ is called "one Lord" in this passage, we should not conclude that Jesus is not God, just as we should not conclude that the Father is not Lord. The use of a title for one person of the Trinity in one context does not automatically rule out its application to another person in another context. As we consult all that Scripture has to say about the Father and Jesus, we learn that the Father is called God (1 Peter 1:2) and

Lord (Matthew 11:25), just as we learn that Jesus Christ is called God (John 20:28; Hebrews 1:8) and Lord (Romans 10:9).

1 Corinthians 10:8—*Did Paul err in stating how many people died?*

Paul affirms that 23,000 died in the incident of the golden calf, while Exodus 32:28 places the figure at 3000. There is no contradiction when properly understood. Exodus 32 records only those killed by the sword. First Corinthians 10 refers to those killed by the sword as well as a plague.

1 Corinthians 11:2—*Are we to hold firmly to traditions in addition to following the Bible?*

Tradition here refers to information Paul personally handed down to the Corinthian believers. As an apostle, Paul communicated God's truth to the Corinthians in person, face-to-face. As yet there were no written Gospels for Paul to appeal to, so such face-to-face transmission of information was necessary up until that information could be permanently recorded in written form (see 2 Timothy 3:15-17). Paul most certainly was not giving justification for a continuing line of oral information passed down from apostles to bishops on up to modern times. He is referring only to the apostolic teachings he had personally delivered to the Corinthians.

1 Corinthians 11:3—*Do the words "the head of Christ is God" mean that Christ is not God?*

This verse has nothing to do with inferiority or superiority of one person of the Trinity over another; rather, it has to do with patterns of authority. Notice that Paul says the man is the head of the woman, even though men and women are utterly equal in their essential being. They are both human, and both are created in God's image (Genesis 1:26-28). They are said to be one in Christ (Galatians 3:28). This indicates that equality of being and social hierarchy are not mutually exclusive. Men and women are completely equal in nature; nevertheless, a functional hierarchy exists between them.

In the same way, Christ and the Father are utterly equal in their divine being (Jesus said "I and the Father are one"—John 10:30) even though Jesus is functionally under the Father's headship (1 Corinthians 11:3). There is no contradiction in affirming both an equality of being and a functional subordination among the persons in the Godhead.

1 Corinthians 12:11—*What are spiritual gifts?*

Spiritual gifts are special abilities bestowed sovereignly by the Holy Spirit upon individual believers for the purpose of edifying the church (the body of Christ). These gifts include teaching, pastoring, evangelizing, the message of wisdom, the message of knowledge, faith, healing, miraculous powers, prophecy, distinguishing between spirits, speaking in different tongues, and the interpretation of tongues (1 Corinthians 12:8-10; see also Romans 12:3-8 and Ephesians 4:7-13).

There is a difference between natural talents and spiritual gifts. Natural talents are from God but are transmitted through parents; spiritual gifts come directly from God the Holy Spirit (Romans 12:3,6; 1 Corinthians 12:4). Natural talents are possessed from the moment of birth; spiritual gifts are received when one becomes a Christian. Natural talents are generally used to benefit human beings on the natural level; spiritual gifts bring spiritual blessing to people and edify believers (1 Corinthians 12:11; Ephesians 4:11-13).

Some Christians (*cessationists*) believe that certain gifts, such as the gift of speaking in tongues and the gift of healing, passed away in the first century. Other Christians (*charismatics*) disagree and believe that all the spiritual gifts are for today.

1 Corinthians 12:28—*Are there apostles and prophets today?*

It is true that God gave the church apostles and prophets, but these gifts were strictly foundational gifts, no longer existent today in the strict biblical sense. We must remember the important principle that Scripture interprets Scripture. When we turn to other passages of Scripture, we see that the church was built on the foundation of the apostles and prophets (Ephesians 2:20). Once a foundation is built, it never needs to be built again. Once the foundation is laid, the foundation is built upon. In like fashion, the building of the church structurally rests on the foundation of the apostles and prophets, but we don't need to build any new foundations.

The New Testament apostles were utterly unique. They were the special objects of God's self-revelation, and they recognized that God was providing revelation through them (1 Corinthians 2:13; 1 Thessalonians 2:13; 1 John 1:1-3). They recognized their divine authority (Acts 20:35; 1 Corinthians 7:10; 11:23). They were handpicked by the Lord or the Holy Spirit (Matthew 10:1-2; Acts 1:26). A key requirement of an apostle is that he had to be an eyewitness of the resurrected Christ (1 Corinthians 9:1; 15:7-8). These apostles were all authenticated by miraculous signs (2 Corinthians 12:12; see also Acts 9:36-42; 20:6-12). They were granted an eternal place of honor, with their names inscribed on the foundations of the New Jerusalem (Revelation 21:14).

1 Corinthians 14:5—*Is the gift of tongues one I should be seeking?*

Personally, I don't think so. Here are the scriptural facts:

- The Holy Spirit is the one who bestows spiritual gifts on believers (1 Corinthians 12:11). Not every Christian has every gift.

- Speaking in tongues is not an evidence of the baptism of the Holy Spirit. Not all the Corinthians spoke in tongues (1 Corinthians 14:5), but they had all been baptized (12:13).

- The fruit of the Holy Spirit (Galatians 5:22-23) does not include speaking in tongues. Therefore, Christlikeness does not require speaking in tongues.

- Most of the New Testament writers are silent on tongues. Only three books (Mark , Acts, and 1 Corinthians) mention it. (Note: Mark 16:17 is not in the two best Greek manuscripts.) Significantly, many of the other New Testament books speak a great deal about the Holy Spirit, but fail to mention speaking in tongues a single time.

- Other gifts are more important than tongues, and these are to be sought (1 Corinthians 12:28,31).

1 Corinthians 15:29—*What is the baptism for the dead?*

Scholars differ as to what Paul means in this passage. Some believe Paul is referring to a cultic practice among the Corinthians, who had many other false beliefs (see 1 Corinthians 5; 12). In effect, Paul would be saying, "If you don't believe in the resurrection, why engage in the practice of baptizing people for the dead? You are inconsistent with your own (false) beliefs."

Others suggest that Paul is simply referring to the fact that baptism of new converts is replenishing the depleted ranks of believers who have died and gone on to be with the Lord. If so, then his sense here would be, "Why do you continue to fill the church with baptized converts, who replace those who have died, if you do not really believe there is any hope for them beyond the grave?"

Still others suggest that Paul is referring to the fact that baptism symbolizes the believer's death with Christ (Romans 6:3-5). The Greek word translated *for* (*eis*) can mean *with a view to*. In this sense, he would be saying, "Why are you baptized with a view to your death and resurrection with Christ, if you do not believe in the resurrection?"

Whichever interpretation is correct, Paul certainly did not urge his hearers to practice the idea, nor did he command it. He merely used the case as an illustration. Also, no other verses in the Bible mention baptism for the dead. Christ does not mention it, nor do any of the other apostles.

1 Corinthians 15:44-50—*Was Jesus resurrected spiritually?*

Paul here affirms that Jesus' resurrection body was a spiritual body.

The primary meaning of *spiritual body,* however, is not an immaterial body but a supernatural, spirit-dominated body. The physically resurrected body is a supernatural body that is dominated by the spirit instead of being under the dominion of the flesh.

It is important to recognize that the apostle Paul often uses the word *spiritual* in 1 Corinthians to refer to something supernatural. Some scholars believe the Greek word translated *spiritual* in 1 Corinthians 15 should actually be translated *supernatural* in this context. After all, this same exact Greek word is translated *supernatural* in 1 Corinthians 10:3-4 (RSV), which refers to the supernatural food, drink, and rock that God provided for the Israelites in the wilderness. Especially in view of the contrasts in verses 40-50 (earthly/heavenly, perishable/imperishable, weak/powerful, mortal/immortal), the translation *supernatural* (as a contrast to *natural*) would fit the context much better than the word *spiritual.*

1 Corinthians 15:50—*If flesh and blood cannot inherit heaven, how can we say that Jesus ascended into heaven in a physically resurrected body?*

The phrase *flesh and blood* is an idiom that refers to mortal humanity. Mortal humanity must be made immortal in order to survive in heaven. The resurrection body will be endowed with special qualities that will make it perfectly adapted to life in God's presence.

2 Corinthians

2 Corinthians 2:10—*What does Paul mean when he says, "If you forgive anyone, I also forgive him"?*

This verse deals with an incident of church discipline in Corinth. The person of whom Paul was speaking had committed a serious offense, and as a result, severe church discipline was imposed upon him. Paul now urged the Corinthian believers to lovingly restore this person to fellowship in view of the remorse the person had shown. The person had repented, so forgiveness was in order. After all, the purpose of church discipline is to restore one to fellowship, not to permanently injure him.

2 Corinthians 3:17—*Does this verse prove Jesus is the Holy Spirit?*

This verse affirms that "the Lord is the Spirit." Most expositors view this verse as saying that the Holy Spirit is Lord, not in the sense of being Jesus, but in the sense of being Yahweh (the Lord God). We know the verse is not saying Jesus is the Holy Spirit, for just earlier the apostle Paul clearly distinguishes between Jesus and the Holy Spirit (see verses 3-6). More broadly, the whole of Scripture indicates that Jesus is not the Holy Spirit, for the Holy Spirit is said to be another comforter (John 14:16). Jesus sent the Holy Spirit (John 15:26; 16:7). The Holy Spirit *seeks to glorify* Jesus (John 16:13-14) and testifies of Jesus (see John 14–16).

2 Corinthians 5:5—*In what way is the Holy Spirit a deposit of what is to come?*

The word *deposit* was used among the Greeks to refer to a pledge that guaranteed final possession of an item. It was sometimes used of an engagement ring, which acted as a guarantee that a marriage would take place. The Holy Spirit is a deposit in the sense that His presence in our lives guarantees our eventual total transformation and glorification into the likeness of Christ's glorified resurrection body (see Philippians 3:21). The Holy Spirit in us is virtually a guarantee of what is to come.

2 Corinthians 5:19—*Does Paul here indicate that all will be saved?*

This verse affirms that "God was reconciling the world to himself in Christ, not counting men's sins against them." Contextually, there is no support for universalism in this verse. Even though God desires to save all (2 Peter 3:9), not everyone will be saved (Matthew 7:13-14; Revelation 20:11-15). Actual reconciliation is only for those who are in Christ, not for all persons (see 2 Corinthians 5:17). If all were saved (as universalism teaches), then Paul's exhortation to be ambassadors for Christ and to plead with the world to be reconciled to God would be meaningless. To interpret this passage in favor of universalism is to say that Scripture contradicts itself, because many other passages clearly teach the contrary (for example, Matthew 25:31-46).

2 Corinthians 5:21—*How could Jesus be made sin when He Himself was sinless?*

Jesus was always without sin actually, but He was made to be sin for us judicially. That is, by His death on the cross, He paid the penalty for our sins and thereby canceled the debt of sin against us. Though Jesus never committed a sin personally, He was made to be sin for us substitutionally.

2 Corinthians 6:14—*Do the words "Do not be yoked together with unbelievers" mean we can't engage in relationships with any unbelievers?*

This verse does not prohibit the inevitable interactions with unbelievers that are a part of everyday life (see 1 Corinthians 5:9-10). In context, the apostle Paul was calling the Corinthians to separate from false apostles. After all, such false apostles would do nothing but lead the Corinthian believers astray (2 Corinthians 11:3). One's best option is to always be yoked with Christ (Matthew 11:29-30).

2 Corinthians 8:9—*Does this verse indicate that financial prosperity is provided for in the atonement?*

Paul affirms that Jesus "became poor, so that you through his poverty might become rich." If Paul in this verse was intending to say that financial prosperity is provided for in the atonement, he was offering the Corinthians something that he himself did not possess at the time. In 1 Corinthians 4:11 he informed these same individuals that he was hungry and thirsty, poorly clothed, and homeless.

In 2 Corinthians 8:9 Paul was speaking about spiritual prosperity. This fits both the immediate context in 2 Corinthians and the broader context of Paul's other writings. For example, if financial prosperity was provided for in the atonement, one must wonder why Paul informed the Philippian Christians that he had learned to be content even when going hungry (Philippians 4:11-12). One would think he would have instead claimed the prosperity promised in the atonement to meet his every need.

2 Corinthians 12:2—*Are there three heavens?*

The Bible refers to three different heavens. The first heaven is the earth's atmosphere (Job 35:5). The second heaven is the interstellar universe (Genesis 1:17; Deuteronomy 17:3). The third heaven is the ineffable and glorious dwelling place of God in all His glory (2 Corinthians 12:2). It is elsewhere called the heaven of heavens and the highest heaven (1 Kings 8:27; 2 Chronicles 2:6).

2 Corinthians 12:7—*What was the apostle Paul's thorn in the flesh?*

The word translated *flesh* is the normal word in the Greek language used to denote the physical substance of which the body is composed.

Whatever Paul suffered from, it was apparently physical in nature. And it hurt.

The word for *thorn* carries the idea of a sharpened wooden shaft, a stake, or a splinter. This gives us at least some indication of the pain Paul was forced to endure—a pain that God would not take away. This was no little prick. Paul had to endure a very serious and grievous suffering. It extended over a period of time, for he said he prayed to the Lord three times that this thorn might be taken away.

Many scholars believe Paul may have suffered from a severe eye disease that lasted a considerable time. We all know how uncomfortable a little dust in the eye can be, but perhaps the idea of a thorn in the eye better captures the kind of pain Paul suffered. Such an eye affliction may be the reason why Paul did not travel alone throughout Asia Minor (see Acts 15:40; 16:1-3). He apparently needed a guide.

Our text tells us that a messenger of Satan was behind this thorn that tormented Paul (2 Corinthians 12:7). The Greek word for *torment* literally means, to strike, to beat, to harass, or to trouble. This is the same word used for the soldiers violently striking and beating Jesus during His trial (Matthew 26:67). Paul's physical ailment was beating him down. Despite this, God's response to Paul's request for the thorn's removal was no. This refusal on God's part was not in any way related to a sin or to any lack of faith on Paul's part. In fact, the affliction was not for punishment but for protection—that is, protection from a self-inflated attitude. Because of this, Paul accepted without hesitation God's verdict on the matter.

Galatians

Galatians 1:8—*What false gospel is the apostle Paul referring to?*

This false gospel was a gospel of legalism that added works to faith. This was not the same gospel Paul had preached and by which the Galatians had been saved. False teachers had apparently been at work throwing the Galatians into confusion on this matter (see Acts 15:24; 20:29-30). These were apparently Jewish false teachers who sought to Judaize these Gentile believers, demanding that they must take an additional step and become Jews through circumcision. This effectively added law to the grace Paul had been preaching.

Galatians 5:16—*What does it mean to live by the Spirit?*

Since the time of Adam and Eve's fall into sin, all human beings have been born into the world with a sin nature. This sin nature is expressed through numerous kinds of sin—covetousness, jealousy, dissension, bickering, and much more. In our own strength, we do not have the power to resist the sinful inclinations of our sin nature. But we can have victory over the sin nature by depending on the Holy Spirit. The word *live* in Galatians 5:16 is a present tense verb, indicating continuing action. We are to persistently and continually walk in dependence on the Spirit. As we do this, we will live in a way that is pleasing to God.

Galatians 5:22-23—*What is the fruit of the Holy Spirit?*

As we walk in dependence upon the Spirit, we enjoy not only victory over sin but also find the fruit of the Spirit growing in our lives. Many theologians have noted that as we look at the qualities listed in

Galatians 5:22-23, we find an accurate profile of Jesus Christ Himself. The character of our Lord is reproduced in our lives as we depend on the Spirit. As we walk in the Spirit, we progressively take on the family likeness (as members of God's forever family).

Ephesians

Ephesians 1:10—*Does Paul teach universalism when he says God will "bring all things in heaven and on earth together under one head, even Christ"?*

No. This verse simply indicates that in the age to come, Christ will be supreme over all things. The issue of the salvation of unbelievers is nowhere in sight. In fact, earlier in this chapter, Paul speaks of those who were chosen "in him before the creation of the world" (verse 4). In keeping with this, the phrase "in Christ" (which occurs throughout Ephesians) is never used by Paul (or anywhere in Scripture) of anyone but believers. Paul emphasizes elsewhere in Scripture that some will go to their eternal destiny without Christ (for example, 2 Thessalonians 1:7-9). Ephesians 1:10 lends no support to universalism.

Ephesians 4:7-13—*What are the gifts of the Holy Spirit?*

See comments on 1 Corinthians 12:8-10.

Ephesians 4:9—*Did Jesus descend into hell ("the lower, earthly regions")?*

There are two views as to where Jesus went the three days His body was in the grave before His resurrection:

The Hades view. One view is that Christ's spirit went to the spirit world while His body was in the grave. Here, some believe, He spoke to the "spirits in prison" (1 Peter 3:19) who were in a temporary holding place until He would come and "lead captivity captive" (Ephesians 4:8 KJV), that is, take them to heaven. According to this view, there were two compartments in Hades (or Sheol)—one for the saved and another for the unsaved. They were separated by a great gulf (Luke 16:26), which no man could pass. The section for the saved was called Abraham's bosom (Luke 16:23). When Christ ascended as the firstfruits of the resurrection (1 Corinthians 15:20), He led these Old Testament saints into heaven with Him for the first time.

The heaven view. This view affirms that Christ's spirit went directly to heaven. In support of this view are the following facts:

- Jesus affirmed that His spirit was going directly to heaven, declaring, "Father, into Your hands I commend My spirit" (Luke 23:46).

- Jesus promised the thief on the cross, "Today, you will be with me in Paradise" (Luke 23:43). Paradise is defined as the third heaven in 2 Corinthians 12:2-4.

- When Old Testament saints departed this life, they went directly to heaven. God took Enoch to be with Himself (Genesis 5:24; see also Hebrews 11:5), and Elijah was caught up into heaven when he departed (2 Kings 2:1). Jesus followed this Old Testament pattern.

- "Abraham's bosom" (Luke 16:23) is a description of heaven. At no time is it ever described as hell. It is the place to which Abraham went, which is the kingdom of God (Matthew 8:11).

- When Old Testament saints appear prior to the crucifixion, they appear from heaven, as Moses and Elijah did on the Mount of Transfiguration (Matthew 17:3).

- Descending into "lower, earthly regions" is not a reference to hell, but to the grave. Hell itself is not in the lower parts of the earth—it is under the earth (Philippians 2:10).

So no evidence suggests that Jesus went in His spirit to hell during the three days His body was in the grave.

Ephesians 4:11—*Does this verse indicate that there are apostles today?*

No. See comments on 1 Corinthians 12:28.

Ephesians 4:30—*In what way are we sealed by the Holy Spirit?*

In ancient times, scrolls or documents sent from one location to another were sealed with wax, and the seal was imprinted with the Roman stamp. The authority of the Roman government protected that document against unauthorized opening. The seal could not be broken until the document reached its final destination.

In the same way, you and I as believers are sealed by the Holy Spirit for the day of redemption. We are sealed by God Himself, and that seal cannot be broken. This seal guarantees that you and I will be delivered into eternal life—on the day of redemption. The Holy Spirit, as our seal, represents possession and security. The Holy Spirit is God's mark of ownership on us. No one can remove us from His ownership until the day of redemption.

Ephesians 5:18—*What does being filled with the Holy Spirit mean?*

Every Christian is commanded to be filled with the Holy Spirit (Ephesians 5:18). More precisely, they are to continually keep on being filled by the Spirit. We know this because the word *filled* is a present tense verb. This indicates continuing action. Day by day, moment by moment, you and I as Christians are to be filled with the Spirit. But what does this mean?

The context provides us with the answer. Both drunk and spiritual persons are controlled persons—that is, they're under the influence of either liquor or the Spirit, and they accordingly do things that are unnatural to them. In both cases they abandon themselves, either to the influence of liquor or to the Holy Spirit. To be filled with the Holy Spirit means that one's life will be controlled or governed no longer by self but by the Holy Spirit. It is not a matter of acquiring more of the Spirit, but rather of the Spirit of God acquiring all of the individual.

The filling of the Spirit is accomplished in the life of a believer when he or she is fully yielded to the indwelling Holy Spirit. This yieldedness results in a spiritual condition in which the Holy Spirit controls and empowers the individual moment by moment.

Ephesians 5:19—*Does the fact that only singing is mentioned mean that musical instruments should not be used in worship services?*

No. Musical instruments are used throughout the Bible in the context of worship. For example, various instruments were often used in producing music as a part of worship in the temple (1 Chronicles 25). It is well-known that many of the psalms were originally designed for musical accompaniment (see Psalm 4–6).

Scripture tells us that "David and all the house of Israel played music before the LORD on all kinds of instruments" (2 Samuel 6:5 NKJV). David affirmed, "I will play music before the LORD" (2 Samuel 6:21). We are told that "four thousand praised the LORD with musical instruments" (1 Chronicles 23:5). We are also told, "The priests sounded trumpets opposite them, while all Israel stood" (2 Chronicles 7:6). The Levites were stationed "in the house of the LORD with cymbals, with stringed instruments, and with harps" (2 Chronicles 29:25). The psalmist proclaims, "On the harp I will praise You, O God, my God" (Psalm 43:4). He exults, "With the lute I will praise you" (Psalm 71:22). Indeed, "Praise Him with the sound of the trumpet; praise Him with the lute and harp! Praise Him with the timbrel and dance; praise Him with stringed instruments and flutes! Praise Him with loud cymbals; praise Him with clashing cymbals!" (Psalm 150:3-5).

Revelation 5:8 indicates that harps will continue to be used in heaven in worship of God. If musical instruments were used in worship of God in Old Testament times and will be used in worship of God in heaven, there is no good reason why such instruments should not be used in our worship of God in the present.

Ephesians 5:22—*Is Paul promoting male supremacy in commanding wives to submit to husbands?*

No, not at all. God equally values both men and women, for both were created in the image of God (Genesis 1:26). Christian men and women are also viewed as positionally equal before God (Galatians 3:28). Further, the four Gospels indicate that Jesus defended and exalted women in a very patriarchal Jewish culture (see John 4).

Paul's instructions about submission reflect the fact that God is a God of order (1 Corinthians 14:33) and arranged His universe in orderly fashion, with an authority structure. Without an authority structure, anarchy would rule.

We must not overlook the fact that husbands are called to love their wives just as Christ loves the church (Ephesians 5:25). I have a feeling that if men were more faithful in loving their wives as Christ loves the church, women would have less of a problem with Paul's instruction. Men should also be cautious not to overlook Paul's instruction that both men and women are to submit to one another (Ephesians 5:21).

Philippians

Philippians 2:6-9—*In what way did Jesus make Himself nothing?*

The apostle Paul, speaking of the Incarnation, said that Christ, "being in very nature God, did not consider equality with God something to be grasped, but made himself nothing, taking the very nature of a servant, being made in human likeness" (Philippians 2:6-7). Jesus, as eternal God, made Himself nothing in three key ways:

First, Jesus veiled His preincarnate glory. Christ never actually surrendered His divine glory (Matthew 17), but it was necessary for Jesus to veil His preincarnate glory in order to dwell among mortal men and not overwhelm them by His glorious presence (see Revelation 1:17).

Second, Christ submitted to a voluntary nonuse of some of His divine attributes on some occasions in order to accomplish His objectives. Christ could never have actually surrendered any of His attributes, for then He would have ceased to be God. But He did voluntarily cease using some of them, on occasion, in order to live among men and their limitations. More specifically, Jesus never used His divine attributes on His own behalf, such as omnipotently and instantly willing Himself from Jerusalem to Bethany. He walked, and He got tired in the process! He did, however, use His divine powers for others in the miracles He performed.

Third, Christ condescended by taking on the likeness (literally, the appearance) of men and taking on the form (the essence or nature) of a bondservant. Christ was thus truly human. He was subject to temptation, distress, weakness, pain, sorrow, and limitation. Yet it must be noted that the word *likeness* suggests similarity but difference. More specifically, His humanity was genuine, but He was different from other human beings in that He did not have a sin nature. Nevertheless,

Christ's taking on the likeness of men represented a great condescension on the part of the second person of the Trinity.

Philippians 2:10—*Does Paul imply that everyone will be saved in the end by confessing Christ is Lord?*

No. Scripture clearly teaches that all unbelievers will eventually confess Jesus is Lord; nevertheless, there is no evidence here or elsewhere that they will be saved. This is evident for many reasons.

First, note that our text tells us that unbelievers confess only *that* Jesus is Lord. There is no reference to their believing in Him, something that is necessary for salvation (Acts 16:31).

Second, even demons believe that Jesus is Lord and that God exists (James 2:19), but they are not saved. Believing that Jesus is Lord will not save anyone. Only belief in Christ will save (James 2:21-26).

Third, numerous passages of Scripture teach that many will be lost forever. This includes the devil and his angels (Matthew 25:41), the beast and the false prophet (Revelation 19:20), Judas (John 17:12), a multitude of unsaved people from all nations (Matthew 25:32,41), and all whose names are not written in the book of life (Revelation 20:14).

Philippians 2:12—*What does Paul mean by "work out your salvation"?*

This verse has nothing to do with assurance of final salvation for individual believers. As a backdrop, one must keep in mind the particular situation of the church in Philippi. This church faced many challenges:

- rivalries and individuals with personal ambition (Philippians 2:3-4; 4:2)

- the teaching of Judaizers who said circumcision was necessary for salvation (3:1-3)

- perfectionism (the view that one could attain sinless perfection in this life—3:12-14)

- "antinomian libertines" (people who took excessive liberty in how they lived their lives, ignoring or going against God's law—3:18-19)

Because of such problems, this church as a unit was in need of "salvation"—that is, salvation in the temporal, experiential sense, not in the eternal sense.

The Greek word for *work out (katergazomai)* is a compound verb that indicates achievement or bringing to a conclusion. Paul was calling the Philippians to solve all the church's problems, thus bringing corporate "salvation" or deliverance to a state of final achievement. Paul would not permit things to continue as they were. The problems must be solved. The Philippians were to work it out to the finish.

Philippians 2:25-30—*Were the apostles unable to accomplish some miraculous healings?*

Yes. As the apostles aged, miracles began to taper off. Philippians 2:25-30 is an illustration, for this passage reveals that Paul could not heal Epaphroditus. Paul was also unable to heal Timothy of his stomach problem (1 Timothy 5:23). Nor could he heal himself of his thorn in the flesh (2 Corinthians 12:7-9). God's time of self-revelation was apparently coming to a close toward the end of the apostles' lives. At the beginning of the book of Acts, many were being healed; at the close of New Testament history, many were left unhealed.

Colossians

Colossians 1:15—*Was Jesus, as the firstborn, the first being created by God?*

No. *Firstborn* does not mean first-created. Rather, the word means first in rank, preeminent one, or heir. The word carries the idea of positional preeminence and supremacy. Christ is the firstborn in the sense that He is positionally preeminent over creation and is supreme over all things. He is also the heir of all creation in the sense that all that is the Father's is also the Son's.

Among the ancient Hebrews, the word *firstborn* referred to the son in the family who was in the preeminent position, regardless of whether or not that son was literally the first son born to the parents. This "firstborn" son would not only be the preeminent one in the family, he would also be the heir to a double portion of the family inheritance. This meaning of *firstborn* is illustrated in the life of David. David was the youngest (last-born) son of Jesse. Nevertheless, Psalm 89:27 says he was God's firstborn. Though David was the last one born in Jesse's family, David is called God's firstborn because of the preeminent position God was placing him in.

Based on such usage, it is clear that when Scripture calls Jesus *firstborn,* He is being recognized as preeminent over all creation. That Christ is the heir of all things is as it should be, since Christ is also the Maker of all things (Colossians 1:16). All in the creation is His by divine right.

Colossians 1:16—*What are thrones, powers, rulers, and authorities Paul refers to?*

In the rabbinic (Jewish) thought of the first century, these terms were used to point to the hierarchical organization in the angelic realm. These appellations point not to different kinds of angels, but simply to differences of rank among them.

Colossians 1:20—*Does God's purpose of reconciling to Himself all things through Jesus teach that all people will be saved in the end?*

No. Paul is referring not to universal salvation but simply to the universal sovereignty of Jesus Christ. In other words, all authority has been given to Jesus Christ in heaven and on earth (Matthew 28:18). By virtue of His death and resurrection, Christ as the last Adam is Lord over all that was lost by the first Adam (see 1 Corinthians 15:45-49).

All persons, saved and unsaved, will one day bow before Christ and acknowledge His universal lordship. But nowhere do the Scriptures teach that all people will be saved. Jesus will say to many, "Depart from me, you who are cursed, into the eternal fire prepared for the devil and his angels" (Matthew 25:41). Luke speaks of a great impassible gulf between heaven and hell, and those who have rejected God are living in torment (Luke 16:19-31). Paul speaks of punishment of the wicked as everlasting destruction apart from the presence of the Lord (2 Thessalonians 1:7-9). These passages clearly show that not everyone will be saved.

Colossians 1:24—*Does this verse teach that Christ's suffering on the cross was insufficient to atone for our sins?*

The apostle Paul stated, "I fill up in my flesh what is still lacking in regard to Christ's afflictions, for the sake of his body, which is the church." This does not mean Christ's atoning sacrifice is not sufficient to pay for our sins. Paul was likely referring to the fact that we too can suffer for Christ because "it has been granted to you on behalf of Christ not only to believe on him, but also to suffer for him" (Philippians 1:29). But in no sense is our suffering for Christ a means of atoning for sin. Only Jesus suffered *for* sin. We suffer because of our sins but never for the sins of others. Each person must bear the guilt of his own sin (Ezekiel 18:20) or accept the fact that Christ suffered for his sin (2 Corinthians 5:21; 1 Peter 2:21; 3:18). When we suffer for Christ, we are undergoing pain as part of His spiritual body (see 1 Corinthians 12:26), the church, but only what Christ suffered in His physical body on the cross is efficacious for our sins.

Colossians 2:8—*Does this verse mean Christians should not study philosophy?*

The Bible is no more against philosophy than it is against religion. Rather, it is against *vain* philosophy, which Paul calls deceptive (verse 8). Likewise, the Bible is not opposed to religion, but only against *vain* religion (see James 1:26-27).

Further, Paul is not speaking about philosophy in general, but about a particular philosophy, usually understood as an early form of Gnosticism. This is indicated by his use of the definite article, which should be translated "the philosophy" or "this philosophy." So Paul was referring to this particular Gnostic-like philosophy that had invaded the church in Colossae and involved legalism, mysticism, and asceticism (see Colossians 2). He was not alluding to all philosophy.

What is more, Paul himself was well trained in the philosophies of his day, even quoting them from time to time (see Acts 17:28; Titus 1:12). Paul successfully reasoned with the philosophers on Mars Hill, even winning some to Christ (Acts 17:17,34). Elsewhere he said a bishop should be able to refute those who oppose sound doctrine (Titus 1:9), something that requires familiarity with philosophy. Peter likewise exhorted believers to "always be prepared to give an answer to everyone who asks you to give the reason for the hope that you have" (1 Peter 3:15).

Colossians 4:16—*What happened to the lost epistle of the Laodiceans?*

Luke refers to other Gospels (Luke 1:1), and John affirmed that there were many other things Jesus did that are not recorded in his Gospel (John 20:31; 21:25). However, only those inspired books that God preserved by His providence were intended to be in the canon of Scripture. Simply because a book is cited in the Bible does not mean that the book belongs in the Bible, even though that book may contain some truth.

Besides, there are some good reasons to believe the epistle from Laodicea is not really lost, but is really the book of Ephesians. Notice that Colossians 4:16 does not call it the epistle *of* the Laodiceans, but the letter from Laodicea, whatever name it may have had. There is evidence that the book of Ephesians did not originally bear that title, but was a kind of cyclical letter sent to the churches of Asia Minor. Some early manuscripts do not have the phrase "in Ephesus" in Ephesians 1:1.

Finally, no epistle of the Laodiceans is cited by any of the early church Fathers, though they make over 36,000 New Testament citations, including every book and almost every verse of the New Testament. A fraudulent epistle of the Laodiceans appeared in the fourth century, but no scholars believe it is the one Paul referred to. Indeed, it is largely a collection of quotations from Ephesians and Colossians that the Council of Nicea (AD 787) called a "forged epistle."

1 Thessalonians

1 Thessalonians 4:13—*Did the apostle Paul teach the doctrine of soul sleep?*

No. The souls of both believers and unbelievers are conscious between death and the resurrection. Unbelievers are in conscious woe (see Luke 16:22-23; Mark 9:43-48; Revelation 19:20), and believers are in conscious bliss (Philippians 1:23). "Sleep" is a reference to the body, not the soul. Sleep is an appropriate figure of speech for death of the body because death is temporary until the resurrection, when the body will be awakened.

1 Thessalonians 4:16—*Is Jesus the archangel Michael?*

No. According to Daniel 10:13, the archangel Michael is specifically called "one of the chief princes." This indicates that he is one among a group of chief princes. How large that group is, we are not told. But the fact that Michael is one among equals proves that he is not totally unique. By contrast, the Greek word used of Jesus in the New Testament is *monogenes,* which literally means one of a kind (John 3:16). Note also that Jesus is never called a chief prince in the Bible. Rather, Jesus is called the King of kings and Lord of lords in Revelation 19:16. This title indicates absolute sovereignty and authority. A King of kings and Lord of lords is much higher in authority than a mere chief prince (who is one among equals). One has absolute sovereignty and authority; the other has derived, limited authority.

As for 1 Thessalonians 4:16, the text never explicitly says that Jesus Himself speaks with the voice of the archangel. It is much more natural and logical to read the verse as saying that when Jesus comes from heaven to rapture the church from the earth, He will be accompanied by the archangel since it is the archangel's voice (distinct from Jesus) that issues the shout.

This is similar to what will happen at the second coming of Christ (seven years after the rapture, following the tribulation period). At the second coming, "the Lord Jesus is revealed from heaven in blazing fire with his powerful angels" (2 Thessalonians 1:7). If the angels accompany Christ at the second coming, then surely the archangel Michael will accompany Him as well.

2 Thessalonians

2 Thessalonians 1:9—*Does everlasting destruction of the soul mean the soul is snuffed out of conscious existence?*

No. "Everlasting destruction" simply indicates living eternally (and consciously) in a perpetually ruinous state. Many lines of evidence support the everlasting consciousness of the lost:

- The rich man who died and went to hell was in conscious torment (Luke 16:22-28), and nothing in the text indicates it was ever going to cease.

- Jesus spoke repeatedly of the people in hell as weeping and gnashing their teeth (Matthew 8:12; 22:13; 24:51; 25:30), which indicates they were conscious.

- Hell is said to be of the same duration as heaven—everlasting (Matthew 25:41).

- The fact that their punishment is everlasting indicates that they too must be everlasting. One cannot suffer punishment unless he exists to be punished (2 Thessalonians 1:9). It makes virtually no sense to say that the wicked will suffer endless annihilation. Rather, the wicked will suffer a ruin which is everlasting—and this is a punishment that will never end.

- There are no degrees of annihilation, but Scripture reveals there will be degrees of suffering among the lost (see Matthew 10:15; 11:21-24; 16:27; Luke 12:47-48; John 15:22; Hebrews 10:29; Revelation 20:11-15; 22:12).

2 Thessalonians 2:9—*What are we to make of Satan's counterfeit miracles, signs, and wonders?*

Although Satan has great spiritual powers, there is a gigantic difference between the power of the devil and the power of God. God is infinite in power (omnipotent); the devil is finite and limited. Moreover, only God can create life (Genesis 1:1,21; Deuteronomy 32:39); the devil cannot (see Exodus 8:19). Only God can truly raise the dead (John 10:18; Revelation 1:18); the devil cannot, though he will one day give breath (animation) to the idolatrous image of the Antichrist (Revelation 13:15).

The devil has great power to deceive people (Revelation 12:9), to oppress those who yield to him, and even to possess them (Acts 16:16). He is a master magician and a super scientist. And with His vast knowledge of God, man, and the universe, he is able to perform counterfeit miracles, signs, and wonders (2 Thessalonians 2:9; see also Revelation 13:13-14). Simon the sorcerer in the city of Samaria amazed people with his Satan-inspired magic (Acts 8:9-11), but the miracles accomplished through Philip were much, much greater (Acts 8:13). The devil's counterfeit miracles do not compete with God's true miracles.

2 Thessalonians 2:15—*Are we today to hold firm to traditions, in addition to following the Bible?*

No. The Greek word for *traditions* (*paradosis*) simply refers to that which has been passed down. Paul had earlier passed down some apostolic teachings about the second coming of Christ to the Thessalonian Christians (the context of 2 Thessalonians makes this clear), and Paul reminds them in this verse to hold firm to those teachings.

Let us not forget that the apostles for a time communicated their teachings orally until those teachings could be permanently recorded in written form. When the apostles committed their teachings to written form and then died, the written Scriptures alone became our final authority for matters of faith and practice (2 Timothy 3:15-17).

1 Timothy

1 Timothy 2:3-4—*Will all people be saved in the end?*

This verse affirms that God "wants all men to be saved and to come to a knowledge of the truth." This passage expresses God's desire that all be saved, but it does not promise that all will be. This divine desire is realized only in those who exercise faith in Christ (Acts 16:31). Scripture is clear that in the end, the saved and the unsaved will experience two different destinies, heaven or hell (see Matthew 13:49; 25:31-46).

1 Timothy 2:4—*If God wants all to be saved, why doesn't He just save them all?*

God has made the provision for all people to be saved through Christ's death on the cross. This salvation is a gift. But the gift must be received by faith (John 3:16; Acts 16:31). If the gift is refused, God will not force a person against his will to receive it. C.S. Lewis said that in the end there are two groups of people. One group of people says to God, "Thy will be done." These are those who have received the gift of salvation by placing their faith in Jesus and will live forever with God in heaven. The second group of people are those to whom God says, sadly, "Thy will be done!" These are those who have rejected Jesus and His gift of salvation and will accordingly spend eternity apart from Him.

1 Timothy 2:13-15—*What does Paul mean when he says women will be saved through childbearing?*

This verse is difficult to interpret. Some Bible expositors believe the verse simply refers to believing women being kept safe while bearing children. Others believe the verse refers to believing women being kept safe because of Jesus' birth. Still others think the verse generally means that the believing woman will find fulfillment in her God-appointed role as wife and mother.

1 Timothy 3:12—*What does Scripture mean when it says an elder of the church must be the husband of one wife?*

This verse has been debated by Christians since the first century. There are four basic suggestions as to what it means:

- The elder must be married only once. No remarriage is allowed, even if the wife dies.

- The elder must be married to one wife at a time (that is, no polygamy is allowed).

- A single person cannot be an elder in the church.

- The elder must be faithful to his wife—that is, he must be a "one-woman man." I believe this is probably the correct view.

1 Timothy 5:21—*Who are the elect angels?*

All the angels were originally created good and holy, just as God made and pronounced all His creation good (Genesis 1:31; 2:3). For God to create anything wicked would be inconsistent with His holy character. Jude 6 affirms that originally all the angels were holy creatures. God did not create Satan and the fallen angels (demons) in a state of wickedness.

Though all the angels were originally created in a state of holiness, Scripture indicates that they were subjected to a period of probation. Some of the angels remained holy. Others did not—following Lucifer's lead, they rebelled against God and fell into great sin.

Once the angels were put to the test to remain loyal to God or to rebel with Lucifer, their decision seems to have been made permanent in its effect. Those angels that passed the probationary test will now always remain holy. Those who failed the probationary test are now confirmed in their evil state.

This is the reason the good angels are called elect angels in 1 Timothy 5:21. They are not called elect because they sinned and then were elected unto redemption (they never sinned during the probationary period). Rather, they are called elect because God intervened to permanently confirm (elect) them in their holiness so they could not sin in the future. Good angels are now incapable of sinning. The lines have been drawn, and the lines are now absolute.

1 Timothy 5:23—*Are Christians permitted to drink?*

Drunkenness is forbidden by God. It is simply not an option for the Christian. In Ephesians 5:18, the apostle Paul explicitly instructs, "Do not get drunk on wine, which leads to debauchery. Instead, be filled with the Spirit." Paul is telling us to be controlled by the Spirit, not by wine. Drinking wine in moderation is permissible (see John 2:9; 1 Timothy 3:3,8), but many wine-drinking Christians today are wrongly assuming that wine in the New Testament is identical to the wine used today. This, however, is not correct. Today's undiluted wine is what the Bible calls "strong drink."

See comments on John 2:9.

2 Timothy

2 Timothy 1:10—*If Jesus has abolished death, why do people still die?*

This verse indicates that the result of Jesus' death and resurrection will be the *eventual* abolishing of death, not the immediate abolishing of death. Another way to look at it is that Christ has abolished death officially, but this will not become actual until the future rapture, at which time death will be swallowed up in victory (1 Corinthians 15:54).

2 Timothy 3:8—*Where in the Old Testament are we told that Jannes and Jambres were the magicians who opposed Moses?*

Not a single Old Testament verse provides this information. It is accurate due to the inspiration of the Holy Spirit, and it is also found in widespread Jewish legends about two of Pharaoh's magicians who competed against Moses and lost (Exodus 7:11; 9:11). This legend appears in Pseudo-Philo, the Dead Sea Scrolls, the Talmud, Targums, and various rabbinical writings. Even pagan accounts—by Pliny the Elder (AD 23–79) and Apuleius (circa AD 130)—record these individuals as magicians of Moses' time. The Pythagorean philosopher Numenius (second century AD) also speaks of these two.

2 Timothy 3:15—*What does it mean to be wise for salvation?*

Timothy's mother started Timothy's training in the Old Testament Scriptures at a very early age and continued this training throughout his childhood. The clause, "You have known the holy Scriptures" is in the present tense in the Greek, which indicates continuous, ongoing action. Timothy's mother didn't just sporadically talk to Timothy about the Scriptures; she regularly spoke to him about the Scriptures. Timothy literally became wise about the things of salvation and became a believer.

Titus

Titus 2:9—*Does the Bible condone slavery?*

No. The practice of human slavery was a way of life among the ancients, including the Egyptians, Sumerians, Babylonians, Assyrians, Phoenicians, Syrians, Moabites, Ammonites, Edomites, Greeks, and Romans.

People could become slaves in any number of ways. For example, enemies captured in war could become enslaved (Genesis 14:21). A person in severe debt could place himself in slavery to pay the debt (Exodus 21:2-6). A thief who could not repay what he stole could be enslaved. A child born into a family of slaves would himself become a slave (Genesis 15:3).

Among most ancient peoples, slaves were considered property without any personal rights. This was not the case among the Israelites. Though slaves were still considered property, they had definite rights as defined under the Mosaic law. In many cases, the slave was treated as a member of the family. Indeed, in many cases the slave was better off as a slave (in terms of having food and other provisions) than as a free person. The law provided that no Israelite (including slaves) could be treated harshly (Leviticus 25:39), and it was unlawful to beat a slave to death (Exodus 21:20). Moreover, if a slave was beaten to the point of mutilation, he was to be set free (Exodus 21:26-27).

Contrary to what some have claimed, the Bible does not condone slavery. From the very beginning, God declared that all humans are created in the image of God (Genesis 1:27). The apostle Paul also declared, "We are the offspring of God" (Acts 17:29), and God "has made from one blood every nation of men to dwell on all the face of the earth" (verse 26). All of us are equal before God. Moreover, despite the fact that slavery was countenanced in the Semitic cultures of the day, the law in the Bible demanded that slaves eventually be set free (Exodus 21:2; Leviticus 25:40). Likewise, servants had to be treated with respect (Exodus 21:20,26). Israel, itself in slavery in Egypt for a prolonged time, was constantly reminded by God of this (Deuteronomy 5:15), and their emancipation became the model for the liberation of all slaves (see Leviticus 25:40).

Further, in the New Testament, Paul declared that in Christianity "there is neither Jew nor Greek, there is neither slave nor free, there is neither male nor female; for you are all one in Christ Jesus" (Galatians 3:28). All social classes are broken down in Christ; we are all equal before God.

Though the apostle Paul urged, "Servants, be obedient to those who are your masters" (Ephesians 6:5; Colossians 3:22), he was not thereby approving of the institution of slavery. He was simply alluding to the *de facto* situation in his day. He was simply instructing servants to be good workers, just as believers should be today, but he was not thereby commending slavery. Paul and Peter also instructed all believers to be obedient to government (even if unjust) for the Lord's sake (Romans 13:1; Titus 3:1; 1 Peter 2:13). But this in no way condones oppression and tyranny, which the Bible repeatedly condemns (Exodus 2:23-25; Isaiah 10:1).

Titus 2:13—*Does this verse refer to Jesus alone or to Jesus and the Father?*

The KJV reads, "Looking for that blessed hope, and the glorious appearing of the great God and our Savior Jesus Christ." This sounds like both the Father and Jesus are in view.

In reality, the verse is referring to Jesus alone. The NIV correctly puts it this way: "We wait for the blessed hope—the glorious appearing of our great God and Savior, Jesus Christ." An examination of Titus 2:10-13 and 3:4-6 reveals that the phrases *God our Savior* and *Jesus our Savior* are used interchangeably four times. The parallel truths that only God is the Savior (Isaiah 43:11) and that Jesus is Himself the Savior constitute a powerful evidence for Christ's deity.

Greek grammarians have taken a solid stand against the view that

Titus 2:13 refers to two persons—God and the Savior, Jesus. Such Greek scholars argue their case based on a detailed study of a number of identical sentence constructions in the Greek New Testament. Greek scholars have thus come up with a guiding principle or rule for interpreting such constructions.

It's a little technical, but here it is: When (1) two nouns in the same case are connected by the Greek word translated *and,* and (2) the first noun is preceded by the definite article (*the*), and (3) the second noun is not preceded by the article, the second noun refers to the *same person* or thing to which the first noun refers and is a further description of it.

In Titus 2:13, two nouns—*God* and *Savior*—are joined together with the Greek word for *and,* and a definite article (*the*) is placed only in front of the first noun (*God*). The sentence literally reads: "the great God and Savior of us." In this particular kind of construction in the Greek New Testament, the two nouns in question—*God* and *Savior*—are referring to the same person, Jesus Christ. The two nouns have a single referent. The presence of only one definite article has the effect of binding together *God* and *Savior* as referring to one person.

Titus 3:5—*Is baptism necessary for salvation?*

This verse affirms that believers are saved "through the washing of regeneration." The Greek word for baptism (*baptizo*) is not used in this verse. Paul did not use this word because he was not referring to baptism. Paul refers to "washing of regeneration" (Greek: *loutrou*) to describe how believers are cleansed of guilt at the moment of salvation. The fact that this is a washing of regeneration indicates that a spiritual washing is in view, not a literal water-baptism kind of washing. Besides, the very words used in this verse point out beyond any doubt that our salvation is not a result of doing things (like getting baptized) but is based entirely on God's mercy.

Philemon

Philemon 16—*Does the apostle Paul approve of the institution of slavery?*

No. A close look at the book of Philemon reveals that the apostle Paul did not perpetuate slavery by his words, but actually undermined it, for he urged Philemon, Onesimus's owner, to treat him as "a beloved brother" (verse 16).

See comments on Titus 2:9.

Hebrews

Hebrews 4:15—*Could Jesus have sinned when He was tempted?*

In the Incarnation, Jesus (eternal God) took on an additional nature—a human nature. In His humanity, He was subject to temptation, distress, weakness, pain, sorrow, and limitation. However, by virtue of the fact that He was also fully God, the temptation stood no chance of success.

See comments on Matthew 4:7.

Hebrews 5:8—*If Jesus was truly God, how could He have learned obedience?*

Prior to the Incarnation, Christ, the second person of the Trinity, had only a divine nature. But in the Incarnation, Christ took on a human nature. It is thus in His humanity that Christ learned obedience. Some theologians point out that Jesus, as omniscient God, intrinsically knew all about obedience—more so than any of us. But it was only when He became a human being that He began to actually experience obedience from the human perspective.

Hebrews 6:4-6—*Can Christians lose their salvation?*

Hebrews 6:4-6 asserts, "It is impossible for those who have once been enlightened, who have tasted the heavenly gift, who have shared in the Holy Spirit, who have tasted the goodness of the word of God and the powers of the coming age, if they fall away, to be brought back to repentance, because to their loss they are crucifying the Son of God all over again and subjecting him to public disgrace."

Those who subscribe to Arminian theology believe this passage indicates that a Christian can lose his or her salvation. If this interpretation is correct, one would also have to conclude that it is impossible to be saved a second time.

Others interpret this passage as referring to people who have an insincere faith in Jesus Christ. They are professed believers but not genuine believers.

Still others interpret this passage as a warning to Christians to move on to spiritual maturity. I subscribe to this third view. Note that the context of Hebrews 6:4-6 is set for us in verses 1-3: "Therefore let us leave the elementary teachings about Christ and go on to maturity, not laying again the foundation of repentance from acts that lead to death, and of faith in God, instruction about baptisms, the laying on of hands, the resurrection of the dead, and eternal judgment. And God permitting, we will do so."

The context clearly deals with going on to maturity. This was an important issue for the Jews of the first century who had converted to Christ and become Christians. The Jews living in and around the Palestine area were under the authority of the high priest, who had sufficient influence to cause a Jew to lose his job, have his kids kicked out of synagogue school, and much more. When some Jews became Christians in the first century, the high priest put some heavy-duty pressure (persecution) on them. This caused some of the Jewish Christians to become a bit gun-shy in their Christian lives. They weren't open about their Christian faith. Perhaps they thought that if they kept quiet about their faith and withdrew from external involvement in Christian affairs (like church attendance), the high priest would lighten up on them.

The author of the book of Hebrews saw this as a retreat from spiritual maturity in Christ. He thus encouraged them to move on to maturity in Christ. Though it is impossible for a Christian to actually fall away from salvation, the author of the book put his warning about moving on to spiritual maturity in strong terms. Hebrews 6:4-6, then, is not saying, "Shape up, or you'll lose your salvation." Rather, it is saying, "In view of the fact that you're already in the school of Christ and have made a commitment, let's move on to maturity. No retreat is allowed." This was a message those first-century Jewish converts needed to hear.

Hebrews 7:3—*Was Melchizedek a preincarnate appearance of Christ?*

There is much conjecture today about Melchizedek. Some say he was an angel who took on human form during the time of Abraham. (This seems not to be the case, however, because the priesthood was a human function, not an angelic function—see Hebrews 5:1.) Others say Melchizedek was a preincarnate appearance of Christ. But Melchizedek is described as being *like* the Son of God, not as *being* the Son of God Himself (Hebrews 7:3). It seems best to view Melchizedek as an actual historical person—a mere human being—who was a type of Christ.

Those who argue that Melchizedek was a preincarnate appearance of Christ usually cite Hebrews 7:3 in support of this view: "Without father or mother, without genealogy, without beginning of days or end of life, like the Son of God he remains a priest forever." No human being, it is argued, can be without father or mother, without genealogy, or without beginning of days or end of life. In response, many scholars believe that this verse simply means that the Old Testament Scriptures have no record of these events. To the writer of Hebrews, the silences of Old Testament Scripture were as much due to divine inspiration as were its affirmations. In Genesis 14:18-20, nothing is said of his parentage, his birth, or his death. He appears as a living man—the king of Salem and a priest of God Most High—and then he disappears. As such he is an appropriate type of Christ.

Scholars are careful to note that the omission of information in Genesis about Melchizedek's parentage should not be taken to mean he had no father or mother. Rather, it simply means that none of those items of information was included in the Genesis 14 account and that they were purposely omitted in order to lay the stress on the divine nature and imperishability of the Messiah, the antitype.

It should be noted that Melchizedek was a type of Christ in other ways besides his imperishability. Melchizedek's name is made up of two words that mean king and righteous. Melchizedek was also a priest. Thus, Melchizedek foreshadows Christ as a righteous king and priest. We are also told that Melchizedek was the king of *Salem,* a word that means peace. This too points to Christ, who is our peace (Ephesians 2:14).

Hebrews 7:25—*Does the fact that Christ prayed to the Father mean that He was not God?*

No. In the Incarnation, Christ (eternal God) took on a human nature. It is thus in His humanity that Christ prayed to the Father. Christ came as man, and one of the proper duties of man is to worship, pray to, and adore God, so it was perfectly proper for Jesus to address the Father in prayer. Positionally speaking as a man, as a Jew, and as our High Priest ("made like his brothers in every way"—Hebrews 2:17), Jesus could pray to the Father. But this in no way detracts from His intrinsic deity.

Hebrews 10:25—*Can Christians skip church?*

Attending local churches is strongly urged in the New Testament. Hebrews 10:25 specifically instructs us not to forsake "our own assembling together." The Christian life as described in Scripture is to be lived within the context of the family of God and not in isolation (Acts 2; Ephesians 3:14-15). Moreover, by attending church we become equipped for the work of ministry (Ephesians 4:12-16). The Bible knows nothing of a lone-ranger Christian. As the old proverb says, many logs together burn very brightly, but when a log falls off to the side, the embers quickly die out (see Ephesians 2:19; 1 Thessalonians 5:10-11; and 1 Peter 3:8).

Hebrews 13:2—*Can angels actually appear as human beings?*

This verse exhorts, "Do not forget to entertain strangers, for by so doing some people have entertained angels without knowing it." Scripture indicates that though angels are by nature incorporeal (nonmaterial) and invisible (Hebrews 1:14), they can nevertheless appear as men (Matthew 1:20; Luke 1:26; John 20:12). Their resemblance to men can be so realistic, in fact, that the angel is actually taken to be a human being. A person who helped you during a time of need in your past could possibly have been an angel that appeared as a human. There is no reason to suggest that such appearances cannot occur today just as they did in biblical times.

James

James 2:16-17—*Is James saying a person is justified by works, thereby contradicting the apostle Paul?*

No. James begins by asking, "What use is it, my brethren, if a man says he has faith, but he has no works? Can that faith save him?" (James 2:14). Notice the oft-neglected little word *says*. Some people have genuine faith; others have an empty profession of faith that is not real. The first group of people, who have genuine faith, also have works to back up the fact that their faith is genuine. Those who make an empty profession of faith show their lack of true faith by the absence of works. So James answers his question by pointing out that you can tell whether a person has true faith by the test of works.

Martin Luther said it best: James 2 is not teaching that a person is saved by works or by personal merit. Rather, a person is justified (declared righteous before God) by faith alone, but not by a faith that is alone. In other words, genuine faith will always result in or be accompanied by good works in the saved person's life.

James 2:21—*Was Abraham justified before God by works and not by faith?*

No. In this verse James is not talking about justification before God but rather justification before men. We know this to be true because James stressed that we should show (James 2:18) our faith. That is, our faith must be something that others can see in our actions (verses 18-20).

James acknowledged that Abraham was justified before God by faith, not works: "Abraham believed God, and it was accounted to him for righteousness" (James 2:23). When he spoke of Abraham being "justified by works" earlier in verse 21, he was speaking of what

Abraham did that could be seen by men, namely, he offered his son Isaac on the altar. Here Abraham proves the reality of his faith by offering up his son. This event with Isaac took place some 30 years after Abraham had first believed in God (at which time he was justified before God).

James 5:12—*Does God forbid taking oaths?*

No. James is simply warning against duplicitous language. Our *yes* should be *yes* in the sense that we tell the truth always, with no need to take oaths as an assurance that we are telling the truth.

See comments on Matthew 5:37.

1 Peter

1 Peter 1:1—*In what way are the elect chosen by God?*

Election is a sovereign act in which God chooses certain individuals to salvation before the foundation of the world. Christians have had two primary views regarding the issue of election.

The first view is that God's election is based on His foreknowledge. This view says that God used His foreknowledge to look down the corridors of time to see who would respond favorably to His gospel message, and on that basis He elected certain persons to salvation. Several arguments are offered in favor of this view:

- Scripture teaches that God's salvation has appeared to all men, not merely the elect (Titus 2:11).

- The Bible teaches that Christ died for all (1 Timothy 2:6; 4:10; Hebrews 2:9; 2 Peter 2:1; 1 John 2:2).

- Scripture includes numerous exhortations to turn to God (Isaiah 31:6; Joel 2:13-14; Matthew 18:3; Acts 3:19), to repent (Matthew 3:2; Luke 13:3,5; Acts 2:38; 17:30), and to believe (John 6:29; Acts 16:31; 1 John 3:23).

- Scripture seems to indicate that election is based on God's foreknowledge of who would respond positively to such exhortations (Romans 8:28-30; 1 Peter 1:1-2).

However, many claim that if election is not unconditional and absolute, then God's whole plan is uncertain and liable to miscarriage. The second view (my view) is that God's election is based on His sovereign choice. A number of arguments are offered in favor of this view:

- Biblical statements support election by choice (Acts 13:48).

- The whole process of salvation is a gift of God (Romans 12:3; Ephesians 1:5-8; 2:8-10).

- Certain verses speak of human beings having been given to Christ (John 6:37; 17:2,6,9), and of the Father drawing men to Christ (John 6:44).

- There are examples in Scripture of the sovereign calling of God upon individuals, like Paul (Galatians 1:15) and Jeremiah (Jeremiah 1:5), even before they were born. He chose Jacob rather than Esau before they were born (Romans 9:10-16).

- Election is necessary in light of man's total depravity (Job 14:1; Jeremiah 13:11; Romans 3:10-20).

- Election is necessary in light of man's inability (Ephesians 2:1).

- Election is compatible with God's sovereignty (Proverbs 19:21; Jeremiah 10:23).

- Election is portrayed as being from all eternity (2 Timothy 1:9).

- It is on the basis of election by choice that the appeal to a godly life is made (Colossians 3:12; 2 Thessalonians 2:13; 1 Peter 2:9).

Two primary arguments have been suggested against this view. First, it is argued that if election is limited by God, then surely the atonement must be limited as well (providing salvation only for the elect). However, this conclusion is clearly refuted by John 1:29; 3:16; 1 Timothy 2:6; Hebrews 2:9; and 1 John 2:2.

Second, it is argued that election by choice makes God responsible for reprobation. However, those not included in election suffer only their due reward. God does not elect a person to hell. Those not elected to salvation are left to their own self-destructive ways.

Whichever view one concludes is the correct one, the following facts should be kept in mind: God's election is loving (Ephesians 1:4-11), election glorifies God (Ephesians 1:12-14), and the product of election is a people who do good works (Romans 11:33-36; Ephesians 2:10; Colossians 3:12).

1 Peter 3:18—*Did Jesus rise from the dead as a spirit creature?*

No. This verse does not refer to a spiritual resurrection of Christ; rather, it refers to Christ's physical resurrection by the Holy Spirit. God did not raise Jesus *as* a spirit but rather raised Him *by* His Spirit. This is in keeping with Romans 1:4, which tells us that it was "through the Spirit of holiness" that Jesus was "declared with power to be the Son of God by his resurrection from the dead."

The uniform testimony of Scripture is that Jesus was raised not spiritually but physically from the dead:

- The resurrected Christ Himself said, "Behold My hands and My feet, that it is I Myself. Handle Me and see, for a spirit does not have flesh and bones as you see I have" (Luke 24:39 NKJV).

- Christ predicted in John 2:19-21 that He would rise physically: "Jesus answered them, 'Destroy this temple, and I will raise it again in three days'…The temple he had spoken of was his body."

- Jesus' resurrection body retained the physical wounds from the cross (Luke 24:39; John 20:27).

- The resurrected Christ ate physical food on four different occasions (Luke 24:30; 24:42-43; John 21:12-13; Acts 1:4).

- The physical body of the resurrected Christ was touched and handled by different people (Matthew 28:9; John 20:17).

- The Greek word for body (*soma*), when used of a person, always refers to a physical body in the New Testament.

- The same body that is sown in death is the very same body that is raised in life (1 Corinthians 15:35-44).

1 Peter 3:18-19—*What spirits in prison did Jesus preach to?*

Some scholars believe the spirits in prison are fallen angels who grievously sinned against God. The idea here is that these spirits are the fallen angels of Genesis 6:1-6 who were disobedient to God during the days of Noah. This same group of evil angels is mentioned in 2 Peter 2:4-5 and Jude 6. According to this interpretation, these evil angels disobeyed God, left their first estate (they forsook their proper realm), and entered into sexual relations with human women.

The Greek word for *preach* (*kerusso*) is not the word used for preaching the gospel but rather points to a proclamation—as in a proclamation of victory. The passage may imply that these evil spirits thought they had destroyed Jesus, but that in raising Him from the dead, God turned the tables on them—and Jesus Himself preached about their doom.

Another possible interpretation is that between His death and resurrection, Jesus went to the place of the dead and preached to the wicked contemporaries of Noah. The preaching, however, was not a gospel message but was rather a proclamation of victory.

Still others believe this passage has reference to Christ preaching through the person of Noah to those who, because they rejected his message, are now spirits in prison. They had 120 years, during which time the ark was being built, to respond to Noah's message. But they refused. They are thus now in prison awaiting the final judgment.

As to Christ preaching through Noah, one must keep in mind that 1 Peter 1:11 tells us that the Spirit of Christ spoke through the Old Testament prophets. And Noah is later described as a "preacher of righteousness" (2 Peter 2:5). The Spirit of Christ may have preached through Noah to these ungodly humans who, at the time of Peter's writing, were spirits in prison, awaiting final judgment.

1 Peter 3:21—*Does the phrase "This water symbolizes baptism that now saves you also" mean that water baptism is necessary for salvation?*

I don't think so. In this context, Peter is dealing with the believer's good conscience, not salvation. The believers to whom Peter was writing were being tempted to compromise their Christianity in order to reduce or avoid religious persecution. Such compromise, however, would wreak havoc on their consciences, for they knew they'd be going against God's will in following such a course of action. Peter therefore urges his readers that the act of public baptism would save them from their temptation to sacrifice their good (inner) consciences merely to avoid persecution. After all, such (external) baptism is a means of publicly and once-for-all identifying with Jesus Christ. Even though persecution would likely continue, at least they would retain a clear conscience before God, which is far more important.

1 Peter 4:6—*Does this verse mean that people can hear the gospel after they die?*

No. We must not forget the clear statement in Hebrews 9:27 that "man is destined to die once, and after that to face judgment." Whatever is meant by "preached even to those who are now dead," it doesn't refer to the possibility of receiving the gospel after the moment of death.

Though evangelical scholars have offered several interpretations of this verse, perhaps the best view is that it refers to those who are now dead but who heard the gospel while they were yet alive. This especially makes sense in view of the tenses used: The gospel was preached (in the past) to those are dead (presently).

2 Peter

2 Peter 1:20—*Are we not to interpret the Bible for ourselves?*

This verse says that "no prophecy of the scripture is of any private interpretation" (KJV). The Greek word translated *interpretation* literally means to unloose. The verse could be paraphrased: "No prophecy of Scripture is a matter of one's own unloosing." In other words, the prophecies did not stem merely from the prophets themselves or by human imaginings, but ultimately came from God, as verse 21 goes on to emphatically state. This passage is not dealing with how to interpret Scripture but rather deals with how Scripture came to be written.

2 Peter 2:9—*Is God holding unbelievers for future punishment?*

This verse affirms, "The Lord knows how to...hold the unrighteous for the day of judgment, while continuing their punishment." The word *hold* in this verse is in the present tense, indicating that the wicked (nonbelievers) are held captive continuously. Peter is portraying them as condemned prisoners being closely guarded in a jail while awaiting future sentencing and final judgment. While God holds them there, He is said to be "continuing their punishment." The word *continuing* in this verse is also in the present tense, indicating the perpetual, ongoing nature of the punishment. One day they will be resurrected and then judged at the Great White Throne judgment, after which time their eternal punishment will begin in the lake of fire (Revelation 20:11-15).

2 Peter 3:8—*In what way is a day like a thousand years, and a thousand years like a day for the Lord?*

God, the eternal one, is beyond the limitations of time. This verse is found in the context of a discussion of the second coming, so the idea would seem to be that we as finite creatures cannot unravel the mysteries of the timing of end-time events, for God does not use our time scale. He is beyond time altogether and will bring end-time events to fruition in accordance with His sovereign plan.

1 John

1 John 3:9—*Does this verse teach sinless perfection?*

This verse affirms, "No one who is born of God will continue to sin, because God's seed remains in him; he cannot go on sinning, because he has been born of God." Earlier in this same epistle, however, John noted the folly of denying that we, as redeemed Christians, are sinful (1 John 1:8). This is one reason John calls us to confess our sins to God (1 John 1:9). So in whatever way 1 John 3:9 is understood, it should not be taken to mean that Christians attain sinless perfection. The apostle Paul, as a redeemed Christian, certainly recognized that sin continued to wreak its havoc in his own life (Romans 7:18-21). If Paul wasn't perfect, who among us would claim to attain what Paul could not attain?

Christians have dealt with 1 John 3:9 in two primary ways. Some believe that in view of the present tenses used in this verse, John was saying that Christians will not have habitual sin. In this understanding, Christians will not be dominated by perpetual sin. Sin will not be a continual pattern in their lives.

Other interpreters explain the verse as relating to the new nature of Christians. We are told in verse 5 that there is no sin in Christ. Then, in verse 6, we are told that those who abide in Christ do not sin. As we move on to verse 9, we find an important teaching regarding our new natures as Christians. The new natures within Christians—which are pure and holy, like Christ—do not sin. Insofar as the believer expresses his new nature in his daily experience, he will not sin. If the believer does sin, he acts against his new nature. This view thus concludes that 1 John 3:9 is a call to a holy life—a call to allow our new natures to so dominate our daily experiences that the result is holiness in daily life.

1 John 4:4—*Can a Christian be demon possessed?*

Christians disagree on this issue. I believe a Christian cannot be demon possessed, and 1 John 4:4 is one good verse to support this view. Because the Holy Spirit perpetually indwells Christians (1 Corinthians 6:19), Christians cannot be demon possessed.

Christians have been delivered from Satan's domain. As Colossians 1:13 puts it, "He has rescued us from the dominion of darkness and brought us into the kingdom of the Son he loves."

The Scriptures never describe a Christian as being demon possessed. For sure, it provides examples of Christians being afflicted by the devil, but not possessed by the devil.

1 John 5:6-8—*Who are the three witnesses in this passage?*

A little historical background helps us understand what is going on in this verse. A false teacher by the name of Cerinthus spread the heretical idea that the Christ (a kind of cosmic spiritual being) came upon a human Jesus at His baptism but departed before His crucifixion. First John 5:6-8 refutes this idea. *Water* is a reference to Jesus' baptism, and *blood* is a reference to His crucifixion. Both of these act as metaphorical witnesses to the fact that Jesus the Christ experienced both baptism and death by crucifixion. The Holy Spirit (elsewhere called the Spirit of truth—John 14:17; 15:26) is the third witness testifying to this fact. The mention of three witnesses reflects the requirement of Jewish law (Deuteronomy 19:15; John 8:17-18).

1 John 5:7—*Does the absence of this verse in modern translations prove that the doctrine of the Trinity is not true?*

The KJV reads, "There are three who bear record in heaven: the Father, the Word, and the Holy Ghost; and these three are one." Modern translations, however, omit this verse. In fact, this verse has virtually no support among the early Greek manuscripts, though it is found in Latin manuscripts. Its appearance in late Greek manuscripts is based on the fact that Erasmus was placed under ecclesiastical pressure to include it in his Greek New Testament of 1522, having omitted it in his two earlier editions of 1516 and 1519 because he could not find any Greek manuscripts that contained it.

Its inclusion in the Latin Bible probably results from a scribe incorporating a marginal comment (gloss) into the text as he copied the manuscript of 1 John. But including it in the text violates almost every rule of textual criticism. Even the NKJV notes the weak support for the inclusion of this text.

The simple fact that this one verse has no manuscript support, however, does not mean the doctrine of the Trinity is not true. Numerous other passages that have undeniably strong manuscript support establish the following:

- There is only one true God (Deuteronomy 6:4).

- While there is only one God, there are three distinct persons within the Godhead. Each of these three persons is called God in Scripture: the Father (1 Peter 1:2), the Son (John 20:28), and the Holy Spirit (Acts 5:3-4).

- There is three-in-oneness within the Godhead (Matthew 28:19).

1 John 5:16—*What is the sin unto death?*

John does not specify what this sin is. Apparently it could refer to any sin that is repeatedly committed such that one is drawn deeper and deeper into the world system, which is portrayed in John's theology as a death-producing system. We might summarize it this way: The more one falls into sin, the deeper one is drawn into the world system. The closer one is to the world, the more likely death is.

2 John

2 John 1—*Who is the "chosen lady"?*

It is likely that this lady was not a human being but rather a church. The church is called a chosen lady because it is made up of God's elect believers. The lady's children are the individual members of the church. The reference to the chosen sister (verse 13) may well point to John's own church congregation.

John probably called the church a lady because of the possibility that the letter could be intercepted by Roman authorities while en route. If that happened, the letter might give these authorities enough information to capture and imprison the Christians (or worse). Calling the church a lady was therefore a simple safety measure.

2 John 10—*Does this verse mean Christians shouldn't allow cultists into their houses?*

Second John 10 does not prohibit Christians from allowing cultists into their homes in order to witness to them. Rather, it is a prohibition against giving cultists a platform from which to teach false doctrine.

In the early days of Christianity, believers had no centralized church building where they could congregate. Rather, many small house-churches were scattered throughout the city. In the New Testament, we see the early Christians "breaking bread from house to house" (Acts 2:46; 5:42) and gathering to pray in the house of Mary, the mother of Mark (Acts 12:12). Churches often met in houses (Romans 6:15; 1 Corinthians 16:19; Philippians 2; Colossians 4:15).

So apparently, John is here warning against allowing a false teacher into the church and giving him a platform from which to teach. Seen in this way, this prohibition guards the purity of the church.

3 John

3 John 2—*Does this verse prove that God desires Christians to be financially prosperous?*

This verse affirms, "I wish above all things that thou mayest prosper and be in health, even as thy soul prospereth" (3 John 1:2 KJV). The Greek word for *prosper* in this verse does not refer to financial prosperity but simply to general well-being. In fact, the NIV correctly reflects this idea in its rendering of the verse: "I pray that you may enjoy good health and that all may go well with you, even as your soul is getting along well." In biblical times the wish for things to go well and the wish for good health were standard forms of greeting. Financial prosperity is completely foreign to both this ancient greeting and 3 John 2.

Jude

Jude 14—*Does the book of Enoch belong in the Bible because Jude cites it?*

No. The apostle Paul quoted from pagan poets (Acts 17:28; Titus 1:12), but this does not mean the writings of these pagan poets belong in the Bible. Nor does it mean everything contained in their writings is true. It simply means that there was a truth in these poets that Paul rendered worthy of inclusion in his biblical book. Likewise, simply because Jude sites a writing from Enoch does not mean the book of Enoch belongs in the Bible. Nor does it mean that everything in the book of Enoch is true or accurate. It simply means that there was a truth in Enoch's book that Jude rendered worthy of inclusion in his letter.

Revelation

Revelation 1:4—*Who are the seven spirits before God's throne?*

Many Bible expositors believe this is a reference to the Holy Spirit, the third person of the Trinity. This is largely based on Scripture verses that list seven aspects of the Spirit of the Lord (see Isaiah 11:2; Zechariah 3:9). The number seven also represents the perfect work of God (see Genesis 2:2-3). In this case, the number seven may represent the perfect work of the Holy Spirit.

Revelation 1:8; 22:13—*Is Jesus the Alpha and Omega?*

Yes. The context of Revelation 1 indicates the verses are referring to Christ. After all, we are told that someone is coming. This someone was pierced. Was the Father pierced? No. Was Jesus pierced? Yes—on the cross for the salvation of humankind. Then, in Revelation 22:12-13, we are told that this same being is coming soon. Dropping down to verse 20, we read, "Come, Lord Jesus." So Jesus, the Alpha and Omega, is coming soon. This is powerful evidence for the absolute deity of Jesus Christ, for *Alpha and Omega* is used exclusively of God in the Old Testament (Isaiah 44:6; 48:12-13).

Revelation 2:13—*Does Satan have a throne somewhere on the earth?*

We know that Satan, a spirit being, is not omnipresent (everywhere-present) like God is, and therefore he must have local existence (he can only be in one place at a time). At the time Christ spoke these words, Satan may have been localized in Pergamum.

Scholars have noted that Pergamum in ancient times was the official center of emperor worship in Asia. Pergamum was among the first cities of Asia to build a temple to a Roman emperor. Other scholars have noted that Pergamum was the city where the temple of Asclepius (a pagan god) was located. The symbol of this false god was a serpent (a term also used of Satan in Scripture—see Genesis 3:1). Also, a giant altar of Zeus overlooked Pergamum. With all the false religion in this city, we should not be surprised to hear Jesus say that Satan has a throne there.

Revelation 3:5—*Can a Christian have his or her name blotted out of the book of life?*

Though this passage may imply that a believer's name could be erased from the book of life, actually it only gives a positive affirmation that their names will *not* be erased. Jesus' statement may thus be considered not a threat but indeed an assurance that saved peoples' names will always be in the book of life.

This seems to be the gist of what other verses communicate about the book of life. For example, in Luke 10:20 Jesus said to the disciples, "Do not rejoice that the spirits submit to you, but rejoice that your names are written in heaven." In Hebrews 12:23 we read of "the church of the firstborn, whose names are written in heaven."

Revelation 3:14 (NASB)—*If Jesus is the beginning of God's creation, is He a created being?*

No. The Bible employs a wide range of meanings for the Greek word *arche,* translated "beginning" in Revelation 3:14 (NASB). Though *arche* can mean beginning, the word is truly unique and also carries the important active meaning of one who begins, origin, source, creator, or first cause. Evangelical scholars agree that this is the intended meaning of the word in Revelation 3:14. Interestingly, the English word *architect* is derived from *arche.* We might say that Jesus is the architect of all creation (John 1:3; Colossians 1:16; Hebrews 1:2).

Revelation 7:4 (see also 14:1-3)—*Who are the 144,000?*

Some modern Christians have taken this as metaphorically referring to the church. However, the context indicates the verse is referring to 144,000 Jewish men—12,000 from each tribe—who live during the future tribulation period (see Revelation 14:4). The very fact that specific tribes are mentioned, along with specific numbers for those tribes, removes all possibility that this is a figure of speech. Nowhere else in the Bible does a reference to 12 tribes of Israel mean anything but 12 tribes of Israel. Indeed, the word *tribe* is never used of anything but a literal ethnic group in Scripture. Apparently these 144,000 become believers during the future tribulation and evangelize all over the world.

Revelation 7:4—*Why are the Old Testament tribes of Dan and Ephraim omitted from this list of Jewish tribes?*

The Old Testament has some 20 various lists of tribes. Most scholars today agree that Dan's tribe was omitted because that tribe was guilty of idolatry on many occasions and, as a result, was largely obliterated (Leviticus 24:11; Judges 18:1,30; see also 1 Kings 12:28-29). To engage in unrepentant idolatry is to be cut off from God's blessing. The tribe of Ephraim was also involved in idolatry and pagan worship (Judges 17; Hosea 4:17).

Revelation 7:4—*Why was the tribe of Levi included in the list of Jewish tribes?*

The tribe of Levi is probably included here because the priestly functions of the tribe of Levi ceased with the coming of Christ—the ultimate High Priest. Indeed, the Levitical priesthood was fulfilled in the person of Christ (Hebrews 7–10). Because there was no further need for the services of the tribe of Levi as priests, there was no further reason for keeping this tribe distinct and separate from the others.

Revelation 13:18—*Why are the numbers 666 used in reference to the Antichrist?*

Bible interpreters have offered many suggestions as to the meaning of 666 through the centuries. A popular theory is that inasmuch as the number 7 is a number of perfection, and the number 777 is a number reflecting the perfect Trinity, perhaps 666 points to a being who aspires to perfect deity (like the Trinity) but never attains it. Ultimately, the Antichrist is just a man, though he is influenced (and possibly indwelt) by Satan.

Others have suggested that perhaps the number refers to a specific man of the past—such as the Roman emperor Nero. It is suggested that if Nero's name is translated into the Hebrew language, the numerical value of its letters is 666.

Of course, all this is highly speculative. The truth is, Scripture doesn't clearly define what is meant by 666. Interpreting this verse involves a lot of guesswork.

Revelation 16:14—*Can demons perform miracles?*

Although Satan has great spiritual powers, there is a gigantic difference between the power of the devil and the power of God. First, God is infinite in power (omnipotent); the devil (and demons) are finite and limited. Second, only God can create life (Genesis 1:1,21; Deuteronomy 32:39); the devil cannot (see Exodus 8:19). Only God can raise the dead (John 10:18; Revelation 1:18); the devil cannot, though he will one day give "breath" (animation) to the idolatrous image of the Antichrist (Revelation 13:15).

See comments on Exodus 7:11 and 2 Thessalonians 2:9.

Revelation 16:16—*What is Armageddon?*

Armageddon literally means Mount of Megiddo. Megiddo is about 60 miles north of Jerusalem. This is the site for the final horrific battle of humankind just prior to the second coming (Revelation 16:16). Napoleon is reported to have once commented that this site is perhaps the greatest battlefield he had ever seen.

Revelation 20:11-15—*What is the Great White Throne judgment?*

The Great White Throne judgment is the judgment that unbelievers must face (Revelation 20:11-15). (Believers will not participate in this horrific judgment.) Christ is the divine Judge, and those who are judged are the unsaved dead of all time. The judgment takes place at the end of the millennial kingdom, Christ's 1000-year reign on the earth. Those who face Christ at this judgment will be judged on the basis of their works (Revelation 20:12-13).

It is critical to understand that they actually get to this judgment because they are already unsaved. This judgment will not separate believers from unbelievers, for all who will experience it will have already made the choice during their lifetimes to reject God. Once they are before the divine Judge, they are judged according to their works not only to justify their condemnation but also to determine the degree to which each person should be punished throughout eternity in hell.

Revelation 21—*What is the New Jerusalem?*

The most elaborate description of the heavenly city in the Bible is in Revelation 21, where we read of the New Jerusalem. The city measures approximately 1500 miles by 1500 miles by 1500 miles. The eternal city is so huge that it would measure approximately the distance between the Mississippi River and the Atlantic Ocean. It is tall enough that from the earth's surface it would reach about one-twentieth of the way to the moon. The eternal city could either be cube-shaped or pyramid-shaped. It may be preferable to consider it shaped as a pyramid, for this would explain how the river of the water of life can flow down its sides as pictured in Revelation 22:1-2. This river of the water of life is symbolic of the abundance of spiritual life that will characterize those who are living in the eternal city. The stream seems to symbolize the perpetual outflow of spiritual blessing to all the redeemed of all ages, who will be basking in the full glow of eternal life.

Revelation 22:12—*Why did Jesus say, "I am coming soon"? Almost two thousand years have passed since He said it.*

Some scholars suggest that from the human perspective it may not seem soon, but from the divine perspective it is. According to the New Testament, we have been living in the last days since the Incarnation of Christ (Hebrews 1:2; James 5:3). Moreover, we read in James 5:9

that "the Judge is standing at the door." Romans 13:12 exhorts us that "the night is nearly over; the day is almost here." Hebrews 10:25 admonishes us to "encourage one another—and all the more as you see the Day approaching." And 1 Peter 4:7 warns, "The end of all things is near." In view of such verses, it would seem Christ is coming soon from the divine perspective.

Other scholars suggest that perhaps Jesus meant He is coming soon from the perspective of the events described in the book of Revelation. In other words, from the vantage point of those living during the time of the tribulation period itself—a seven-year period of trials that culminates in the second coming (see Revelation 4-19)—Christ is coming soon.

Revelation 22:16; Isaiah 14:12—*How could the title* Morning Star *be used in reference to Jesus in one verse and in reference to Lucifer in another verse?*

Context always determines the way words are to be understood. Revelation and Isaiah have two different contexts and communicate two different meanings. In Revelation 22:16, the term *Morning Star* has a messianic sense related to Numbers 24:17, which promised that "a star will come out of Jacob." The star thus became a symbol of the coming messianic king, who was Jesus. The word *morning* communicates the idea that a spiritual dawn is right around the corner. The cold dark night of spiritual lethargy is nearly over with the coming of the Morning Star (Jesus).

In Isaiah 14:12, the term is used metaphorically to refer to a fall from great glory. Lucifer was the mightiest, most magnificent, most beautiful, and most splendorous angel, and yet he sinned and fell from his great glory. We thus read, "How you have fallen from heaven, O morning star."

Some believe "morning star" may be part of a taunt against Lucifer in his fall from glory. The idea would be something like this: "How you have fallen from heaven, O pretended messiah!"

A Select Bibliography

Archer, Gleason. *Encyclopedia of Bible Difficulties.* Grand Rapids, MI: Zondervan, 1982.

Arndt, William. *Bible Difficulties and Seeming Contradictions.* St. Louis, MO: Concordia, 1987.

Boa, Ken and Larry Moody. *I'm Glad You Asked.* Wheaton, IL: Chariot-Victor, 1994.

Geisler, Norman and Thomas Howe. *When Critics Ask.* Grand Rapids, MI: Baker Books, 1992.

Kaiser, Walter and Peter Davids, F.F. Bruce, and Manfred Brauch. *Hard Sayings of the Bible.* Downers Grove, IL: InterVarsity Press, 1996.

McGee, J. Vernon. *Questions and Answers.* Nashville, TN: Nelson, 1990.

O'Brien, David E. *Today's Handbook for Solving Bible Difficulties.* Minneapolis, MN: Bethany House, 1990.

Rhodes, Ron. *What Does the Bible Say About...?* Eugene, OR: Harvest House, 2007.

Richards, Larry. *Bible Difficulties Solved.* Grand Rapids, MI: Revell, 1993.

Index

If you have any questions or comments, feel free to contact Reasoning from the Scriptures Ministries.

RON RHODES

Reasoning from the Scriptures Ministries

PHONE: 214-618-0912
E-MAIL: ronrhodes@earthlink.net
WEB: www.ronrhodes.org

Free newsletter available upon request

Other Great Harvest House Reading

by Ron Rhodes

To learn more about books by Ron Rhodes
or to read sample chapters, log on to our website:

www.harvesthousepublishers.com

HARVEST HOUSE PUBLISHERS

EUGENE, OREGON